James Duke was born in Ipswich in 1946. After a degree in Englis.
at Sussex University he became House Manager at the Royal Court
Theatre, and then went on to work for a major theatrical agency,
forming his own business in 1974. His first play was produced at
the Soho Poly in 1976 and in 1991 he gave up the agency to concentrate on his writing career full time. His biography of Robert
Shaw has received widespread critical acclaim.

Contents

Author's Note

The word 'actor' is used throughout this book to mean both actor and actress (except in Chapter 4) in order to avoid frequent and irritating repetition. I am only too aware that this may lay me open to charges of sexism.

In fact, unlike words such as chairman or barmaid, it seems to me that the word 'actor' is not gender specific. Originally, indeed, it was used to mean both sexes (Samuel Pepys in 1666: 'Doll Common doing Abigail most excellently and Knipp the widow very well and will be an excellent actor I think.').

Women did not make their first appearance on the English stage until 1660 when Margaret Hughes appeared in a production of *Othello* as Desdemona and it was not until the eighteenth century that the word 'actress' (from the French *actrice*) became current, frequently in a pejorative context ('To stop the trade of love behind the scene/Where actresses make bold with married men,' Dryden, 1700).

'Actor' is today used widely, though not universally, within the acting profession to denote performers of both sexes, so all in all I do not think there is much need for me to apologise for using the word in this way myself.

More contentiously, I have generally opted to use 'he' throughout the text when referring to individuals (actors, producers, directors, etc.) who could be of either sex. This is because I find the alternatives misleading ('she') or cumbersome ('s/he', 'she/he'). It is also true, however regrettably, that many of these jobs (directors and producers particularly) are still predominantly carried out by men. My use of 'he' may reflect this reality – but it does not intentionally endorse it.

Preface

As far as I know this is the first book written by someone who has been a 'theatrical agent', as I was for well over fifteen years, working in an office that represented actors at every level, from the most exalted to the most lowly, from international film stars to young actors just out of drama school. Of course, the word 'theatrical' (frequently used to describe the profession as well as its agents) is a misnomer. The entertainment business did once consist solely of productions mounted for the stage, but cinema, radio and television have changed all that. Now the new media are at the forefront of scientific discovery and they change so rapidly it is sometimes difficult to keep track of precisely what system is being used to disseminate each production to its audience. Satellite, cable, DAT tapes, interactive laser discs and wide-screen television will soon be followed by high-definition television and no doubt, in time, holograms. The impact of the new digital transmission systems has yet to be properly assessed. In the words of a feature film contract, copyright in a performance is granted for all existing systems of distribution and for those 'yet to be invented'!

Being a theatrical agent required a working knowledge of all the agreements that related to the various media, the terms and conditions and the special circumstances that differentiate, say, film from the theatre. But, more importantly, it was necessary to try and develop an understanding of how each branch of the media operated as a business and what were their specific requirements for the employment of actors.

However it is not just this invaluable experience that has helped me write this book. Before I began my career as an agent I worked at the Royal Court Theatre and in later years I had plays produced at various fringe venues (Soho Poly, King's Theatre, Bridge Lane Theatre) and, in an attempt to help clients develop their careers, I helped to produce a West End musical, two straight plays and a major feature film, as well as representing award-winning television directors and a noted British film producer, and setting up a sub-section of the agency to deal with film technicians.

Consequently I saw both sides of the fence. I saw the difficulties and problems confronting an actor wanting to get a job and how their attitude and demeanour affected their chances. But I saw the other side as well, the difficulties for the employer of raising the money to fund a venture, and/or of trying to find a market for the product. And I also saw the separate struggle of directors, casting directors and freelance producers to secure employment for themselves.

To some extent, whenever competition for selection gives one group of people power over another, there is going to be an attitude of 'us' and 'them'. Inevitably employers, though a large and diverse group, are seen by actors as 'them'. The demands and concerns of employers in all the various media are not the same as the demands and concerns of an actor. This often leads to actors feeling that they are being exploited or taken advantage of, especially in relation to levels of pay.

It's hard to tell if this is true or not. Undoubtedly actors and – since the various changes in the law affecting the operation of a 'closed shop' – technicians have been exploited by producers simply because they work in an industry crammed with competing talent: salaries are squeezed, and an actor, holding out for a particular level of pay, may find he is simply replaced with the second choice. Very frequently the offer made is a simple take-it-or-leave-it, and this tends to mean that prices for actors have remained stable or have even been driven down. Equity, the actors' union, negotiates yearly increases on minimum wages and non-negotiable standard fees, but these do not compensate for the overall determination of producers to pay actors as little as they can get away with.

The key words here are 'get away with'. The price pendulum swings dramatically in the opposite direction once the actor becomes well known and is in demand. The producer's perception then changes. He comes to believe that the actor is important to his production and will, in the theatrical sense, 'put bums on seats'. The actor is then able to do some exploiting in his turn, demanding sums which may be out of all proportion to his actual contribution to the project. Fair enough, you may say, but the amount of money available for, say, film production is finite and if $10 million is paid to Arnold Schwarzenegger to star in one film, there is no guarantee that the box-office receipts will cover his cost, let alone the total cost of the film. That $10 million is therefore lost to the industry, further cutting down the amount available for other productions. Hollywood stars whose potential at the box office is perceived to be important – often against overwhelming evidence to the contrary – have removed hundreds of millions of dollars from the industry as a whole.

But it is not only over money that the 'us' and 'them' psychology exists. Indeed, it is in other areas that it is most prevalent and ultimately most destructive. In an interview or audition, where the person sitting behind the desk or in the stalls has the power to make decisions that may dramatically affect the actor's life in the short and possibly even long term, it is natural enough that an actor should think of 'us' and 'them'. The incredible tension that can develop in such situations – even if comparatively small roles are at stake, especially when an actor has not worked for some time – can be channelled into this sort of attitude, reinforcing it and increasing the antipathy felt for the people who make the decisions.

In an actor's life there are going to be many such encounters, with casting directors, directors, producers and agents. An 'us' and 'them' attitude on these occasions is very unhelpful. It generates a feeling of hostility, however well disguised. It makes an actor defensive and less ready to respond flexibly to what may be required. Worse, it gets in the way of a proper understanding of what is actually going on, the processes that lie behind the ultimate decision. If you can put yourself in the shoes of the director facing you and see what his problems are, then you will be better placed to fit yourself to those requirements. (The circumstances with an agent should be different, but the same rules apply – see Chapter 8.) Not only will this help you to get the job, but if you don't get it, it will also help you see why, which in some ways is just as important.

There are unfortunately some casting directors, directors and producers who seem to take great delight in putting actors through hell. They are rude, unsympathetic, inconsiderate and demanding. They regard themselves as infinitely superior. Generally speaking they are not among the top flight: possibly they are compensating for their own inadequacy by self-glorification at the expense of others. A well-known British film director, for example, kept an actress waiting for an hour outside his office, eventually called her in and then, before she could utter a word told her she was entirely wrong for the part because she needed to get her teeth fixed. Fortunately such horrors are the exception rather than the rule.

Most prospective employers are careful of feelings and considerate. But this can be misleading. A show of friendship may make it seem that the part is as good as offered, when all the director is in fact doing is taking care to put the actor at ease in the interview or audition. Many directors go out of their way to make an actor feel at home and relaxed and give them twenty or thirty minutes, though, in fact, they may have no intention of actually employing them. The director's friendliness is no guarantee of success.

It may be unrealistic to advise against looking at employers as 'them'. But it is important to realise that often employers and actors are on the same treadmill. Casting directors, directors and even producers nowadays (with the severe reduction in the numbers of 'in-house' radio and TV staff) are freelance just like actors, and they will experience very similar processes in order to get employment for themselves. Demo tapes will have to be compiled, CVs written, interviews attended. The director you face in an interview will have been selected from a short list, his or her agent will have done whatever they could, his or her work will have been reviewed, and a decision made by a producer, in exactly the same way as the director makes a decision about you.

Does an agent belong to 'us' or to 'them'? Some agents make it clear, right from the beginning, that they regard themselves as lined up with 'them'. Others, often ex-actors themselves, sit firmly on the side of 'us'. The truth is that a good agent should actually be neither. The agent is after all paid by the actor. In the end the agent should be prepared to go into battle for the rights and privileges of his client. That is what agents are paid for. But nevertheless, for an agent to do the job properly it is necessary to be just as understanding of the employer's difficulties as of the client's. What an agent hopes to give his client is an edge on the competition. If this edge is arrived at by friendship with a producer, by understanding and co-operating with a producer's specific requirements at any one time, that is fair enough. If, however, in trying to ingratiate himself with an employer, an agent compromises or prejudices his client, then that is beyond the bounds of proper behaviour. (Which is not to say it doesn't happen.)

In my view agents who behave as though they are surrogates for the employers, who tell a client what they are going to do and what they must accept – and many do – should be avoided, just as much as those whose sole purpose seems to be sympathising with the woes and difficulties of the clients. The best agent sits on the fence between the two – though it is a fence that should ideally lean towards 'us'.

Much of an agent's day-to-day work is exactly as an actor might imagine it. There is a great deal of routine activity: gathering information; a lot of telephone calls to attempt to get clients seen for specific roles; a lot of begging of favours. But much of an agent's time is also spent listening to and dealing with the reactions of clients to interviews and auditions, and talking them through rejections and disappointments (as well as celebrating their successes), discussing the direction of their career and sorting out their contracts. Most of all a good agent will be aware of the complexity involved in negotiating a contract, where psychological factors can often be as important as rational arguments.

In my own time as an agent, I have heard literally hundreds of different accounts of interviews and auditions, of where the actor thought he had gone wrong or what he did right and subsequently the explanations from the other side as to why a job was not forthcoming or, alternatively, why the actor was so delightful they were employed on the spot. I have interviewed hundreds of actors with a view to representing them, seeing for myself how their performances differed, how some would be immensely impressive, while others, perhaps better qualified and more experienced in terms of acting, performed badly in the interview. I have listened to the reactions of casting directors, directors and producers to letters, CVs, video tapes and particularly photographs, and made lists (always short) of the phrases used as reasons for rejection. I have seen the ways a part, sometimes a small part, can catch the public imagination and catapult an actor to sudden success, while other roles, bigger and better and more financially rewarding, make no impact whatsoever and disappear without trace.

All this, not to mention years of discussion on the subject with actors and colleagues and other agents, has given me very definite views which have led me to write this book. My main aim has been to try and dispel the many myths that surround the business of getting a job. It is my view that a clear understanding of the processes involved, of what is expected of you as an actor outside the field of acting, will not only make you better prepared, better-motivated and more likely to succeed, but just as importantly, will also help you cope with the rejections and psychological knocks that the profession you have chosen will inevitably deliver.

1 A Working Actor

THIS BOOK IS INTENDED primarily for the actor setting out on the first steps of his professional career; for the actor who may have been in the business for some years but has not had a great deal of success in establishing himself in full employment; and for the actor who may have been successful for a period of time but who has slipped, once again, behind that invisible line.

It is *not*, generally speaking, a book for someone who wishes to become an actor, and who is thinking about how they should go about it and which means of entry into the profession they should choose. So it is a book not about how to become an actor, but about how to *succeed* as an actor – 'success' here defined as being a 'working actor'.

There is an invisible line drawn in the career of every successful actor. It comes at a different time for each individual, sometimes at an incredibly early age (as with Michael Crawford, Marcus Sewell or Janet McTeer), sometimes much later in life (as with Richard Wilson). This line separates the period when an actor is constantly looking for work and worrying about where the next job is going to come from, and the time when calls and offers start to be received regularly, and employment stretches ahead in long sequences, with smaller jobs fitted in between the longer commitments. Availability checks are received constantly, as the actor finds he is in demand from employers who believe he has something unique to bring to their production. That is the definition of success in professional terms – though it may not be what the public thinks of as 'stardom', which is an entirely different matter.

It is how to cross this invisible line and stay across it that is the subject of this book.

Drama schools are designed to give courses in the art and craft of acting but, unfortunately, include little on the art and craft of getting the opportunity to act. This is not surprising in a sense, since they are staffed largely by ex-actors or professionals who have not been involved in the business side of the profession at all, or, if they have, only at the receiving end and possibly with limited success. Their experience is therefore almost as limited, in this respect, as that of their students.

Nor is there much written on the subject and what there is can be misleading. Successful actors' autobiographies don't give much guidance on how to emulate their achievements. The many fictional accounts in books, television, film and theatre (*Chorus Line, 42nd Street, Fame, Star!, Funny Girl* and *The Entertainer*, to name only a few) may make good drama, but, relying as they usually do on the 'plucked from the chorus line' cliché, they are hardly a practical guide to the way ahead. Indeed they can be positively unhelpful in encouraging the belief, even among professional actors who should know better, that becoming successful is merely a question of waiting for the opportunity to be in the right place at the right time.

THE ART OF ACTING AND THE BUSINESS OF A CAREER

In the course of most people's careers they may have six or seven interviews for a job or promotion in their working lives. An actor, though, may have that number in a week, almost certainly in a month. Everyone who works or wants to work has to think about their career and how best to promote it. But the job of being an actor is unique in that it requires, on a daily basis, positive application and consideration of the prospects of employment. In a very definite sense the job of being an actor is in fact *two* jobs. Firstly there is the art and craft of acting, delivering performances that audiences can appreciate and enjoy and respond to, and working on that talent or ability to train and develop it to its full potential. But the second job is no less important, and this is the art and craft

of selling the product that results from the training and performances, namely, oneself.

This book does not deal with the first aspect of being an actor
(the assumption is made that you are already doing everything you
can to perfect your craft), but is entirely concerned with the second. To borrow a line from the Dustin Hoffman film *Tootsie*, 'an
actor *acts*'. It is absolutely no good honing and shaping your talent
unless someone is given the opportunity to see the result in performance. An actor needs an audience. Getting that audience, and
getting the chance to perform in front of increasingly large audiences – from twenty people in a pub theatre, to a thousand people in
the Stratford Memorial Theatre, to seven million people watching
a television drama, to two hundred million people all over the
world who may see a major feature film – is what selling yourself
is all about.

It is not easy. In some ways the two aspects of an actor's life are
inimical to each other: art and business do not always go comfort-
ably together. The act of creation involved in forming a well-
rounded and believable character is far removed from the detailed
work involved in keeping up to date with what is going on where
and with whom. But this is a dichotomy that has to be resolved.
The freedom to act, to create, is entirely dependent on attention to
business. However talented you are as an actor, unless you are able
to cope with the rigours of the business side of the profession, you
will not get the opportunity to act, and realise your potential. It is
as simple as that. Waiting around to be 'discovered' – however
many stories you hear to the contrary – is not a formula for a
successful career.

SELF-RELIANCE

It is a mistake to think you can satisfactorily assign the business
side of your career to someone else: i.e. an agent. An agent can be
most helpful (or very unhelpful – see Chapter 8) but generally
speaking their uses are greater the more successful you have become. You should certainly not believe that getting an agent is
somehow mystically going to help you cross the 'line'. In the end

it is your own responsibility to control and influence your career. Declaring, as some actors do, that they are not suited to dealing with such problems ('that's why I have an agent') is not an option you should entertain. An agent is one of many tools available to help you advance your career, but it is up to you to use that tool wisely. Abdicating your responsibility, failing to show an interest in your career, will inevitably lead to your agent showing less interest in it too. Finding an agent is certainly not the be-all and end-all of an actor's responsibility in shaping his own success.

LUCK

If you are not prepared to work as hard at promoting and selling yourself as you are on the artistic and creative side, you will undoubtedly be frustrated in your amibitions.

It would be ridiculous to deny that luck does not play a part in an actor's career. But since it is, by definition, not something that can be predicted or relied upon, there is absolutely no point in sitting back and letting good fortune shape events. You have already, if you care to think about it, experienced good and bad luck. It is a question of interpretation. What is essential is that you do not foster the idea that all you need is luck, that somehow, one day, you will be lucky, that you will get a lucky break, and that all you have to do is wait for it. That is merely an excuse, and a poor one, for inactivity. And if that is going to be your attitude you will definitely not have the success you feel you deserve. The watched kettle never boils: the awaited telephone call will never come.

SELLING YOURSELF

Essentially the business side of the profession of acting amounts to one thing: salesmanship. You are simply selling a product like any other. The only difference here is that the product happens to be YOU.

For most working people the occasions when they have to sell themselves, as opposed to other people or things, are limited to the number of job applications they write and the interviews they have as a result, combined with various interviews for promotion purposes. Even these rare occasions most people find difficult to cope with and extremely stressful. Most people are reluctant to push themselves forward and sing their own praises or blow their own trumpets. This reluctance is deeply ingrained. It is also regarded as polite and well-mannered. But it is an inhibition that has to be overcome by the actor.

It is interesting that in America, where actors apply themselves much more thoroughly to the business side of acting, the psychological and social barrier is much lower. Americans are much more comfortable with the idea of promoting themselves and are better at it. They are not embarrassed to speak about their lives and their achievements in a way that the English might describe as aggressive and pushy. Obviously to come on too strong is just as bad as not to come on at all but there are lessons to be learnt from the American example.

However uneasy you are talking about yourself you must learn to become good at it; you must learn to become *very* good at it. In a sense it should not be difficult. It is like creating a role. The person walking into the interview is as much a character as a part in a play, though a complex and difficult character and one in which it is essential to appear relaxed and 'natural', and which moreover requires you to write your own lines. Obviously the more you understand about the situation into which you are walking the better you can create dialogue and a character to match expectations. Like any experienced salesman you will want to understand as much about a potential customer's requirements as you can. Then your sales pitch can be angled to tally as far as possible with those requirements. If, for instance, a salesman selling fridges knows his potential customer is very ecologically minded, he will be prepared to stress the line of models that use least CFCs. Similarly if an actor knows that the director he is going to see is specifically looking for a very athletic performer, he can emphasise his physical prowess.

UNDERSTANDING THE INDUSTRY

A basic understanding of the many and diverse areas of what is loosely called 'show business' is essential to an actor. It will, for instance, help you prepare properly for an interview. That is why it is important not only to find out as much as possible about the part you are being auditioned or interviewed for, but also everything you can about the background and circumstances of the production. You may think that a knowledge of how the business works is irrelevant to presenting yourself as the right actor for a particular role. You would be mistaken. For instance if you think that all feature films are big budget, well-paid, glitzy productions you could give the wrong impression to a director of a small budget, shoestring project (of which there are many) that nevertheless has a good role for you. He will be looking for an actor who is prepared to muck in, who is not over-concerned about the size of his salary, and who understands the privations involved. Similarly with a theatre job. There may be a production which will involve little money but is being presented at a theatre which happens to be frequented regularly by other directors, writers, casting directors and the press and where, therefore, a part has greater significance than simply the amount of money on offer.

The entertainment industry is not one monolith but several different businesses each with its own requirements and *raison d'être*. It ranges from two or three actors and a stage manager putting on a play in the upstairs room of a pub and sharing the proceeds, to a crew of sixty photographing a major feature film on a 330-foot sound stage at a cost of £150,000 a day. Between these two extremes there is a continuum: from pub theatre to theatre productions on a bigger scale, repertory companies, commercial theatre, West End theatre, the television industry, films for television, and feature films with very limited budgets, up to full-scale feature films with multi-million dollar budgets and international stars.

Like it or not, in today's world, this continuum is a business. Even at the bottom, in the pub theatre, business is the key. A clever and intelligent and well-acted play in the upstairs room of a pub may not find an audience at all unless it is well marketed and well publicised. The quality of the product may be exceptional but unless people get to hear about it, that quality is wasted. Relying on traditional word of mouth may not be enough. In this case lack of profits is less important than the fact that the performances will then not be seen by prospective employers, the real aim of the exercise (a bit like a supermarket's 'loss leaders', sold under the cost price in order to attract customers into the shop). In a major feature film, at the other end of the spectrum, where millions have been spent and profit is the clear motivation, marketing is very much the key to success also. But even heavily subsidised theatres need to show healthy box office returns in the current climate. A theatre putting on an interesting and high quality season – at great cost to the public purse – will not attract further public funds for long if the percentage of seats it manages to fill is, ultimately, low.

However regrettable this may seem there is no getting around the basic principle. The entertainment industry in the UK is a business and you as an actor are part of that business. Acting is, and has to be, a business too.

MARKETING

Modern business is based on marketing, researching and defining a market for a particular item and designing, packaging and presenting a product to meet those specific market conditions. You may not imagine that the concepts used in selling motorcars, for instance, have any application to what you have to do as an actor. But there are certain essential features that apply as much to marketing oneself as to selling a car.

A car, like most products, has features of design and construction that can be measured precisely. A car's horsepower can be scientifically established, as well as the load it is capable of bearing, its consumption of petrol per mile, or how frequently it will need servicing. All these objective factors and many more give the prospective buyer a basis for comparison between one car and another which will influence their eventual choice of which model to buy.

There are also other equally important factors which cannot be quantified. These are questions of quality and are entirely subjective. How a car feels when it is driven; the impression its exterior design gives – whether of sleek power or sturdy roadworthiness; how the interior design registers – whether it is fussy and effete, or understated, or plastic and cheap, or walnut and leather with the air of something valuable and distinguished. All these factors will vary in importance from one customer to another. It is a matter of taste, and taste is not quantifiable. Taste is also dynamic and changes with the passage of time. What was once regarded as elegant and fine can now be seen as ugly and crude.

The actor's situation is different in that no one single part of his product (i.e. himself) can be measured objectively or scientifically. Appreciation of all his qualities is subjective and a matter of taste.

Oddly enough, something of this problem faces many manufacturers. Although their products can in part be quantified objectively, if all the competing products within a certain market have virtually the same technical specifications, and they therefore have to rely on qualitative factors to distinguish them from the competition. Back to the example of the car. In any one category, there are at least four or five cars from different companies that are more or less the same: the same number of doors, seats, the same petrol consumption, acceleration and top speed. In this market each of the competing companies therefore relies on establishing an image for their product which is based on qualitative performance – the way it looks, the way it feels to drive – and individual taste. Naturally this image is not chosen at random. Careful market research indicates what the public wants in these areas from a car.

This is precisely what an actor has to do. In the face of overwhelming and equally talented competition, the actor who will get the job is the one who makes the prospective employer (his market) feel he is someone of quality, that he looks right, that his looks match his ability and that his overall image corresponds with what the prospective employer is in fact looking for. Companies spend huge amounts of money in creating an image and no detail is too small to be considered. The logo on the stationery, the colour of company vans and cars, even the shape and size of business cards: all are carefully calculated. The same must apply to an actor. Everything you do, the paper you write a letter on, the clothes you wear, the way you brush your hair, the language you use, says something about *you*. Every detail has, therefore, to be carefully considered in developing the profile and image you want to create.

Unlike the car manufacturer, however, your image will vary from job interview to job interview. Casting directors and directors are not known for their imagination, so creating an image to match the part (and the circumstances of the production) is an essential ingredient to success. Which is why it is crucial to make sure you find out as much as possible about what each prospective employer actually wants.

ADVERTISING AND PUBLICITY

Of course the major difference between selling a car and selling an actor is that an actor cannot afford the huge advertising and publicity budget that a car manufacturer uses to ensure his product is seen by the people who are likely to go out and buy it.

But once again the general business principle is the same. Somehow or other an actor has to advertise and publicise his product, even on the smallest scale. The first step, and the most basic, is placing a photograph in *The Spotlight* casting directory. Getting an agent who will spread photographs and CVs around the business and send out letters to prospective employers is another means of advertising. Getting into the newspapers with reviews of productions, or news features about a particular project, is another. It all helps to establish or re-establish your name, your presence, your face and your profile.

To take another leaf from the pages of industry, what advertising is done and where (in what media, in what papers or magazines) is not a random choice. Potential markets are carefully researched to establish what advertising will most effectively reach the specific target group. And here an actor can follow the example of normal business practice. An enormous amount of time and trouble has to be put into this area of endeavour.

There are literally hundreds of jobs available to be filled every day. It is a question of finding out where they are and how to get access to them.

Obviously there are limits to the amount of research that an individual can do. Endless telephone calls are prohibitively expensive and may not be all that constructive. But information can be obtained from newspapers and magazines, especially the trade press. In addition many projects are based on books or plays which have been published and can therefore be obtained from the library to see if there are any appropriate parts.

INFORMATION REFERENCE SYSTEM

In Part Three of this book is a basic information reference system, a guide to principal employers throughout the industry. It has been deliberately constructed so it can be added to and revised. The entertainment industry is highly dynamic and changes extremely rapidly, especially in the relatively new world of independent television production – a *very* important source of employment. Companies formed in a partnership can break apart through a clash of personalities, or lose their contract from a crucial commissioning contractor, or make a programme or series that fails badly in the ratings. These are only a few of the many reasons for change.

There will often be changes in the large broadcast television companies, too. A recent report suggested that of the current television franchise holders, there will be only four in ten years' time. The BBC Charter is due to be renewed in 1996 and will undoubtedly be drastically changed, adding to the already enormous alterations that have overtaken the Corporation – especially in drama production – in recent years.

There are almost constant changes in personnel throughout the industry, both promotions and demotions. Producers and directors are hired and fired with surprising rapidity. Senior management positions, like Head of Drama, are also subject to frequent change.

For all these reasons it is important to constantly update the reference system. But you will also come across new companies in all the various media, each of which you should note in the appropriate section. There may well be new media to keep track of as well. At the moment, for instance, there is no production purely for the video market. Videos of films or television programmes are hired or sold, but it is conceivable that, if the video market continues to expand at the current rate, it will be economically viable to produce, say, a drama series (a 'soap') aimed exclusively at the video market and sold only through video outlets.

Also included in the reference section is a list of theatre, film and television directors with some of their credits, with the aim of giving you background to their work and a basis for discussion (see Chapter 9). This should be expanded and kept up to date by adding credits to the work of a particular director, and also adding directors to the list. There is a constant stream of new directors entering all three media.

It is essential to have as much information as possible on the group of individuals and the companies who define your market. Once you have established a basic reference system – whether using the model at the back of this book, or creating one of your own – and made it as comprehensive as possible, you need to decide how best to approach the task of targeting it (of advertising yourself), and suggesting that you are the right person for the part they have in mind.

While the reference system in Part Three will help you sift through and calibrate the information you acquire as well as giving you raw data, Part One of the book ('Employers') aims to help you understand the varying business requirements throughout the different media, and the parts played by the individuals (casting directors, producers, directors etc.) within them.

In fact the entertainment business is vast, a huge canvas of varied activity, and the better you understand the way it works the better you will be able to go about the task of seeking employment. The difficulties of this, and the many aids and organisations offering help, is the subject of Part Two ('Actors').

DOING SOMETHING

All these things, however – research, building up a reference system, understanding the profession in which you work, carefully considering how you want to present yourself and to whom, and working out where your best opportunities lie – are important not only from the point of view of obtaining employment. They have another, more fundamental, importance. They mean you are actually *doing* something.

'An actor acts', but when not employed on a production, when not actually 'acting' (which at the beginning of a career may be most of the time), keeping in touch with what is going on in the industry at large is an important psychological factor.

Being an actor calls for two essential traits that have to become ingrained in the personality: self-motivation and the ability to cope with rejection. The two go hand in hand. Without the ability to, 'Pick yourself up/Dust yourself off/And start all over again . . .' you will not be able to motivate yourself to try and try again.

DEALING WITH REJECTION

However successful you are, you will have been and will continue to be regularly rejected. And this rejection is at a very basic level. When a director turns you down for a role he is rejecting *you* – or so it appears.

It is very difficult to cope with this rejection precisely because there is no distance between you and the thing that is being rejected. If it were something you'd made or written or were trying to sell, 'no thank you' would not be so personal. But when the 'thing' is you, yourself, you cannot help but feel that somehow you are at fault, that what is being rejected is you as a person, not you as an actor, and the rejection is a devastating psychological blow.

The truth, of course, and essential to remember in dealing with the numerous rejections you will receive, is that it is not you as a *person* who is being rejected but you as a *product* – the product you have packaged and created and targeted at the particular employer. In the end what is rejected is this product, something you have made, not you yourself. You must try always to remember that.

Some interviews and auditions are brutal and bruising. The actors are herded in like cattle, looked at and prodded and herded out again. There may be as many as five hundred actors involved. Rejection is swift, with no attempt to soften the blow. But here again what the director is looking for is a particular product and, in the case of a mass audition (usually for commercials or musicals), a product that he will recognise in a matter of seconds.

In a sense it is more difficult to deal with rejection based on a one-to-one interview, in which the director or producer has spent time and trouble telling you about the production and has given you the opportunity to read the script. The more you have been asked about yourself and the more you have revealed then obviously the more hurt you will feel when you do not get the job. But though you may feel personally upset, the truth is that the rejection is no more personal than the casual dismissal at a mass audition. The director is looking for a particular type to fit into a whole cast of characters. The word 'chemistry' is often used in this context. It is the director's job to balance the chemistry of the cast to get the right mixture. He is actually looking at you as a potential part of that mix. He may feel you are a good and strong actor but that your presence in the cast will in some way overbalance the overall impression he is trying to create.

However you deal with it, rejection has to be dealt with. If you allow it to colour and sour your attitude it will affect your ability to get employment and you will have trapped yourself in a vicious circle. If you turn up at an interview with the attitude that you are really wasting your time, or appear surly and sarcastic, you will definitely *not* get the job. An attitude like this will also affect your ability to re-motivate yourself, which is the other psychological trait you need to cultivate.

PERSISTENCE

You will hear from many actors that one of the most soul-destroying aspects of the profession is being out of work for long periods of time, maybe five or six months at a stretch, maybe as long as a year or eighteen months or even more. Even a comparatively successful actor can experience these periods of unemployment. It makes life very difficult. 'An actor acts.' Not acting for month after month not only affects your confidence and belief that you can actually do what is required, but leaves an emptiness and feeling of uselessness which goes beyond questions of professional competence.

The drop-out rate of actors in the profession is high (and highest among women – see Chapter 11). The acting profession is over-crowded, especially between the playing ages of 18 and 35. As actors get older, there are more parts and generally less competition. It may not be a comforting thought for a younger actor, but the number of actors over 80 who can perform competently is very few indeed, and with a comparatively large number of parts to cast they are very much in demand!

Persistence is necessary. In order to fill the void, in order to counter the feeling of uselessness, you have to *do* something. On the creative side it is possible to take lessons and classes to hone skills and develop new ones – improve your singing or learn some special skill like fencing or riding, for example – which will keep you in touch with your talent and professionalism. But if you make an effort every day conscientiously to find work, you will be surprised what benefits that brings, not only by way of getting auditions and inter-views, but just as importantly in making you feel that you have a constructive and positive role to play in advancing your own career.

There are many stories, some apocryphal, some true, of actors (and even people who have never acted in their life before) being approached by a director or casting director on the street, given a screen test and subsequently playing a leading role in a series or feature film. (Zeffirelli was famous for approaching his casting in this way.) Generally speaking, however, an actor's career follows a set pattern. It is like a stone thrown into the still water of a pond. The ripples start small, but gradually get larger and larger, en-compassing an ever greater area. Unlike throwing the stone into the pond, however, not only does it take a hefty shove to get the actor's career started in the first place, but the ripples need to be constantly encouraged in their journey outward. There is abso-lutely no point in waiting for someone to come along and throw the stone in for you, or in expecting the ripples, once started, to travel on by themselves. You have to do these things yourself.

STARTING AGAIN

Most of what has been said above applies to actors at the begin-ning of their careers. But it applies equally to actors who have been in the business for some time and may, indeed, have had some success, but now find themselves in a situation where the offers have dried up. There is no guarantee of consistency of employment for anyone in the theatrical profession. Unlike some countries that honour their actors and where prominent actors are made life members of the national theatre (in Israel, for example, and until very recently in Ireland) thus guaranteeing them a certain social status and income, in the UK an actor's success is judged purely in terms of his last job. Even sparkling careers can come to a premature end or hit a dead patch. There are many different reasons for this but the main one is type-casting, when directors begin to think of an actor in a particular way and for a very limited range of roles, and do not want to make the effort to imagine that he or she is capable of doing anything other than this one type. Eventually, having played a particular character over and over again (sometimes the same part in a series, sometimes different parts but of the same type), the actor becomes totally associated with it. When that character becomes overexposed, or the actor gets older and no longer fits the role he once played, or the fashion for a certain type of character changes, or a long-running series comes to an end, the actor is left high and dry and has virtually to start again from scratch. Trying to convince prospective employers that you can play a different type of role is often as difficult as finding employment in the first place.

Directors work under a great deal of pressure, especially in television and film: in these fields, time is money. The more quickly a production can be mounted and completed the better. In terms of casting this usually means that a director will opt for an actor whom he has seen before in a similar role. Not only does this involve less risk, but it saves time. It is the lazy option, of course, but finding out that an actor who, for instance, has always been thought of as a 'heavy' can also do a light comedy role may come well below a director's many other priorities in putting together a production.

It is for this reason that it is vitally important to try and play as many different sorts of character as possible. In the age of casting by videotape, the more evidence of your versatility that you have the better. Clearly the more types you play, the wider your field of employment.

This is a counsel of perfection, more easily said than done. The business may not allow you such choice. But wherever possible it is worth looking for diversity; perhaps accepting a role you might not normally have considered, purely because it offers you the chance at playing, for instance, a comic part. And make sure, if possible, that the performance is recorded on tape.

Certainly the best way of re-launching a career that has already achieved some success but has subsequently slumped badly is to play a part quite different from the sort of thing you have been known for in the past. Dudley Sutton, for instance, once cast as a 'bovver' boy and later as a Cockney heavy, had a considerable period of unemployment before he was cast in *Lovejoy* as a fusty, bow-tied and rather pedantic antiques dealer. And Gudrun Ure, known once as a lovely young ingénue, re-emerged as the energetic and sprightly grandmother of *Supergran*.

Such opportunities are rare, of course, but a sense of direction, a feeling of what one would like to do, a target to aim for, is important. And indeed if the opportunity does not come through the normal channels, then endeavours should be made to prompt and prod employers by mounting a fringe production of a play which contains an appropriately different and contrasting role to the ones for which you are normally known (see Chapter 10).

Type-casting is not the only reason why careers falter. There are many others. Sometimes a promising start is blighted by a series of productions which simply do not find an audience. Sometimes a series is side-lined by the company that made it, or transmitted late at night or early in the afternoon, or even cancelled altogether due to some coincidence of a real-life event making it unsuitable for transmission. And sometimes it is simply a case of a relatively well-known actor being overlooked by directors and thereby suffering a long sequence of unemployment. All these factors can explain a lack of consistency and all can be corrected, at least partially, by application and energy in re-establishing your name and your profile among prospective employers. It is never too late.

AN ERA OF CHANGE

The point has been made that the entertainment industry is a business and depends, like any other business, on the exigencies of profit and loss, turnover and cash flow. There are obvious exceptions to this rule, areas where it is simply impossible for a company to make a profit and where, therefore, state and regional subsidies make up the shortfall of box-office receipts. Most notable among these are the Royal Shakespeare Company, the National Theatre and the regional repertory companies. This is not entirely due to the profligacy of the companies in mounting productions. Sometimes the totally inappropriate buildings in which it is decided they should work cost so much to run and maintain that this could never be covered by the sale of tickets, even if every performance played to a full house! The window-cleaning bill alone, for a civic edifice of glass and steel designed by an architect more used to buildings used by commercial concerns, can account for ten per cent of box-office receipts.

But of course there are other factors. A regional repertory company has an obligation to provide more than cover productions of West End shows. It has a cultural and educational function within its remit as well as the provision of entertainment. In this country (unlike Germany and France) these cultural and educational responsibilities are not seen as being of great importance and are therefore not generously funded. But for a regional theatre to live on its box-office income, especially if it is to include productions of 'classics', is simply impossible. The value society in general, and a region in particular, puts on its cultural life in relation to theatre is therefore accurately expressed in the amount of funding it is prepared to provide for its repertory theatres.

Considering the number of theatres that used to be supported by box-office takings alone, with no subsidy of any sort, it is perhaps surprising that this is no longer a possibility. But there has been a sharp decline in theatre-going since the turn of the century, and even more so since the end of the Second World War and the rise of television.

Over the last thirty years there is no doubt that the amount of available employment for an actor has shrunk, and this shrinkage is almost entirely due to the growth of television as the prime entertainment medium for most people in the UK.

Historically, this is part of an established pattern: live theatre, which was flourishing at the start of the century, with even the smallest towns in Britain supporting one or more repertory theatres, was dealt a vicious blow by the advent first of silent films and then of talking pictures in the 1930s. Now the cinema in turn is in decline in this country, with only four major studios and twenty large sound stages operating in 1993, and cinema audiences in 1992 effectively at only 6 per cent of the attendance figures for 1946. So while films were responsible for the decline of the live theatre, television has been responsible for the decline of the cinema.

Between 1945 and 1960 there were still large numbers of theatres accommodating touring productions and twice weekly repertory, there was film production at all levels and the development of 'live' television productions. By 1970 theatres and cinemas had closed by the hundred. At the time of writing there is a slight resurgence in the number of film attendances (not enough to be able to finance a film on a British audience alone) but there is no increase in the number of theatres, arts funding is under severe pressure which may well lead to the closure of some subsidised theatres, the remaining film studios are on the brink of extinction and film production is at an all time low, whether with British or American finance.

It might be thought that the huge expansion in television drama production and the entirely new employment prospects offered by television commercials largely replaced the job opportunities lost in film and theatre. Unfortunately, though of course new jobs were created, there was nothing like the number of parts previously cast in theatre and film. Drama is a very small proportion of the output of television and often not its most successful. It is also the single most expensive item to produce. Exactly as theatres economised by producing small-cast plays, so television companies rapidly learnt that they could buy in feature films much more cheaply than they could produce their own large-scale drama, and therefore concentrated on comparatively small-scale productions of situation comedy and soap operas which, fortunately for them, proved to be enormously popular. The costume dramas and classic serials of the

BBC drama department (from *Pride and Prejudice* to *War and Peace*) have almost become a thing of the past. Recent work such as *Scarlet and Black* and *Middlemarch* is dependent on international financing for its production.

The tremendous expansion of soap operas (*Eastenders, Coronation Street, Families, Emmerdale Farm, Take the High Road, Children's Ward* and *The Bill* currently) has been disastrous for employment prospects. Soaps employ very few guest actors. With an average cast of twenty, the current crop therefore only represents 160 jobs (plus perhaps two guests per episode) for what amounts to four and a half hours of television. Situation comedies are equally constrained. Often they employ no more than four or five actors per episode with guest parts restricted to one- or two-line parts.

Obviously television commercials have represented a real expansion in employment but there again the trend is to use actors less and less. Animatronics, animation and computer graphics (including the developing field of 'morphing', i.e. getting a computer to construct a real person from its picture memory) are used increasingly.

The emergence of Channel Four and the development of so-called 'independent' television production companies (a misnomer if ever there was one, since they are all totally dependent on a television franchise holder to broadcast their material) has not improved matters either.

A decision was taken within Channel Four from the beginning, perhaps influenced by its then chairman Richard Attenborough, that the main drama budget should be concentrated not on television drama but on *film* production, with the idea that this would help to relieve the ailing British film industry. While the merits of this decision are debatable, what is not in question is that this had a further effect on the number of acting job opportunities available on television. By necessity the budgets made available to film makers were small by film standards (though not by those of television production) and the films were correspondingly small in scale. The number of parts they offered actors was therefore small too, certainly in comparison to the number that would have been available had the money been spent on studio-based television drama. The budget of a feature film of two hours would produce six hours of television drama. The inception of *Film on Four* also had another effect: it persuaded the BBC, for whatever reason, that it should follow suit. More money from television drama budgets was diverted into film production with the creation of *Screen Two*, and with similar results.

The development of independent television production companies and television franchise holders, who now mainly commission rather than produce programmes, has had another effect on the acting profession. Independent production companies make their profits by delivering a programme to a television franchise holder at a set price. Clearly the more cheaply the programme can be made, the more profit will be involved.

Whenever a budget is under pressure, the most vulnerable elements are squeezed first. The most vulnerable element in drama production is the actor. Though there are minimum rates of pay, salaries above the minimum are liable to be cut to the bone in an attempt to save money. And as competition is fierce, there is always another actor who will play the part for less money.

Overall, employment prospects for an actor in the UK may look fairly gloomy at the moment, but it is possible that things will improve. A change of government or of government policy might increase arts funding and thereby stimulate new productions and re-open some subsidised theatres. It might also bring positive action to revive the British film industry by providing the tax 'shelter' schemes so long advocated by film finance experts. (The Canadian and Australian governments created a huge pool of film production virtually overnight by instituting such measures.) In television, fashions change and the popularity of 'soaps' may decline while the success of drama series like *Inspector Morse* may lead television companies back into the production of comparatively large-scale series. The so-far negative effect of satellite broadcasting, taking advertising revenue away from terrestrial stations and thus further reducing their drama spend, may be reversed. It is possible that given a sufficient income BSkyB would begin to make, or at least commission, its own dedicated drama production. The revival, in the West End theatre, of the musical over the last ten years has certainly had a positive effect on employment prospects as musicals, generally speaking, require large casts.

For the time being, however, it is necessary to deal with an extremely competitive situation. Realism is essential. It is necessary to be aware of the difficulties of the business you are in or are about to join. The purpose of this book is to give you a framework for coping with and overcoming those difficulties by addressing them positively and by understanding precisely what they are.

Part One
Employers

2 The Individuals – Who Does What?

HERE CAN BE a great deal of confusion in an actor's mind about what exactly the people he is writing to or being interviewed by actually do. It is fairly obvious what the director's job is, but how does his function overlap with the responsibilities of a producer or executive producer? Who has the ultimate power? And where does the casting director fit into this power structure? These are not just matters of general and passing interest. In an interview, knowledge of who does what may help you relate more effectively to the people you are facing: in letter writing, it may help you to compose the right letter and send it to the right person. This knowledge may also help you understand how decisions, particularly negative decisions, are reached. Understanding the power structure will help you understand what went wrong if you are subsequently rejected.

The titles given to the various occupations in each of the media are virtually the same: however the jobs these titles represent vary according to whether they are in film and television, theatre, television commercials, or radio, where the jobs carry different responsibilities and different weight.

FILM AND TELEVISION

Executive Producers

The executive producer on a feature film is usually the person at the top, who has found or developed the script, raised the money to finance the film and is in overall control of the whole production. Or, if the film is financed by a major American studio, the executive producer will be the person who controls the project and liaises with the producer and director on the studio's behalf; again, he or she has the final say. In the latter case the production will have a separate producer who will have brought the project to the studio in the first place, but in the former, where the executive producer has raised independent finance to mount the film, a separate producer may be hired to be responsible for the day-to-day running of the film.

To what extent an executive producer controls the decision-making on a project is a matter of individual choice. Some wish to be consulted on every decision, others only on the major ones (like choice of director and leading actors), leaving everything else to their producer and director.

In television the executive producer credited on a production is invariably the Head of Drama for the television company which has commissioned the programme. He or she will therefore be in overall charge of the project and will be consulted on all major issues (choice of director, writers, cast, and budget). The degree to which this power is exercised varies greatly, and sometimes amounts only to a power of veto.

Producers

The producer in film is either the person who created the project and took it to a studio for financing and has subsequently put it into production, or someone hired specifically to control all the production aspects of the film, but under contract just like any other member of the production team. (In the latter case they are called 'line' producers within the profession, though this rarely appears on the credits.)

In the former case the producer will certainly be responsible for decisions on who writes and directs the project and who is cast in the leads (and even, if they are experienced, who the casting director is). A line producer will probably only be partially involved in these decisions, but he or she will certainly choose the production manager who will 'crew' the film, and may influence the choice of director, if a director has not already been appointed.

In television the producer is the person who is in overall charge of the production of the programme and makes the decisions involving choice of writers and director and major technicians like lighting cameraman and production designer, sometimes – though not always – in consultation with the director.

The primary responsibility of the producer in both television and film is control of the budget and seeing that the production is brought in on time. This involves careful overseeing of the day-to-day running of the production, especially during the shooting period when costs can mount rapidly due to overruns. If a film goes over schedule and over budget it may be the director's fault, but it is up to the producer to try and remedy the situation and work out ways to cut corners in order to get back on track.

Directors

The director is the person who is responsible for the 'creative' control of the production – that is, how the script is going to be translated from the written word into the final product. It is his job to conceptualise the writer's work in visual terms, which of course includes deciding which actor's appearance and ability best match his conception of the writer's description of each character, and how each actor will inter-relate with the others (the famous 'chemistry'). It is also his job to see that the actors he has chosen are given an environment in which they can work and to encourage them to produce performances in line with his overall conception of the production, while at the same time giving them the chance to add qualities of their own in the way they perform their roles.

Once the shooting is completed the director must carry this vision through into the editing suite in deciding how the production should be cut together and what should be used and what left out.

In television the producer will be consulted on all these matters and the director will argue his corner if they don't see eye to eye. But generally speaking, since the producer has chosen the director in the first place and has been consulted about major casting, it is most likely that an amicable consensus will be reached on the creative aspects of the programme.

In films things can get a little more heated. Unless the director is of great renown, he will not, for instance, have the right to the final cut of the picture. He will be able to deliver a first or second cut, but the final cut is at the discretion of the executive producer. Obviously a film is in the market place much more than a television programme, dependent for profit on finding an audience. It will be the studio financing the film or the person who has raised the money independently who will know best – or at least feel he knows best – where the market for the film is.

Similarly a director will not have a free hand in casting. Indeed frequently the major roles, contrary to popular belief, have been cast long before the director is hired. The 'stars' are necessary to obtain finance, the director is not. The director's decisions on casting are reduced to supporting roles. If this is the case a casting director, appointed by the executive producer or producer, may also be in place before the director arrives, to help with the early casting of the starring roles.

Casting Directors

Despite their title, casting directors never actually cast anything. Their job is to make suggestions to the producer and/or director, having read the script, and to act as intermediaries between the production companies and the actors, usually through the actor's agents, checking availabilities, taking suggestions for the parts, both by phone and letter, and doing the deals for the contracts of the actors who are finally chosen for the production (though not the stars, whose contracts are handled directly by the producers) both in terms of money and billing.

As the casting director looms so large in the life of an actor, taking on an almost mythic significance, it is worthwhile reviewing the way their profession has developed in the UK over the last thirty years.

The first casting directors in this country were employed only on films. Never numbering more than a dozen (of whom the most famous were Miriam Brickman, Maud Spector, Mary Selway, Irene Lamb, Gerry Walker, Rose Tobias Shaw, Irene Howard, Ronnie Curtis and Tony Arnell) their names can be seen on the credits of countless British films. The term 'casting director' was itself a grade in the ACTT (the film technicians' former trade union) and as work in films was at that time regulated by a 'closed shop' agreement, there were very few new names to contend with.

As the British film industry declined, the British television industry expanded, and the newly franchised television companies in the 1960s, like Associated Rediffusion, Granada, and ABC, decided that they should set up casting departments of their own. These casting departments were needed to deal with not only drama production but also the then large output of what were called 'variety' programmes, i.e. programmes like *Sunday Night at the London Palladium*, which featured 'acts' as well as singers and dancers.

The BBC viewed this development with suspicion and firmly refused to follow suit. Its vast drama production, both on television and radio, as well as its variety shows, were all individually cast by the producer or director of each show (and for some time, to complicate matters further, what are now called directors were first called producers – a term borrowed from theatrical production).

It was not until the mid 1980s, with the introduction of Channel Four and the radical review caused by the introduction of 'independent' television production, that this policy changed. Channel Four was set up as a 'commissioning' or 'publishing' station with no production facilities of its own. All its programming was to be made by third parties. A review of the BBC recommended that a proportion of the BBC's production – for reasons of economy – should similarly be made by 'independents'.

The development of independent producers meant that all the television stations could cut back on their huge resident staffs and farm programming out to independents who could hire staff on a freelance basis. The huge and costly casting departments were quickly reduced, and most of their staff used their redundancy money to set up as freelance casting directors. As this development coincided with the demise of the ACTT and the 'closed shop' under the Thatcherite legislation of the 1982 and 1988 Employment Acts, there was nothing to stop anyone, however inexperienced, setting up in business as a casting director. From the dozen or so working in 1970, the number has now grown to over a hundred working in the London area.

The best of the casting directors are very good at their jobs. They conscientiously go to shows and watch television and film productions, noting actors of merit for future reference. They sift through the letters and photographs that actors send in, and keep up-to-date files. They are aware of the development of many actors' careers and watch their progress with interest, and they go to drama school 'showcase' productions regularly in the search for new talent.

A good casting director will look at a script, get a feel for what the producer and director have in mind, and offer recommendations which will help shape and mould the production – very much in the same way as the production designer will recommend particular locations and designs for the visual aspects of the film. David Puttnam said of his casting director, Patsy Pollock, that she 'brings as much to a film as the producer or the director'.

There is unfortunately a negative side. A casting director has a great deal of power over an actor's career, especially that of a young actor, and some of them can behave in a high-handed and rude fashion, showing little concern for the actor's feelings. A casting director for one of the major television companies, known for her love of cats, was visiting an actress after her performance in the television studio, as were two of her actor friends. One of these actors happened to make a disparaging remark about cats. The casting director turned on him immediately. 'What's your name?' she demanded. The startled actor mumbled his name. 'Well,' the casting director continued, 'you can be sure of one thing; you'll never work for me or this company in your career.'

Similarly, some casting directors take very little trouble to try to make interviews humane, especially interviews for television commercials. Whereas the best casting directors will frequently try to restrain the excesses of a director intent on dismissing actors in seconds, others make no attempt to do anything but get the maximum number of actors seen in the shortest possible time. Neither do they perform any sort of quality control, simply calling in any actor in roughly the right age range and type.

Fortunately, most casting directors are conscientious and hardworking. If they form an opinion that you are right for a particular role they will often go to great lengths to convince the director and/or producer. But it is important to remember that the final decision is not theirs. The casting director merely advises; it is the director/producer who chooses.

Writers

The role of a writer in most film productions is to be heard but not to be seen. Once the script is delivered, a writer's contribution is minimal and he or she will therefore have very little to do with the casting process. In most cases the writer on a film is the equivalent of a draughtsman on a building project: they sketch out what should go where and in what order, but take little part in the actual construction.

In television the situation is very different. Even in the production of 'soaps' the writer is frequently present and consulted on dialogue changes. In a one-off play or screenplay made for television the writer is regarded as a key member of the creative team and will almost certainly be consulted on casting. Sometimes, of course, he or she will have written a role with a specific actor in mind and will say so. Sometimes, the writer will have very strong ideas about who should be cast and these will be taken into account by all concerned. The more *au fait* a writer is with the acting profession, the more he knows about actors and their careers, the more his views will be considered. A writer may by no means be at the centre of the casting process, but he may be an important factor in it. He may even attend casting interviews.

Some writers, through the success of their work, have gone on to become directors and producers of their own material (Dennis Potter and Harold Pinter, for example).

THEATRE

In the theatre the directors (to confuse matters theatre directors used to be called 'producers', and very occasionally the term still persists) traditionally did all their own casting. Theatre directors rarely used casting directors, though in the West End the theatrical managements would usually have an assistant or secretary who tended to do all the 'availabilities' (checking whether actors would be available for the period required), set up meetings or auditions, and generally liaise with agents. In repertory theatres this function usually devolved on to the artistic director's secretary.

More recently, however, some repertory theatres have followed the example set first by Leicester Haymarket and later by the Royal Exchange in Manchester, and have set up their own casting departments (the Royal Exchange, incidentally, was the first to put its casting director on the main board of the theatre). Some other theatres now use freelance casting directors to cast their seasons.

West End theatre managements use casting directors more frequently, as do commercial touring productions, but it is by no means a universal rule. Generally in theatre production a great deal of casting is still done by the director of the play – who in repertory is often also the director of the theatre – and his or her assistant.

The role of theatrical producer in a commercial theatrical management company, producing plays for the West End or for tours or both, is the same in some respects as in film and television. Primarily they control the budget, raise the finance, choose the director and are consulted about all major decisions including the lead casting, but, unlike film and television, the producer will not employ anyone (with the occasional exception of a star actor) before the director has agreed. In the theatre the director is the final arbiter.

The position of the writer in the theatre is ambiguous. Clearly if he is a 'star' writer his collaboration will be sought at every turn including the casting. Indeed Arnold Wesker felt so strongly about the talents of Nicola McAuliffe that he wrote a one-woman show (*Annie Wobbler*) for her which helped launch her career. But less well-known writers may have their influence confined to arguments about dialogue – arguments that they may well find themselves losing.

TELEVISION COMMERCIALS

The roles of producer, director and writer can cross over in television commercials, with one person fulfilling all three roles, or there being at least two producers, one acting for the advertising agency and one for the production company which has been given the job of producing the commercial, with at least two (sometimes more) writers. (There have even been cases, surprisingly considering the money being spent, when there is barely a writer at all, and the dialogue is left to be made up on the spot by actor and director.)

There is also another element in commercial casting decisions: the client, i.e. the manufacturer of the product to be advertised. Often the client is present at auditions. It is quite possible that an interview for a commercial may be in front of a panel of people, including representatives from the advertising agency and the production company, the director and casting director and the client. Alternatively the interview/audition may be videotaped and the decision taken by a committee at a later date.

Commercial casting is rarely a question of an actor's talent or ability but purely of whether his face and appearance fit the overall requirements, the detailed profile that the advertising agency will have developed from its market research. That is why commercial interviews often call in so many actors and why, frequently, the interview itself is very short. If your face doesn't fit, it cannot be made to fit.

The role of casting directors in commercials is therefore very limited. They will, if asked, merely compile a list of the numerous actors who fit the general description and slot them into short interviews throughout the one- or two-day session. But they often include actors they know and indeed some actors (David Firth and James McCarthy, for instance) have become specialists in the field, working in commercial after commercial. If an actor makes an impact in a commercial, particularly with a comic performance, he will frequently be called to commercial interviews though not, of course, for products of the same type. (The manufacturers of Carling Black Label would not want to use an actor already appearing in an advert for Carlsberg.)

RADIO

On radio there is total confusion between the roles of director and producer. All directors on radio used to be called producers, following the example of the theatre. Now sometimes the director of a drama production is called a 'director' and sometimes a 'producer', with apparently little to choose between them. Fortunately for casting purposes the distinction is not important. Whether described as a director or producer, the person with that title does the casting. There are no casting directors on radio.

PRODUCTION ASSISTANTS

There is one job that is virtually the same across all the media: the production assistant. The PA is not usually thought of as being part of the casting process, but often this is a mistake. In certain circumstances a production assistant can be crucial to the development of an actor's career. In television, for instance, a project starts its life in an office with the producer and a production assistant. If you or your agent call in for information, it is most likely that the production assistant will take the call. It is the production assistant who will liaise with the casting director over the script and the interview schedules. And it is the production assistant who will often deal with the actor's worries and concerns during the actual production.

In the selection of actors, therefore, a production assistant can have a very positive input and one that should not be ignored. If a production assistant has worked with and liked an actor on a previous production, or has met an actor socially, or has been impressed by a performance in the theatre or on television, it is quite likely that they will suggest that actor, if there is an appropriate part, right at the beginning of the casting process, at the moment the script first comes in from the writer, and perhaps even earlier if the script is an adaptation of another piece of work. It is the best possible time for an actor's name to be mentioned, at the point when the whole approach to the script is being shaped. Of course, the opposite also applies. If a production assistant does not like an actor, perhaps because they have worked together before and got on badly, then the PA can exert a strong negative influence. Again, right at the seminal point, when the script is first discussed, an 'Oh, not him' can have a devastating impact, just as a positive 'I think she's really excellent' can be very helpful.

The same applies to the other media but perhaps to a slightly lesser extent, because the production assistant on a film or a theatre production may not be taken on until after the casting process has started. But that does not mean that the person who fulfils the PA's role by proxy – usually a secretary or assistant to the producer – in the early days of a production when it is being set up cannot have an equally important impact with his or her views on casting at the crucial first stages.

It cannot be emphasised strongly enough, as has been said already, that it does not pay to make enemies in what is basically a very small business. The secretary you are rude to on the phone because she refuses to give you the information you want may be sitting in a meeting three weeks later when your letter and photograph come up for discussion. The production assistant you fell out with on your last production because you were not given a script on time may be the person who is asked whether you would be a good idea as they've worked with you before.

Not only that. Because the business is so small, word of mouth spreads across the whole spectrum of production very fast. Like it or not, gossip is one of the major occupations of the entertainment industry, and bad news travels at the speed of light.

Don't therefore make the mistake of thinking that the opinion of a junior member of the production team does not count. It does. Most productions are egalitarian. So be very circumspect in all your dealings with production companies and their staff, however junior. This does not mean that you should be servile, merely that you should act with courteousness and consideration. It will pay dividends.

3 The Companies – How They Work

AVING DEALT WITH the individuals who are involved in casting, let us now look at the various companies which employ actors on a regular basis. Understanding how these companies work, how they are financed and run, is essential to understanding employment in the various media.

FEATURE FILMS

The production of a feature film is a major enterprise. Even the cheapest production will involve a budget of over £200,000 and at the top of the scale budgets now regularly exceed $50 million. That is only the negative cost (i.e. the cost of producing the negative) and at least two-and-a-half times that sum will have to be spent in distributing the film to pay for the costs of prints (the copies of the film) and advertising. Raising this kind of finance is far fom easy and there are many different ways for this feat to be accomplished. Even the most successful films may take years of endeavour to get into production. The script of *One Flew Over the Cuckoo's Nest*, for instance, was circulating in London in 1969 – looking for a star to take its central role – before it was finally produced six years later in 1975.

There is a definite hierarchy in film finance. Each major American studio, based in Los Angeles (strangely enough mostly outside the Hollywood district), produces approximately twelve films a year. When a script is accepted by a studio, this means that its producer needs to look no further for his financing. American studios all used to have offices in Britain and pick scripts specifically to be made here with British crews and British actors. Indeed there were British studios – notably Rank and EMI – producing films for an international market. Unfortunately this structure was all swept away with the decline of the film industry, and all that remains of it is the possibility that an American studio will make a picture in the UK either because of its subject matter or because the dollar/sterling exchange rate makes Britain cheaper to work in than the USA. (The *Superman* films for instance, though archetypally American, were all made in English studios, as was the first *Batman* film.)

If the film fails to get studio finance it falls into the 'independent' category (not to be confused with independent television). This means that its producer or executive producer (q.v.) will have to raise the necessary resources himself. Occasionally a studio will offer, say, half the cost in return for the rights to a particular territory (for instance the rights to distribute the film in North America), but the producer still has to find the rest of the money. In Britain currently producers are being offered a percentage of the costs in this way by Channel Four or the BBC in return for the rights to broadcast the film in the UK within twelve months of its 'theatrical' (i.e. cinema) release.

In order to make up the difference, or perhaps to finance the whole film in the absence of such a deal, the producer will have to establish a great patchwork of interlocking contracts to raise the money, each promise of finance dependent on the others. This is the main reason that film financing takes so long. A producer may get all his money in place and then, at the last moment, one of the parties will withdraw bringing down the whole house of cards, unless the other participants are prepared to increase their investment.

The source of this independent finance is varied. The money comes from individuals, companies, even countries. Most of it is channelled through extremely complicated tax arrangements, particularly if the film is going to be made in a country where it is difficult to 'export' local currency.

Whatever the source, however, what is crucial to the producer is to set up a 'package' to present to the various financiers and studios in order to attract them to put up the money. This package will include the script, the rights to the book or play if the script is based on another piece of work, a director and, most crucial of all, one or two major star actors. The difficulty about the latter is that a star actor – especially a major star – will only look at a script if it is offered on a 'pay or play' basis, meaning that if he accepts the offer, he will either play the role – or be paid if the package collapses. In effect this means that once the producer has made the offer to the agent and sent a script, and the actor has accepted, then a contract exists in law, even though the agreement may only be verbal. (Such a contract was recently upheld against Kim Basinger when she withdrew from *Boxing Helena*.) These arrangements imply that the producer has got his finance, though often the finance is dependent on the producer finding a star. Producers therefore contrive to attach star actors to their scripts for the purposes of getting finance, sometimes without the star being aware of or ever having seen the script. This web of mystery and intrigue further complicates matters and further delays the eventual production.

So how do all the enormous difficulties facing the would-be producer of a feature film affect employment prospects for actors in general? It should be evident that the difficulties of getting money to make a film make the chances of leading parts going to non-'star' actors very small. The old studio system, both in England and America, allowed the development of young up-and-coming actors through feature parts into films designed specifically to test them as star material, but so few films are now made that the studios are unwilling to risk any of their product in the cause of developing a new star. There are exceptions of course, mostly when, due to the nature of the part, an unknown is essential (Amanda Donohoe in *Castaway* and Christopher Atkins in the 1980 remake of *Blue Lagoon*) but they are rare.

Films financed with smaller budgets in the UK, usually through the BBC or Channel Four, do not have this constraint and although they often cast well-known actors (Daniel Day Lewis – much less well known in 1985 than now – and Gordon Warnecke in *My Beautiful Laundrette*, and Antony Higgins in *The Draughtsman's Contract*) these are not heavyweight stars. Pictures financed in this way have usually been pre-sold – sold before the production begins – to television distribution and the money is therefore not at risk.

But though the leading parts in films may be too much for non-'stars' to hope for, certainly the featured parts are as available in films as they are in television. The casting director is the key figure here, especially if the film director is an American or someone not familiar with British actors. Many of the older film casting directors developed a stable of actors whom they would regularly line up to be interviewed for key roles in American productions. Now more casting directors are working in the field, things are much more open and if you have impressed one with your performances you may well find yourself in line for an interview.

A few years ago it was possible to contemplate making a career in films. In the British film industry in the fifties and sixties there was what could almost be described as a repertory company of actors (Richard Attenborough, Victor Maddern, Lionel Jeffries, Bryan Forbes, Gerard Sim, Ralph Michael, Bernard Lee) working exclusively in films – a second company worked in the *Carry On* films. Some used it as a basis for producing and directing; others fell on hard times when the film industry went into terminal decline, even believing it a mistake to contemplate going into television (Lionel Jeffries and Gerard Sim were both determined not to take television roles). Others found experience in films led to better parts and eventually to stardom. (Burt Reynolds and Donald Sutherland both initially worked in England in very small parts, and Michael Caine made 35 films in minor roles before he starred in *Alfie*, the film that, with *Zulu*, changed his career.)

But today it is simply not realistic to think of making a career solely in films in the UK. There just aren't enough of them. In 1992, for instance, there were only seventeen productions with significant budgets and only eleven with budgets of less than £2 million. If you feel you want to orientate your career in this area then you should certainly gather all the information you can on likely productions. But if your ultimate goal is to become a film star, whereas working exclusively in films certainly used to be the best way of going about it, today such a course of action is not possible.

TELEVISION

The television industry in the UK has changed more dramatically in the last ten years than at any other time since ITV was established in the fifties. The creation of Channel Four initially and the recent changes in its financing (including allowing it to sell its own 'air-time'); the ITV contractors' franchise 'auction' resulting in the biggest upheaval in the independent sector since the system began (including the loss of the biggest ITV company, Thames Television); the subsequent decision of the government to allow mergers and takeovers among licence holders (resulting within a week in the merger of Carlton and Central Television); and the amalgamation of BSB and Sky to form BSkyB, resulting in the beginnings of profit for satellite television transmissions after a long period of considerable loss; all have brought about major change. The next few years will see further change, a reduction in the number of franchise holders as a result of mergers (such as the LWT – Yorkshire take-over battle in early 1994) and, of course, the effects of the new BBC Charter to be introduced in 1996. Technical change is likely to happen too, with digital communications allowing an expansion of the number of frequencies available to television transmission.

At present, however, British television can be divided into seven major elements: BBC; ITV regional franchise holders; Channel Four; satellite television (which here includes cable); and the 'independent' television production companies commissioned by all broadcasters actually to make programmes, in addition to their own in-house production. The sixth element is the production of television commericals; the seventh is the as-yet undeveloped Fifth Channel and other future projects.

BBC

The BBC is a vast organisation producing programmes on everything from aardvarks to zymurgy, but for the purposes of this book only one part of its operation is of interest: the production of drama. It is important to remember that though drama – plays, films, serials, series and situation comedies – is a high-profile activity receiving a lot of publicity, it actually represents only a small part of the work the BBC undertakes overall and an even smaller part of what it transmits.

The production of drama is the responsibility mainly of two departments within the BBC: Light Entertainment and Comedy (headed at the time of writing by James Moir) and Drama Group (headed by Charles Denton). In the Light Entertainment and Comedy department the Head of Comedy (currently Martin Fisher) is directly responsible for the production of situation comedies and various comedy programmes in different formats. The Drama Group, on the other hand, is sub-divided into Drama Series, Drama Serials, Screen One and Screen Two, each with its own head of production. In all these departments production is divided into internally produced programmes and programmes commissioned from 'independent' television production companies who are given a set price (which sometimes includes the use of BBC facilities, i.e. studios, equipment and construction) to deliver the finished product.

These are the main sources of television employment for an actor at the BBC, but by no means the only departments there which use actors regularly. Children's Programmes, Drama Documentaries, and Arts and Features all produce programmes that feature actors in various capacities from time to time. *Crime Watch*, for instance, is a big employer in its reconstruction of crimes. Schools Broadcasting also has a large drama output (and has a special contract) as do some regular non-drama series like *Timewatch*. Even religious broadcasting has been known to produce drama.

The Open University uses the BBC as its prime source of programming. Within its curriculum some of the set texts are often dramatised or read, and production of this work is controlled from Milton Keynes, the headquarters of the OU. Again there is a special contract under which they operate, which allows transmissions over a much longer period than is normal elsewhere. This means, of course, that the life of a production is extended and the OU only undertakes new productions when it is absolutely necessary, which effectively limits their output.

There is a further complication in the BBC structure – the

regions. Some drama productions will originate from outside London. These will either be within the confines of one of the drama departments already mentioned (for instance *Howard's Way* was a BBC project made in Birmingham under the control of Drama Series in London, but set on the South Coast of England) or entirely outside it. BBC Birmingham and BBC Glasgow each has its own budget for drama and its own Head of Drama – BBC Glasgow also has its own comedy department. They take their own production decisions and are not reliant on London: they do depend, however, on the central organisation for a transmission 'slot' if the programmes are to be networked, i.e shown across the UK rather than just in the regional transmission slots available in off-peak times.

In all departments the decision as to what programme is to be made rests firstly with the head of the department in which it is to be produced. Programme ideas will be submitted from various sources – producers, writers and agents. Once the head of department has decided what he or she regards as suitable, this will then be presented to an 'offers' meeting at which the other departmental heads and the controller of the channel (either BBC1 or BBC2) decide what is actually going to be made. Only after this meeting will contracts be issued and a commitment entered into with the various creative elements of the proposed programme.

The producers then assigned to the programme, or already attached to it, whether staff or independent, will be responsible for choosing its writer(s) – if it does not already have one – and its director and casting director. On a one-off film in the Screen One or Two slot, the director will be of prime concern and a casting director will be appointed only with his approval. On the other hand, in the production of a drama series (like *Casualty*) or drama serial (like *Eastenders*), the casting director will be dealing with several episodes and will be in place before the directors, of which there will be several, arrive.

On situation comedies the producer frequently directs the programme himself and usually appoints a casting director for the whole series.

Most drama production within the BBC structure is now carried out by independent television companies though, to be frank, you would never know it. Some 'independent' production is more independent than others. Though the credits of the programme could read 'produced by The Working Actor Productions for the BBC', the programme may have used BBC contracts and BBC facilities. Other independent producers use the independent contract and may even make programmes in external studios, some owned by ITV companies.

In Part Three of this book the BBC structure is laid out, showing the principal departments and the current head of each. The BBC is, without doubt, the biggest single employer of actors in the UK. It is obvious, therefore, that keeping up to date with its plans for productions is essential. But outside the main drama departments there are also a lot of jobs being cast every day, usually on budgets so small as to preclude the employment of a casting director. The best source of information for these is watching television. Don't confine yourself to watching and noting the independent companies that are making mainstream programming. Watch the television in the morning and the afternoon and late at night. Note the jobs available in schools programmes and in the other transmissions that go out at all sorts of odd hours. Take the producer's and director's name and add them to the reference system at the back of this book.

There is one other oddity to be noted about the BBC: the booker. Before the days of independent production, when the BBC still produced all its own programmes, all actors were 'booked', i.e. given contracts, by a 'bookings assistant' or booker. Bookers now deal only with productions which are being made under the BBC contract, which nevertheless still represents a large proportion of their output.

The BBC booking system is very formal and regimented. An index is kept of all artistes who have ever worked for the corporation and the fee offered by the booker will be rigidly based on that. In order to get an increase in this offer you or your agent will have to prove to the booker that your position in the business has improved considerably since your last employment with the BBC, or that the part under offer is very much bigger than the last part you played for them. If you have never worked for the BBC before you will be offered a little above the minimum unless you can prove you have had earnings well above the minimum for other television companies.

Because it is the sole responsibility of the booker to issue art-istes' contracts, an offer made by any other member of the BBC staff, like the producer or director, is not legally valid until it is repeated by a booker. Once the booker has made an offer, though only verbally, that represents a binding legal contract if the offer is then accepted by the actor or his agent. To illustrate this, a few years ago an actor received an offer to take part in a one-off play. He had not met the director or producer or anyone else in connec-tion with the programe, nor did he know them from any previous work. Delighted to receive the offer, however, he accepted it through his agent. The deal was done. An hour later the booker phoned back to say that the director had made a mistake and asked her to book the wrong actor. The booker made no attempt to withdraw the offer, though, knowing she was legally bound by it, and the actor received the fee that had been agreed, even though he did not appear in the programme.

Independent Television Contractors

The odd thing about a commercial television contractor holding a franchise to broadcast to one of the ITV regions is that, unlike almost any other company, the less product it makes, the greater will be its profits. A television company's revenues come from sell-ing 'air-time' for commercials – the time available per hour regulated by the Independent Television Commission. This air-time is auctioned to the highest bidder. The revenue is collected and used to run the company and make, commission and buy pro-grammes, covering everything from local news to sports events and feature films and American series. Clearly the less money the com-pany can spend while still maintaining its service to the consumer, maintaining its audience share and not falling foul of ITC quality thresholds, the greater will be its profits.

The most expensive type of programme to make is drama; the cheapest, a quiz show. Situation comedies are the cheapest form of drama, having a small cast and usually a limited standing set. They can also be enormously popular, thereby increasing the price an advertiser will pay to have his commerical shown before or during the programme. Quiz shows are also very popular. Serious drama, one-off plays and plays dealing with serious social issues (like the sort of plays done in the *Armchair Theatre* seasons) are not popular and have virtually disappeared from the commercial television output.

Major drama series (like *Inspector Morse*, the Ruth Rendell *Wexford* series and *Taggart*) are extremely expensive and could not recoup their cost solely from air-time sales. Fortunately they are widely sold abroad, and are sometimes even produced in co-production with a foreign television station. Drama series (the 'soaps') are not of the same order of expense and are enormously popular, which accounts for their prevalence on ITV.

The 1991 franchise auction awarded fifteen regional franchises to Granada, London Weekend, Carlton, Meridian, Yorkshire, Tyne Tees, Central, HTV, Ulster, Channel Islands (the smallest), Anglia, Border, Grampian, Scottish Television and West Country. There is also a franchise to broadcast across the whole network from 6.00 a.m. to 9.25 a.m., but GMTV produces no drama for it.

At the time of writing the government has decided it will allow franchise holders to merge and Carlton and Central have announced their intention to do so. Granada has taken over LWT. The effect on drama production of this change will probably be minimal.

In terms of drama production Granada, LWT, Carlton, Yorkshire and Central produce most, with Meridian, Anglia, Scottish and HTV producing some but on a much more limited scale. As with the BBC, much of the production is now farmed out to independent production companies, but to a far greater extent since the franchise holders are not burdened with the public service broadcasting functions that are dealt with in-house at the BBC. Carlton, Meridian and West Country are what is known as 'publisher only' broadcasters, which means they commission all of their programmes from independents, exactly like Channel 4.

This change, from all major drama production being produced in-house by the contractors themselves in their own studios with their own permanent staff, to the majority being made at least notionally externally (notionally because often the old in-house producers have merely set up a production company to make the programme, but still use all the contractor's facilities), has meant a considerable cost saving for the contractors. Instead of having to employ a large technical staff on a permanent basis, the contractor offers a set price to the independent company commissioned to make the programme, which in turn hires freelance staff as and when required.

This has also had an effect on the casting departments. Ten years ago the major contractors all had casting departments with three and sometimes four casting directors. Now a company like LWT only has one and some, like Meridian and Scottish, have no casting department at all. Casting for drama series and films is all done by the freelance casting director hired by the independent production company. The work of the casting department in most television contractors has now diminished into booking artistes for quiz shows and personal appearances.

The latest franchise round also produced some anomalies that might lead to confusion. The *Minder* series, for instance, was originally made by Thames Television. Thames created its own independent television company, Euston Films, which then produced *Minder* for Thames. When Thames lost its franchise in 1991, Euston Films was commissioned by Central Television to make *Minder* for them instead. *The Bill* had similarly to be transferred into the independent sector when Thames lost its franchise.

The 1990 Broadcasting Act which established the principle of the franchise 'auction' meant that each independent television contractor had to pay the Exchequer a large sum of money each year in return for its franchise (with the exception of Central, whose bid was unopposed and which therefore made a ridiculously low offer). Many of the contractors are now paying millions of pounds a year for the privilege of broadcasting, further reducing their margins. This is not good for drama production. In Australia, where a similar system was introduced, the results on drama production were catastrophic. The easiest way for a television company to save money is to axe a major drama series, and with it fifty or sixty acting jobs. The next few years is definitely going to see a contraction of the variety and scale of drama seen on ITV.

Under the heading of commercial television, since it is financed by selling air-time, SC4 should be mentioned, particularly as a matter of interest to Welsh-speaking actors. SC4 is a joint venture between the BBC and Channel Four to provide Welsh language broadcasting. It does produce some drama in Welsh and is therefore, in common with HTV, an employer of Welsh-speaking actors. As this is such a speciality, it will certainly pay any Welsh-speaker to keep in touch with the output of this company both in drama and more general areas.

Channel Four

Apart from continuity announcements, Channel Four does not produce any of its own programming whatsoever. The sole function of its commissioning editors is to buy in foreign programming and commission programmes suggested to it by independent television companies on a whole range of subjects from sport (like Italian football) to gardening, including drama and situation comedies. Unlike the ITV companies, it has a special responsibility to produce programmes for ethnic minorities and minority groups.

The drama output of Channel Four is small in terms of employment. Its biggest commissions are for the *Film on Four* series. Apart from this it commissions some situation comedies, usually with an ethnic content (e.g. *Desmond's*), and contributes to the cost of major international co-productions (*Traffik*), getting in return for its contribution the right to transmit the programme in the UK.

As all its programming is made by independents, Channel Four has no casting department, no studios, and no technicians (other than those used for continuity and engineering). All Channel Four programmes will be cast by the freelance casting director hired by the independent television company holding the commission.

Satellite and Cable

There is very little drama production on satellite or cable television and that is likely to remain the case for some time. Cable, which mostly relays satellite programming via a cable rather than an aerial dish, is the same. Unlike ITV, satellite television, which effectively means BSkyB, is not solely dependent on advertising revenues. It is a subscription service and charges subscribers different amounts for different services, just as the cable operators charge for each station they make available – such as Sport, Movie

Channel or UK Gold. At the moment, because of enormous start-up costs, lack of subscribers and the reluctance of advertisers to re-direct advertising spend away from guaranteed audiences on ITV, BSkyB is a long way from being able to afford the luxury of its own drama production.

But there is a definite increase in the number of people subscribing to satellite, and the day will eventually come, probably sooner rather than later, when it can afford its own drama. When that day does come, it is likely that satellite will follow example of ITV and opt for commissioning independent companies to meet its requirements.

Independent Television Production Companies

The first independent television companies were set up by the main television franchise holders to make programmes for the ITV network and were hardly independent at all. They were mostly created for financing and tax reasons and were wholly controlled by the management of the television contractor that owned them.

It was the arrival of Channel Four on 1 November 1982 that really created a truly 'independent' sector for production companies. Literally hundreds of independents were set up overnight by former producers, directors, editors and production assistants in the hope of 'pitching' an idea to Channel Four that would be picked up by one of their commissioning editors. ITV contractors also began to see the advantages of farming out their programming, and the BBC were in turn obliged by the government to commission 25 per cent of their output from independents.

The impact of these three related events created an independent production industry almost overnight. There is now a bewildering number of companies, with new ones formed every day. Some are extremely large, providing a wide range of programmes to the various commissioning broadcasters (BBC, Channel Four and ITV), and backed up by a major ITV company. For others the reverse process was true; SelecTV was an independent production company before becoming part of a consortium which won the Meridian franchise. There are other large companies with no such backing: Noel Gay Television, Cinema Verity, Warner Sisters and

Talkback among them. But most independents are small, sometimes one-man, businesses and dependent on one commission from one broadcaster. Frequently if the commission is withdrawn the company will find itself out of business. As a general rule the smaller companies work in the area of documentaries, factual programmes and political analysis, leaving the larger companies to make the more expensive drama productions.

It is difficult to sift through this mass of companies to determine which are likely to employ actors. Though some may not be involved in drama they may still require actors as announcers, for voice-overs or in many other ways. A list of principal independent companies is given in Part Three, but this, more than any other field, will need to be constantly updated. Whenever you are watching television be sure to note down any production company that has used an actor in no matter how small a capacity. The company may be listed in the reference system already, but if it is not then it should be investigated further. Production companies may have been formed by people you have worked with in the past or got on well with, which will give you a good point of contact, so try to find out who the directors of a company are. In addition some of the bigger companies may be prepared to give you information about their future plans before they get to the stage of appointing a casting director.

Don't be surprised if the company is not particularly co-operative, however. They may be chary of announcing their plans before actually getting the commission signed and sealed, only wanting to go public when things are definite – and in television that can mean a great deal of negotiating. Television executives are notoriously unreliable and often change their minds at the last minute, or even after the last minute. (A series based on the life of Clementine Churchill was cancelled by Thames Television after well over a quarter of a million pounds had been spent on it.)

Besides casting there is another good reason to keep track of independent companies. They are the conduit you will need if you have an idea for a programme yourself or if you are trying to get your one-man show or fringe production on to television.

Independent production companies make their money from commissions from the broadcasters. They are therefore constantly on the look-out for ideas to 'pitch' to the broadcasters. The bigger companies will employ executives whose job is specifically to search for such ideas, reasoning that the more programmes the company makes, the bigger its profit will be. An idea for a programme, whether drama, documentary, feature or quiz show, is likely to get a better reception from an independent company than from a broadcaster.

If you have any sort of idea it should be well presented, neatly typed, and the idea should be clear from a couple of written pages. If the idea is in fact a script it might be better to send in a précis than the whole script, at least to start with. If you are trying to get a fringe production or one-man show on to television, then a synopsis and a set of the reviews will be essential. From your notes on watching television you will get a fair idea of what independent companies produce what sort of programme. Most have some speciality or other. Diverse Productions, for instance, tends to specialise in arts features production, while Warner Sisters likes drama connected to women's issues. Be sure therefore to send your project to an appropriate company.

The chances of your having an idea for a major drama series accepted are slim. The amount of money involved will mean television contractors will only commission such a series from an independent with a good track record, and they in turn will be looking for star writers, directors and actors to present as part of their 'package'. But Channel Four's requirements mean that there are programme ideas for short programmes – fitting into five- and ten-minute slots – that might be accepted.

This is not to say you should immediately sit down and work up ideas for television programmes. Don't forget there are large numbers of professional producers doing just that already. But if, in the course of your work, something occurs to you, you are certainly better placed that an ordinary member of the public to do something about it. You may like to involve a television director or a producer you have worked with, who could help you present the idea, with the possibility that their name may provide additional 'clout'.

In fact, the relationship between independent production companies and actors has developed in a similar way to film production in the early days of Hollywood. Then, as stars evolved through the system they gradually became producers themselves, finding scripts and suggesting them to the studios, very much in the same way as some actors are now setting up production companies and suggesting projects to the television contractors and the BBC. (Lesley Grantham with *Paradise Club* and Jimmy Nail with *Spender* are two notable examples.)

The Future

In 1992, the Independent Television Commission invited applications to create a Fifth Channel to begin transmission in 1994 on a frequency previously used to tune video recorders to television input. The two bids that they received were deemed inappropriate, largely because the commission felt neither bidder had the financial resources to meet the huge cost of adapting all domestic video recorders to operating on a different wavelength. The creation of the Fifth Channel was, therefore, temporarily shelved.

Undoubtedly, however, there will eventually be a Fifth Channel. In the current political climate there is certainly no reason to believe this would be funded other than by advertising revenue and, equally certainly, it will follow the Channel Four mould and operate on a national (rather than a regional) basis and with a commissioning system for programmes, rather than having its own production facilities.

Whenever the Fifth Channel does come into operation it will certainly further expand the independent production sector. It is unlikely, however, that in its first years of operation it will significantly increase the amount of drama production, as the start-up cost of changing the frequency of video recorders will be huge.

The development of digitally encoded transmission systems, currently being tested, may provide a way of transmitting extra channels on already crowded wavebands, but as yet there are no firm plans for this. (This development may also provide possibilities for genuine 'inter-active' television.)

In recent years another major development in the entertainment industry has been the dramatic expansion of video shops hiring out and selling pre-recorded videos. The growth of this business has been extraordinary: from rentals of £300 million in 1985, and 'sell-throughs' of £50 million, in 1991 £540 million was spent on rentals and £444 million on sales.

Though a great deal of this business has been concentrated on releases of feature films, popular television programmes have also been stocked and some (like *Fawlty Towers*) have been enormously successful. It is conceivable, if the trend continues, that a drama production could be financed out of the rental and sales of a video without prior theatrical release or transmission, especially if the tape included advertisements or had commercial sponsorship.

If this did occur, it would once again be the independent production sector, which already has all the necessary expertise, which would make such a drama once the financing was secured.

TELEVISION COMMERCIALS

The number of television commercials being made at any one time is a good indicator of the nation's economic health. In a recession advertising budgets are pared back. Rather than not advertise at all, advertisers prefer to use their budgets to repeat existing commercials as opposed to going to the expense of making new ones. When times are more expansive and revenues are increasing, companies spend more on advertising and commercials become obsolete more quickly. The number of new commercials on television at any one time is therefore a good guide to how the economy is doing and to the level of confidence of the many companies who use television commercials as a means of publicising their products.

In the making of a television commercial there are three companies involved: the company manufacturing the product (the 'client'), the advertising agency, and the film production company. The advertising agency negotiates a budget with the client and is paid a percentage of the budget in return for its services. If part of the campaign involves a television commercial, the agency will then hire a specialist film production company which will be paid a set price for delivering the commercial – or series of commercials – as required.

The making of a television commercial is probably one of the most specialised aspects of the whole entertainment industry.

Using the techniques of feature film or video and often plagiarising concepts from mainstream production (pastiches and send-ups of popular films and television shows), a 15-, 30- or 45-second commercial has to convey a precise and carefully researched message. Before the camera starts to roll an enormous amount of market research has been carried out to establish the profile of the people at which the product is aimed, and everything in the commercial will be geared to that target audience and what it is perceived to want. The script – perhaps no more than fifteen words long – will have been written and re-written to conform to these exact specifications: the design and choice of everything in vision will be similarly meticulous. And of course the actors will be scrutinised and eventually selected with just as much precision.

Almost without exception television commercials are cast by casting directors – indeed, they provide a large percentage of casting directors' income. Again almost without exception a great many actors will be seen so that the director can try to get an exact match for the 'brief' given to him by the advertising agency. Unlike other interviews it is probable that you will be called in, not because of your previous experience, but because, quite simply, you look right; i.e. your photograph in *Spotlight* looks right. That does not mean you will not be required to show considerable talent. Some commercials, particularly those with a comic theme, require a great deal of concentrated energy and an ability to establish an instant rapport with an audience, through the medium of the camera lens. This is the reason that most auditions/interviews for commercials are now shot on video. The director is not looking at you but at how you can interact with the camera. It is also a means of checking the casting with the advertising agency and client, who are usually consulted before any final decision is made.

Though an advertiser will not want an actor who has been in a commercial advertising a rival product, experience in commercials is often regarded as an advantage, showing that an actor is able to communicate effectively in a short space of time and get the message across. If the commercial is too successful, however, the actor may become heavily associated with one particular product and will find resistance to employing him in other ads.

At the beginning of commercial television, acting in commercials was very much looked down upon by 'serious' actors and employers, and for a star actor to turn up in a commercial was largely regarded as evidence of desperation and an admission of failure. It was felt that the sort of familiarity that the constant and intense exposure that a commercial gives would breed contempt and make it impossible, ever again, for the actor to be cast in a 'proper' part on television or in the theatre. This meant that for the first ten to fifteen years of commercial broadcasting in this country the actors appearing were in effect an under-class. There was also a very careful stricture by the IBA as it then was against transmitting commercials during programmes in which the same actors appeared.

This attitude was slow to change. The appearance of several star actors (who were also paid large sums of money) began to remove the stigma that was associated with commercials. Now it seems that an extremely lucrative commercial contract, often running to six-figure sums, has become an accepted norm in a successful actor's career, and is part of the icing on the cake. The contract is usually exclusive, tying the actor to making commercials for one particular product for a set period of time, but the scale of compensation reflects this inconvenience. Mel Smith for British Telecom shares, Leonard Rossiter and Joan Collins for Cinzano, George Cole for the Leicester Building Society, Larry Hagman and Patricia Hodge for British Gas, Denis Waterman for Scottish Widows Amicable Society, Tom Conti and Nigel Hawthorn for Vauxhall, Dudley Moore for Tesco and Robert Lindsay for Mercury mobile phones are among an ever-growing list. None apparently feels that their participation involves any loss of prestige.

The attitude to familiarity has changed too. Whereas once frequent appearance on television was seen as a disadvantage, now those actors whose faces were first seen by the wider public (and, more importantly, by the casting community) in television commercials are more likely to be cast in television in general. This may be a reflection of the increasing sophistication of commercials where the dramatic or comedic situations are more and more subtle and require an increasing level of performance from their actors. Whatever the reason, no stigma is any longer attached to commercials today, and experience in them can have a very positive effect on an actor's career. It also has to be said that the financial rewards of a relatively small campaign can be worthwhile and even, for an extensive campaign involving a series of commercials, substantial.

There is one further area of commercial activity that has to be touched on: the 'voice-over'. Most commercials are either narrated or introduced by the voice of an actor who is not one of those on screen. It is felt this gives the shortness of the film a perspective and depth.

Like everything else about the commercial, a great deal of thought goes into what sort of voice is to be used; gruff and working-class, soft and velvety, upper-class and comic. The voice-over is added to the commercial in a special studio once the film or video element is complete. The 'voice' is cast, just as the performers in the film have been, by a casting director, though sometimes the film production company will know exactly who they want and book a performer direct.

As voice-over work is very lucrative (repeat fees on even a comparatively small campaign can amount to at least £1000, and on a major series to well over £10,000 for thirty minutes' work in a Soho studio) there are a lot of actors who would like to get into this field. There are voice-over agencies (see Chapter 8) specialising in the provision of voice-overs. But unless you have a particularly distinctive voice it is, to be honest, extremely unlikely you will break into what is a very esoteric world. Voice-over work is highly specialised and dominated by either star actors or virtually unknown performers who have made this their speciality. Both have become expert in delivering exactly what is required in a minimum amount of time.

Like any other production a television commercial can be very successful and appeal to the public or can be a total failure and intensely disliked. Among the former are the Strand Cigarette commercial, 'You're never alone with a Strand,' (which though incredibly popular with viewers did not increase the sale of Strand cigarettes because it associated them with loneliness and isolation), the Volkswagen commercial showing the car dropping to the ground and, more recently, the series of commercials for Gold Blend coffee and the Yellow Pages commercial that made J. R.

Hartley a household name. Nowadays these successes can have a dramatic impact on an actor's career. Of course there is nothing an actor can do to influence a commercial's success, but it is certainly an avenue for career advancement that was not available some years ago.

NON-BROADCAST TELEVISION

With the development of comparatively cheap professional video cameras and the corresponding availability of VHS recorders there has been an expansion in the use of video in industry and commerce. Once only the largest companies could afford the expense of a film crew to record aspects of their work for promotional or training purposes: now there are many production companies specialising in producing video for industry, either as an aid to training or as an exhortation to success or to establish in their staff a sense of corporate identity and loyalty. Some big organisations (such as Barclays Bank and the DSS) have even set up in-house video production with their own staff and extensive video editing suites, believing in the efficacy of video training.

The standard of non-broadcast video varies tremendously as does its subject matter. Sometimes it involves no actors at all, showing only company activities and company employees; at other times it can include top-class performers (like a series produced by, written by and starring John Cleese) in quite complex situations intended to train employees in customer relations.

To some extent this activity is also subject to recessionary economic pressures as it is something a company can easily cut if times are hard. But against this some of the training programmes instituted on video have been so successful in saving the company money or in eradicating mistakes that they have been continued come what may.

Several directors and producers with broadcast television experience have set up companies to exploit the industrial video market with varying degrees of success. There are certainly one or two well-established companies in the field.

Non-broadcast television is definitely an avenue that should be explored and one where most agents will have little expertise, so it is an area which an actor can profitably explore by himself. The work is not particularly well paid but it is a valuable stop-gap. Often to save costs the companies do not use casting directors, so it can be difficult to find out who is doing what. One possible approach is to ring some of the bigger companies and find out from them if they use industrial videos and, if so, who produces them. In this way it is possible to build up a list of such companies who can be called regularly. It is likely that if you are used once in such a production you will be used again.

Another benefit of this sort of work is that it does give you experience in front of the camera in a relaxed and fairly unpressured environment. It gives you an opportunity to adjust your performance knowing that the result is not going to be seen by all and sundry. If you feel your efforts warrant it, the company can often be prevailed upon to give you a copy of the tape, so if you have not been on television you will at least have something to satisfy casting directors' seemingly insatiable desire to see something on video.

RADIO

Effectively there is only one source of employment for actors in radio in the UK and that is the BBC. Some independent radio stations have experimented with 'soap' dramas but with little success. It is possible that they may do so again and that should obviously be looked out for, but at the moment the BBC stands alone.

BBC Radio works in very much the same way as television. It has a drama and a comedy department, both producing programmes which employ actors, in one-off plays, series and serials, and in situation comedies and 'sketch' shows. Its features departments and documentaries also use actors' voices from time to time. There are also specialist slots for which books and stories are read (*A Book at Bedtime, Morning Story*).

Again like television, BBC Radio has a regional structure, and plays, serials and series are all produced in various regions. The

BBC Radio Repertory Company is based in London. It employs actors on a yearly contract to 'play as cast', playing roles across the whole spectrum of drama production, but usually not in the leading roles.

Radio frequently uses the same actor over and over again even to such an extent that there are radio 'stars' billed above the title in the *Radio Times* but not known to the same extent elsewhere. Though the work is not enormously well paid, it does not require a script to be learnt and can be done comparatively quickly and is therefore very popular with actors. As recording is usually done during the day it is also the sort of work that can be combined with, say, a run in the theatre or a break in filming for a television series. Though the basic salary is not large, if the contract is for a number of episodes or is repeated (or relayed on World Service), the money can mount up.

Though there are radio productions that use actors outside the main drama orbit, especially in the regions, an attractive aspect of radio drama is that the majority of productions are cast by a small handful of producers (or directors, whatever they happen to be calling themselves), whose names can be obtained from the *Radio Times*. Each individual producer casts his or her own project, which effectively means that the job of checking availabilities devolves on to the production assistant. Similiarly the production assistant will deal with enquiries for information on future productions.

If you are particularly keen to get into radio drama, it may be worth making up an audition tape to send in with a brief recording of yourself reading something appropriate. Another way of gaining entry into this rather esoteric world is by suggesting a story or book to one of the producers of the programmes that use such material. It may be that you would also suggest that you abridge the work – abridging would be inevitable – yourself. Here again a taped extract might be helpful.

One source of employment that independent commercial radio offers which the BBC does not is radio commercials. Though these tend to be dominated by established star voices, usually the same voices used on television commercials, there are some exceptions to this rule. A tape of your voice reading an advertisement from a paper could be an effective means to sell your voice to a casting director looking for a particular type of approach – soft sell, hard sell, Cockney, straight, character, comic, etc.

Radio commercials, like their television counterparts, are meticulously cast and are invariably placed in the hands of a casting director.

THEATRE

The theatre in all its many forms is probably the most diverse source of employment for actors in the UK, and arguably is still the biggest employer. As there are so many different types of theatrical employment it is perhaps better to attempt to break them down into categories and deal with each in turn. Excluding fringe theatre (which will be dealt with separately in Chapter 10) the basic categories are TIE companies, regional subsidised theatres, national subsidised theatres, commercial theatre outside the West End, and West End theatre.

TIE Companies

Theatre-in-Education (TIE) companies are small groups run by one or more individuals whose purpose is to offer local education authorities the chance to have live drama performed in their schools. Their finance is therefore totally dependent on local authorities and sometimes local sponsorship as they receive no money from ticket sales.

A TIE company involves a unique training for an actor in dealing with audiences who may be less than enthusiastic. It also represents an opportunity to become involved in teaching and community activity. Many TIE companies require the actors not only to act but to participate in the way the material is devised and directed, which is also good experience in dealing with improvisation and in setting up your own productions. They may also require – or offer the opportunity to develop – teaching skills.

Children can make extremely demanding audiences. If they are not interested in a performance, their boredom will become immediately obvious – and will be hard to overcome. On the other hand, if they are interested, they can be utterly rewarding to perform to. Few actors who have performed good work to children at close quarters, and who have seen the rapt attention with which it is received, will ever forget or regret the experience.

Most, though by no means all TIE companies are attached to repertory theatres (e.g. Belgrade Coventry, Wolsey Ipswich, Dukes Lancaster, Thorndike Leatherhead). In addition to TIE, there are also Youth Theatre groups, which have the aim of involving young people in theatrical production. Many of these belong to SCYPT (Standing Conference of Young People's Theatre) and receive funding not only from local authorities but from government grants for training and re-training schemes, and from sponsorship.

TIE and Youth Theatre is a good way to gain professional experience and to earn a salary – though not a substantial one – from acting. From an overall career point of view, though it is unlikely that the shows will be covered by casting directors or other prospective employees or agents, it is possible that some of the directors or writers you work with in Youth Theatre may well move on and subsequently employ you again in other areas in the future.

There may be bad news on the way, though. Equity has recently estimated that due to the pressure on local authority finances by central government, the amount of money available to TIE and YPT companies has been reduced by £900,000. A reduction of this amount will noticeably affect employment in this area, and there are serious fears at the time of writing that all the remaining TIE companies in Britain may be threatened with closure in the course of 1994.

Subsidised Regional Theatre

There are two sorts of subsidised theatre working in the regions: those with a permanent home base, and those who have no base theatre but solely tour.

The latter is, in career terms, a small step up from youth theatre, and often get its funding from similar sources. These companies tour various venues across the country, ranging from conventional theatres to community halls and arts centres, often performing classic plays (on the A-level curriculum) and visiting places that do not have a local theatre. Their funding is a combination of sponsorship, Arts Council grants and local authority subsidies. With the current state of arts funding in this country, these companies are most vulnerable to cuts. They rarely employ casting directors – they cannot afford it – and are a good example of an area where an actor can usefully find out for himself what is going on. Few agents will have much information on anything but the larger groups.

The second type of regional subsidised theatre is the most well known: repertory companies. There has been a decline in the number of repertory theatres operating since the Second World War, but most towns still regard it as a mark of civic pride to have a theatre in their midst. In the late sixties and early seventies there was a huge boom in theatre building, millions being spent on vast new theatres, some combined with arts centres, and with little thought given to the cost of maintaining these edifices to municipal pride. Sheffield Crucible, Leicester Phoenix, Birmingham Repertory, Derby Playhouse, Bolton Octagon, Royal Exchange Manchester, Wolsey Ipswich, Churchill Bromley, Redgrave Farnham, Yvonne Arnaud Guildford, Thorndike Leatherhead, West Yorkshire Playhouse in Leeds and Theatr Clywd; all were completed in the seventies and eighties to join the sixties buildings at Nottingham, Coventry, Southampton and elsewhere in an enormous financial and social investment in theatre building. Other more traditional theatres were re-built, renovated and sometimes extended to include new 'studio' theatres.

The openings of some of these theatres were used to launch grandiose plans for plays in repertoire and seasons of classical plays combined with new plays in the studio theatres. Unfortunately the political climate that had initiated these projects did not last for long enough to fund the elaborate productions for which most of the theatres had been designed, and under the Thatcher government many theatres had severely to restrict the scope of their enterprise. The cost of maintaining some of the steel and glass structures was soon outstripping the cost of ambitious plans for productions, and it was the latter that had to be sacrificed in the face of the former.

The situation has deteriorated further in the nineties. With a deepening recession and 'rate-capping', many councils have been forced to cut their arts subsidy to their local theatre rather than cut social services. The government's insistence that arts funding should be provided by private sponsorship as much as possible may perhaps work for a high-profile and high-status national company like the RSC (and that is debatable considering the trouble they had in 1993 when Royal Insurance withdrew, only to be replaced at the last minute by Allied-Lyons), but for a small local theatre sums of money from sponsorship are unlikely to replace a proper grant.

This lack of funding has led to the closure of some theatres completely, the introduction of 'dark' weeks at others, and a general policy of restricting the choice of shows to West End hits, small-cast plays, well-established classics and school curriculum plays, with very few new plays. In order to make ends meet all subsidised theatres have had to resort to the safest options available, so as to keep the audience levels high.

Naturally the effect of all this on the number of jobs available to actors has been catastrophic.

There are two ways in which a repertory theatre casts its productions; either hiring actors for a season of plays, or for one play at a time. The latter is now much more common than it was. In the days of large-cast productions, casting across the season was more economical, enabling a theatre to use actors from one production in another, it being cheaper to pay an actor to rehearse during the day and play at night, than to pay two actors, one on rehearsal pay, the other on performance salary. Now, with smaller casts the difficulties of cross-casting become too great and more and more theatres are casting each play individually.

Some of the larger theatres now employ casting directors in-house. Some others employ a London casting director to do a whole season. At others again, the casting on a production may be the responsibility of the director who has been brought in for that one show, or, if the production is to be directed by the theatre's own artistic director, as is frequently the case, the artistic director's office will handle the casting.

Keeping track of repertory theatre casting is helped by the printing deadlines on theatre brochures etc, which means that their productions are announced in good time, sometimes as much as six months in advance. In addition most of the work they do will be of plays already performed and published (if only in *Plays and Players*), so it will be possible for you to read the play beforehand to see if there is anything suitable for which you can suggest yourself. Repertory companies are used to getting letters direct from actors and will not treat them differently from an agency letter.

For an actor who already has some experience and who is trying to re-launch his career, it is important to keep up with repertory casting, but it may also happen that a regional repertory theatre is now being run by someone you worked with in the past who knew and respected your work. If this is the case it may be possible to suggest a play, particularly if it is or has been a West End hit, or is on a school curriculum, in which there is a part suitable for you. Artistic directors of theatres are often very open to ideas of this sort.

The production of a play in the repertory theatre may not be the end of the story. Some repertory theatres, like Liverpool and Leatherhead, have permanent tie-ups with West End managements. Others, like the Nuffield in Southampton and the Royal Exchange in Manchester, have established a track record of transfers to the West End. It is important to remember that a job in a repertory theatre may, if the production is exceptional, lead to a transfer to another theatre and possibly to the West End. It may not be a commercial transfer for the 'run of the play'. It may be a run for a limited season at a venue like the Donmar Warehouse or the Lyric Hammersmith. But wherever it goes it clearly creates opportunities for you to be seen in London by casting directors and directors and will undoubtedly receive press coverage.

Sometimes the possibility of a transfer comes out of the blue, based on the sudden dramatic success of the production out of all proportion to what was expected, the play having caught the public's imagination. More frequently the possibility of a transfer is mentioned at the time of the initial contract and sometimes this can cause confusion. In order for the show to transfer anywhere another management will have to be involved and another contract made in addition to the rep contract. This second contract will have to be negotiated on different terms and conditions, salary, billing and period of employment. Some managements will negotiate and sign this contract before the production opens, especially if it is a play by a well-known writer, or directed by a renowned director, or cast with one or two star actors, or any combination of these factors. But mostly they will state their intention to take the production 'in' but will put everything on hold until after the opening night. This is where the confusion arises. A promise, in this context, is not the same as a signed contract, and many actors have felt let down when the play is not the hoped-for success and the contract negotiations do not materialise.

There is a further way in which the run of the play at a repertory theatre can be extended, and that is by means of a British Council tour. British Council tours of various regions of the world go out every year with the purpose of 'promoting British culture abroad'. They are always based on a particular company and usually involve two or three productions but may involve just one. The theatre, for instance the Palace Theatre, Watford recruits a special company for, say, productions of *The Way of the World* and *Much Ado About Nothing*, cross-cast as much as possible. The plays rehearse in Watford and open there for a three or four week run before the company packs up and heads off to the dates around the world that the British Council has arranged. The contract for the actor involves the usual repertory rates for Watford and a special rate for the tour including all travelling expenses and a *per diem* allowance which is usually generous.

Some tours will be as long as six months and go to as many as ten or twelve countries. Hospitality in each country is lavish, with the British Embassy arranging receptions and expatriates keen to entertain visiting actors. It is a marvellous way to see the world, a good experience of playing to a variety of audiences and adapting to a variety of venues and an opportunity to work with a company of actors over a longish period of time.

There is, however, a cautionary note in relation to tours of any type. A tour is work and, as has been said, it is better to work than not to work. But a long tour, whether of the UK for a commercial management or of the world for the British Council, is, by definition, away from London where the majority of casting is done. Being at Birmingham Repertory for ten weeks does not mean you cannot return to London for castings, but being in Beijing does.

Before accepting any tour therefore you should be careful to check whether there are any possibilities of other jobs. A tour will help you pay the bills and may give you the chance to develop a productive relationship with another director, so widening the circle of people who, hopefully, are likely to employ you again, but a tour does not represent a positive step forward in your career in any other way. It is unlikely that casting directors will cover a tour or that the production will be reviewed in the national press.

'There is a tide in the affairs of men,/Which, taken at the flood, leads on to fortune.' One of the things you must be conscious of is when things are going well for you, there may be a number of possibilities opening up, perhaps as a result of your having been seen in a television play or film or theatre role. If this is the case, then taking a six-month British Council tour of the world, however much you want to travel and see the sights, would be a mistake. By the time you come back the impetus will have been lost. Memories are short – the next sensation and the next after that will have arrived (and possibly become established) and your performance, which created all the interest, will be forgotten. You will have to start from scratch again.

On the other hand, what if all the possibilities remain just that, possibilities never converted into offers? The problem is an old one: is the bird in the hand worth two in the bush? So what is the answer? Be realistic in your assessment of the situation and try to make the decision, in consultation with your agent if you have one, on the basis of all the available facts. There is only one thing worse than turning down the opportunity of six months' lucrative work for the prospect of a job that does not materialise: and that is missing the chance of a part that would represent a definite step up for your career and your profile, not to mention your finances.

National Subsidised Companies

Unlike most European countries the UK has only two centrally funded theatre companies: the Royal National Theatre on the South Bank, and the Royal Shakespeare Company at the Shakespeare Memorial Theatre in Stratford and the Barbican Theatre in London. Both companies are subject to the vagaries of Arts

Council grants and government support for the arts. Both have enormous costs in maintaining their respective buildings. Both need sponsorship to maintain their level of productions and both are frustrated by lack of funds in what they would actually like to do. The RSC in particular has recently gone through a period of enormous crisis over funding, initially caused by the cost of running seasons at the Barbican Theatre as opposed to its old base at the Aldwych Theatre, which has only just been solved by the intervention of Allied Lyons.

Both companies have casting departments. And both companies, though the RSC more extensively than the National, cross-cast across a season of plays. As with repertory theatres the print deadlines mean that decisions in relation to what plays are done when (and in the case of the RSC where) have to be taken well in advance, so information on the coming season is readily available. Both companies have 'studio' theatres designed for more experimental work (the Cottesloe at the National and the Swan, the Other Place and the Pit at the RSC) and therefore do a higher proportion of new plays than regional repertories; the main body of their work is, however, in the 'classics'.

The standard of work, the renown of the directors, the public visibility of the productions and the amount of press attention they receive means that, rightly, the competition to get into these companies is perhaps the fiercest for any employment within the acting profession.

In recent times there has been a tendency for both companies to cast as a result of performances seen on television. In the sixties and seventies especially with Olivier's National Company at the Old Vic, and the astonishingly successful productions of the RSC at the Aldwych, many actors were developed with the companies over a number of years and later became extremely well known in other media. From the National came Ronald Pickup, Edward Petherbridge, John McEnery, Derek Jacobi, Edward Hardwicke, Maureen Lipman, Kate Nelligan and Ian Richardson, among others. The RSC was even more prolific, helping develop the careers of Glenda Jackson, Helen Mirren, Ben Kingsley, Norman Rodway, Ian Hogg, Susan Fleetwood, Patrick Stewart, David Warner, Michael Williams and Patrick Magee, to name only a few.

It may be a subjective impression but nowadays neither company seems to be as interested as before in loyalty to their respective company members, and only Michael Gambon is a notable graduate of the eighties. The leading actors currently engaged with both companies have, in the main, come from playing major roles on television (Peter Sproule, John Nettles and David Cater, for example).

The extent to which these companies should, as part of their remit, foster and develop an actor's talent (or can afford to) is debatable. What is not in question is that they are certainly a showcase for an actor, and even a 'play as cast' contract at the National or the RSC is an important step for a young actor of limited experience. For an actor of more experience, however, a contract with the RSC or the National, even one which specifies named parts, can be a frustrating and ultimately unfulfilling commitment. However prestigious the venues, the employment itself does not *guarantee* anything more than a weekly salary for the period of the contract and it is as well to remember that. Many actors, especially actors with a great deal of experience but who have never worked for either company, have entered into a contract with high hopes only to find that what they hoped for does not materialise. Actors in this position can feel that they have been used only to be discarded at the first opportunity, with parts in new productions which they could have played being given to actors outside the existing companies – at greater expense – rather than being given to them. Even the protection of having parts named in the contract has failed to provide any sort of guarantee of success, with the plum part – the part that persuaded the actor to take the other lesser roles – suddenly relegated to a production in one of the minor venues or even, in one case at the RSC, played by another actor altogether!

As always, regular employment in such a competitive business is not to be sniffed at, but a degree of realism as to what the end results of a season at the National or RSC may be could well avoid disappointment and frustration.

Though the Royal Court is not a 'national' company in the true sense it should be mentioned in this context because its funding depends on the Arts Council and it is certainly national in the impact of the work it produces. The Court does not have a company in the sense of cross-casting – it could not afford it – but casts from play to play for both of its theatres (the main house and its studio, the Theatre Upstairs). It has its own casting director and competition for work there is certainly as fierce as for the National and the RSC because, though each period of employment is short (usually not more than eight weeks – four weeks rehearsing and four weeks playing), the press attention is great and many professionals, casting directors, directors, producers and agents will come to see the show, due to the reputation of the theatre. As at the National and RSC, productions are publicised well in advance. But unlike the other two companies, most of the Court's productions will be new plays so it will be more difficult to get a breakdown of the parts available.

The National, the RSC and the Royal Court all transfer successful productions into the West End from time to time. It is obviously easier for the Royal Court to transfer a play as it can be moved lock, stock and barrel from one theatre to another, with only the minor difficulty of reconstructing the set and negotiating new contracts for the actors. The National and RSC have the problem of extracting the members of the cast of the transferring play from their other commitments in the season. This is usually done by a combination of re-casting and waiting until the leading actor's commitment to other plays is over, though this does mean losing some of the impetus created by the initial reception of the play.

A West End transfer represents a considerable success for a production and its cast. It will mean that the production will be seen by a great many prospective employers and re-reviewed in the national press. It is also financially rewarding, as the West End salary for what will become a normal commercial production once transferred into a West End theatre is going to be much greater than the levels of salary in the subsidised company production.

Occasionally a production may not go into the West End but be transferred elsewhere, either on tour in the UK or just to one particular venue. Tours abroad have also been arranged and productions have even gone to Broadway (where the RSC's *Nicholas Nickleby* broke all box-office records) with the agreement of American Equity.

Commercial Theatre Outside the West End

There are a number of productions in the theatre which are funded solely from ticket sales ('box-office returns') and not from any state or local subsidy. A number of provincial theatres are privately owned (though some are owned by local authority trusts) and hired out to touring managements on a normal commercial basis. The theatre manager will be offered various productions and will have to decide which he wishes to have in his theatre, a decision based on his judgement of what the local audience wants and is likely to pay for. As the rental of the theatre will include a percentage of the box-office receipts, the more accurate his judgement, the more the theatre will make.

In order therefore to secure good 'dates' the touring management will not only want to put on a popular and well-tried play (often a thriller in the Agatha Christie genre or a farce of the Ray Cooney variety) but also cast it with as many stars – mostly from television; occasionally from British films – as can be persuaded to join the company and the budget can afford. These ingredients should persuade theatre managers that the production will attract audiences. If the package is good enough the theatre manager may even offer the production a guarantee, a sum of money against the box-office returns, to secure the production for his theatre.

From the touring management's point of view, the longer the tour the better, as it gives a chance for the production costs, director's fees, rehearsal salaries, and set construction costs, plus advance publicity and advertising, to be amortised, or spread, over a longer period. Tours usually run for a minimum of eight weeks but can easily stretch to twelve, and even as many as eighteen to twenty weeks is not unknown.

The decline in theatre attendances has hit commercial provincial theatres hardest and consequently the number of commercial tours has declined sharply. Older actors will remember what were called 'number one' tours. There were also 'number two' and 'number three' tours. The idea of there being various circuits, one more prestigious than another, has now largely disappeared, and there is only a single touring circuit for commercial plays.

Casting of tours varies from management to management but most are cast from the manager's office personally and not through a casting director. The weekly trade paper, *The Stage*, is a good source of information about which managements are going to be doing which plays, and sometimes it is possible to work back from information given out by the theatres themselves. As the play will almost certainly be a revival, it will be easy to get a copy from your local library or Samuel French's bookshop to see if there are any suitable parts.

What I have said earlier about long British Council tours and their effect on your availability for other work obviously applies also to tours within the UK. A tour can provide work at a reasonable rate of pay – though touring expenses are far from generous, and finding somewhere to live at each date can eat into your salary – but it is unlikely to be a major step forward in your career. There is, however, the possibility of persuading casting directors to cover the production on the dates that are within easy reach of London – Richmond Theatre, for instance.

There are two other sorts of commercial production that operate on the same principle as tours, despite being based in only one theatre: summer shows and pantomimes. Again usually run by touring managements, these shows are put together with a collection of star names (in the case of summer shows mostly singers, bands, and comedy acts) and play one venue during the summer season or at Christmas, paying the theatre rental and a percentage of the box-office take in the same way as a touring production.

Although there are no straight roles in summer shows, there are in pantomime, which in recent years is the one area of theatrical production that has shown a sharp increase. Now almost every theatre in the UK wants to host a pantomime over the Christmas period, mainly because they run to 95 per cent occupancy rates. Pantomimes are usually cast in May or June to secure the star performers. They are invariably cast by the individual managements from their offices. Clearly they do not represent a major source of employment, but particularly if you are a good singer or dancer, they may provide a lucrative job over the Christmas period when other forms of employment traditionally close down.

West End Theatre

Productions of plays in the London theatres collectively referred to as the 'West End' are undertaken either by ad hoc management companies formed specifically for the purpose of producing one play, or by established theatrical managements (e.g. Michael Codron, Michael White, The Really Useful Company) who have produced many successful productions and some of whom own or permanently lease one or more West End theatres. Most West End theatres, however, are privately owned and are hired out for each individual production at a rent negotiated between the theatre owners and the theatrical management. The rental will be a set sum of money plus a percentage of the gross box-office receipts. Every contract includes what is called a 'get out' figure: if the weekly 'take' falls below a certain level then the theatre owner can give the management two weeks notice to 'get out' – on the theory that the next production waiting to come in may be more profitable. If no productions are queueing up, the theatre owner may allow the show to continue, assuming the management can still pay the rent – and even sometimes rent free – in the hope that audiences will improve.

Very much like the situation that exists with independent film producers, there are many producers in the West End looking for sources of finance to launch a West End production, not all of them with experience and professionalism. The frequent disasters in the West End, from *Troubadour* at the Cambridge, to *Which Witch* at the Piccadilly, *Bernadette* at the Dominion, and *Leonardo* at the Strand, have often been produced by relatively inexperienced producers who have been lucky enough to raise the production costs, but have not had the necessary expertise in selection of a script or control of the creative side of the production. There is often talk of a quality threshold insisted upon by West End theatre owners, but faced with the alternatives of a 'dark' or unoccupied theatre, and the prospect of being paid at least some rental, more basic commercial considerations come into play.

Not that established theatrical managements don't fail too. Finding a play that will run in the West End is as difficult as backing the right horse in the Grand National, with just as many runners in the field. Even seemingly sure-fire certainties – established star actors in a play by a star writer – can fall at the first fence. But for a management running two or three shows at the same time, profits from one show should help to balance losses from another.

A West End production, even of a straight play, is expensive. A set must be constructed, lights and sound equipment hired, costumes bought or made, the theatre rental paid, director's and designer's fees and rehearsal salaries for all the performers paid, and the most substantial cost of all is in advertising the production in the national press. The expense of this is enormous, with small ads an essential requirement in most of the quality dailies and Sunday papers, and display advertising certainly necessary in the build-up to the first night and the week or two afterwards.

Naturally enough with the huge costs involved, it is likely that the producer will want the reassurance of at least one or two star names in the cast, names who will, at least in theory, put 'bums on seats'.

Casting for West End plays is done in a variety of ways. Some of the biggest producers employ casting directors to cast (and re-cast in the case of long runs) all their productions. Others cast from their own offices and maintain an in-house casting director. But you should remember that almost half the plays in the West End are transfers from elsewhere, from a repertory or fringe theatre (The King's Head in Islington, for example), or from the National, RSC, or the Royal Court, where the original casting would have been done. Bear in mind also that plays produced specifically for the West End often have a short tour beforehand at commercial touring venues. This tour will be part of the West End contract and does not mean that the production will be cast by the theatre presenting the first performances.

Every six or nine months (even sometimes once a year), a successful play will be re-cast. If you have seen a play in which you think there is a good part for you, it is always worth bearing it in mind and watching to see if it has a long run. A call to the management will establish when re-casting is going to take place and, assuming you are suitable, you should be successful in getting an audition. Nor is this merely a stop-gap. If one of the stars of the production is leaving at the same time as the re-casting, and an equally well-known replacement has been found, the press may well re-review the play and casting directors be tempted back for a second look.

As a result of the contraction of funding for the theatre across the whole range of productions, there has been a dramatic drop in the employment of understudies. Some years ago every tour and repertory production would have understudies for all the leading roles. Now such luxury is rare. Actors are expected to soldier on regardless of illness or injury. The only exception (apart from the National and the RSC) is the West End theatre, where the indisposition of a leading actor is not allowed to lead to the cancellation of a performance and consequently the massive loss of takings, which, with average ticket prices of £20, could arise from refunds of £20,000 or more.

The archetypal fantasy (the plot of *42nd Street*, and many other films and stage shows) of the understudy becoming a star the instant the leading lady is struck down by illness should be firmly discarded. Being an understudy is not a direct road to stardom. In recent years there is not one example of an understudy's assumption of a role proving crucial to their career. In fact taking over has become something of a way of life. Some musicals now advertise that the star will only be performing on certain nights, say five or six performances a week, so understudies are hired with this in mind. In long-running shows it has also become common for the stars to take holidays.

The chances of actually performing in the West End are therefore greatly increased by understudy work, and an offer to understudy should be taken seriously if you are a young actor. It gives experience of the West End, a chance to widen the circle of people who know your work, and, not least, a salary. Another advantage is that some of the longer running productions are now adapting the Broadway model of staging a special matinee before an invited audience of casting directors and agents, when the parts are swapped round and understudies are given a chance to play all the leading roles. This 'showcase' is an excellent opportunity to be seen in a demanding part, and often these performances are well attended. There is no guarantee, of course, that the show you are offered will mount such a matinee.

Another advantage of understudying is that you are in London and available for other work and castings. Commercials and short television engagements may well be possible during the run.

There is, however, a danger in understudying too frequently. Some actors have become known among managements as good understudies and are offered nothing else. Too much understudying work leads only to more understudying.

One phenomenon of the eighties which looks set to continue well into the nineties is the emergence (or re-emergence) of the West End musical along the lines of the Broadway genre. Largely due, it is fair to say, to the success of Andrew Lloyd Webber, London has seen what was once a dying breed, the home-grown musical, take not only the West End but Broadway by storm. The bemoaning of the lack of skill of British actors in singing and dancing compared to American expertise has given way to amazement at the depth of native talent and professionalism in these areas, of a standard that has quickly come to rival the American model, so poignantly portrayed in *Chorus Line*.

Chorus Line is, of course, about auditioning for a musical. And what it has to say about the process is a distillation of what is an extremely difficult and disheartening process. Many West End musicals start with an open audition where there may be two or three hundred actors. This is quickly cut down to fifty and then further to the twenty or thirty required. Unless you are among the chosen few it can be an alienating and dispiriting experience.

There are in some musicals parts which require dancers and singers as opposed to actors. But generally speaking, though singing and dancing may be demanding, most roles require some acting expertise. Particularly if your singing is at an advanced level, it would certainly be worth concentrating your efforts on musical casting (and re-casting of long-running shows). Musicals employ a lot of actors and there are usually one or two big productions being set up at any one time, so make sure your singing and dancing technique is maintained and that you have practised your audition pieces. A good part in a musical provides lucrative employment which is seen by many prospective employers and can greatly increase your profile in the business.

Despite the development of television, the West End theatre still has a special allure to many actors. Setting foot in a dressing room – possibly with a star on its door – in a West End theatre often seems like a dream come true. The West End's associations with glamour and the high life are not entirely without foundation: a West End production is usually surrounded by national press coverage, and the first-night party may well be a glamorous event attended by the glitterati and a popping of photographers' flash-guns. Certainly during the first weeks of a run, celebrities may well come to see the play and visit backstage after the show. Families and friends, too, can be entertained backstage and taken out to late-night restaurants after the show.

But however intoxicating this atmosphere may be, it should not allow you to gain the impression that appearing in the West End is an open passport to future success. It *may* be. It may be that you will receive offers of all kinds. But if you do not, make sure you use your engagement to good purpose by ensuring that people know what you are doing: make sure you collect the names of everyone who has seen the production, and continue to maintain contact with all the other media. Lots of people will come to the show: try to meet as many of them as possible. If there is a production coming up for which you are suitable, don't forget when writing to the director or producer to invite them to the show. This is another way of putting your employment to good use.

4 How Much Should I Be Paid?

I N ANY FREELANCE profession, where future employment is not guaranteed, and there is no regular salary, the amount paid for each engagement takes on a crucial significance. It has to take into account the periods of unemployment when there is no money coming in. But of course working alone, and not being able to consult other members of the cast, it is difficult to know what the going rate is and whether the money you are being offered is a fair rate for the job. This is one of the reasons agents are used, because they should have a knowledge of the prevailing rates of pay and of how much more an employer can be persuaded to pay. But not all agents are equally good at negotiating fees, and whether you have an agent or not, it is a good idea to understand precisely the various contracts that apply to the offers you will receive in the various media, so that you can make an informed decision about how fair or not the offers are.

Each sector of the industry has a different contract, different pay scales and different criteria, all arrived at to meet the specific working conditions of that medium. In film, for instance, with the need to keep film schedules as fluid as possible, the contractual start date is flexible, whereas in television, because most of the work is studio based, the contract specifies an exact period of work.

Understanding the way the contract is structured is important, not only so you know clearly what you are committed to, but because it will sometimes enable you or your agent to get a better deal. For instance, a fee for a previous engagement at the BBC may appear low in comparison to a fee on ITV, but by working out the number of days involved it can turn out actually to have paid more per day. Using this figure as a basis, it can then be pointed out to the casting director at ITV that their offer is lower than what you were getting at the BBC on your last job, and hopefully this will lead them to increase their offer.

All the details that follow are based on the official Equity contracts negotiated with the various employers' organisations. You may be offered a contract or agreement which is not in this form, and if you are, you should think very carefully about whether you accept it. Firstly it is unlikely that it will make allowances for all the various residuals and royalties written in to the Equity agreements, but secondly, and more importantly, in the event of a breach of the agreement or an industrial dispute, you may not be covered by Equity's legal service. A production company wishing to cut corners, and therefore costs, in this way, may also be cutting costs in other areas and may not have appropriate accident insurance. It is even possible that they will not have the money they are promising to pay you. If you are in any doubt whatever about these points, consult your agent or Equity, or both, before agreeing to the offer.

A word of warning: the details in this chapter (and elsewhere in this book) of rates of pay and terms and conditions are given in good faith, but all such details are subject to periodic change. If you need up-to-the-minute information (for instance on minimum rates of pay), you should again consult Equity.

FILMS

Actors are employed for feature films under the 1989 Equity, BFTRA (British Film and TV Producers' Association) and IPPA (Independent Programme Producers' Association) contract. This is in the process of renegotiation, largely because the two producers' associations have now merged into one body (PACT, or Producers' Alliance for Cinema and Television), reflecting the disappearance of the distinction between production companies making feature films for theatrical release and companies making television films. (Nowadays a company may make a one-and-a-half hour production for television use in one market and theatrical distribution in another.) At the moment, however, until the re-negotiation takes place, a production company making a film not intended for television will offer a contract based on the old agreement.

A film contract is either on a daily or a weekly basis. For a short part of no more than three or four scenes and certainly no more than three days' work, a film company will offer a daily contract. Since the daily rate is one quarter of the weekly rate, if the part is likely to take more than three days then the film company will offer a weekly contract. The fee for the film will thus be expressed as either so much per day or so much per week depending on the type of contract offered. Minimum rates are provided for each.

Since 1981 film contracts have followed the example of American films and included provision for residual payments, on top of the daily or weekly salary. These 'use fees' (fees for showing the film in other parts of the world or transmission on television), which are calculated as percentages of the salary, are then paid in the following four categories:

Theatrical
    (i) USA/Canada   50%
    (ii) rest of the world   50%
Free television
    (i) USA major network   45%
    (ii) USA other than major network   20%
    (iii) rest of the world   15%
    (iv) UK (3 transmissions in 5 years)   20%
          (additional transmissions)   10%
Pay television
    (i) USA   30%
    (ii) other (including UK)   8%
Videograms (worldwide)   25%

Of these the theatrical use for either USA/Canada or the rest of the world *must* be pre-purchased; i.e. the money must be paid for the usage at the same time as the salary. All the other uses are optional, though it is usual for a producer to 'buy out' one or two as well as the obligatory theatrical use, particularly for UK television.

The intention of the introduction of residuals to film agreements was to stop the long-protested arrangement under which, once an actor had been paid his fee, he did not share at all in the subsequent success of the film. The change was obviously intended to increase actors' fees overall, and this has proved only partially successful. Though it is clear that if the film is very popular and sold worldwide the actor will benefit in the long term, producers have worked out the cost of a residual 'buy-out' of the territories they require and have simply reduced the fee they would have paid under the old agreement accordingly. The principle of sharing in the film's success, however, is an important one.

The contract also specifies the guaranteed period of employment. If the actor's role overruns, payment will be made at a quarter of the weekly salary per day (or, on a daily contract, the daily salary itself) excluding all usage fees. In the event that the overruns last longer than the original guaranteed period, a new contract will have to be negotiated; in other words, if you are engaged for two weeks and your part overruns by three weeks the final week becomes subject to an entirely new agreement.

Daily overtime is paid at the rate of one-third of the daily rate per hour and becomes due after a ten-hour day (including a one-hour break for lunch). Other provisions deal with matters that arise from the unpredictability of film scheduling and suspension of filming (through *force majeure*, or unforeseen circumstances) due to sudden illness of the leading actor, for example, as well as payment for days on which you are called but do not work.

The film company is also obliged to pay a *per diem* rate for expenses if the actor is required to work at a studio more than 20 miles from Charing Cross, or on location more than 30 miles away, for a London-based film. (There are comparable provisions for films not based in London.) The company is also required to provide transportation or expenses in lieu of transportation. On location, film companies provide generous catering facilities for breakfast, lunch and, if shooting at night, dinner and late-night food.

On a weekly as opposed to daily contract, there is one aspect of a film contract that is unique; the start date. A specific start date is given in the contract, but this can be varied either backwards or forwards by the number of days specified in the guaranteed period, up to a maximum of seven days. In other words the company has the right to call the actor up to seven days before the specified start date or seven days after, giving a total maximum latitude of two weeks to allow for the unpredictability of circumstances affecting filming.

The contract does not specify a stop date. Within the proviso that the contract cannot be extended beyond the original length of the guaranteed period (i.e. beyond four weeks if that is the guaranteed period), the stop date will come whenever the company has finished with your services.

But if you have another job waiting for you the question of the stop date can be crucial. You or your agent will have to talk to the production manager and find out from him when, roughly, he expects to be finished with your services. He will give you a good idea, and tell you if any problems are anticipated (for instance, whether the production is on schedule or running late). But he will not release you until he is absolutely sure that your role has been completed, because he knows that once he has given you an official release the production can no longer call on your services except for post-production looping and post-synchronisation on a second-call basis. And equally you are not free to accept another job until you have such a release.

Similarly you have to be officially released at the end of each day's filming, a function usually performed by the first assistant director. You must not just walk away assuming that your scenes are finished. Until you hear you can go, stay. If in doubt, ask. You will definitely not be popular if you leave the studio or location without being told that you are released and the director, perhaps trying to make up time, decides to work in another scene that involves you.

After the guaranteed period ('first call') you can be asked to come back and complete 'post-synchronisation' sound recording, on what is called a 'second-call' basis, which means that you can refuse if you have another professional engagement and delay until you have time free (but only for 'professional' reasons). Post-synch usually means 'looping'. If, for some reason, the natural sound during a take was bad and is not audible, the piece will be re-voiced on a tape 'loop' while the visual shot is running in a dubbing studio. You are then asked to 'lip-synch' your lines to the picture; that is, to match the new recording exactly to your visible diction on-screen. This work is paid at the rate of half your daily salary for a period of up to five hours and a whole daily rate if more than five hours is involved.

On a long picture it is possible for the producer to engage an actor on two contracts with two guaranteed periods thus saving himself the cost of keeping the actor on call for the period of principal photography (the principal action of the film).

TELEVISION

BBC

BBC TV contracts are offered on the basis of an agreement which came into operation on 1 July 1992. The offer is based on the 'category' or length of the final transmitted programme, and there are four categories in all: i) up to 35 minutes; ii) up to 60 minutes; iii) up to 90 minutes; and iv) anything over 90 minutes. The fee for each programme category carries an entitlement to a number of days' work. For the first category of up to 35 minutes the BBC is entitled to call the actor for six days' work. For the second category it is two weeks' work; for the third, three weeks; and for the fourth, four weeks, with a week defined as five working days.

It is possible for the BBC to offer a contract which is 'de-categorised'. This means that if you have been given a part in a Category Three programme (of up to 90 minutes), but the part is small and will only take a week to complete, you will only be offered a Category One fee. This is usually done on productions made on a 'rehearse/record' basis (i.e. when a scene or shot is rehearsed immediately before being recorded, as for a film) and the actor therefore does not have to wait around until the end of the rehearsal period for the production to go into the studio to be recorded.

The fee negotiated will be either for a one-off programme or for a series. Since a series of programmes will all be the same length, whatever the basic fee it will be multiplied in the contract by the number of episodes on offer. So an offer for, say, five episodes of a situation comedy will be for five Category One fees, while that for a full-length Screen Two film will be for one Category Four fee.

The basic Category One fee offered to you determines all your other fees, whatever the category. If your Category One fee is £400 (the minimum at the time of writing is £345), your fee for a Category Four will automatically be £1600 (4 × £400) and vice versa. Whenever there is a negotiation and your fee is changed for one particular category, the other category fees will correspondingly change. In some cases, however, if the part under offer is smaller than you would usually accept, or there are other special circumstances, it can be stated in the contract that the fee is a 'Special Low'. This means that it is below your usual basic fee and the next offer you receive will return to the former level. Equally a 'Special High' can be negotiated if, for instance, the part is a leading one or particularly important. A 'Special High' means that the next offer you will receive will disregard the higher rate and return to your 'normal' fee.

With the exception of overtime, and additional days and costume fittings, the fees offered cover all work, whether rehearsing or recording, doing away with a distinction that used to exist in all previous BBC contracts.

The new agreement also provides for a daily contract for a part that can be rehearsed and recorded within a single day (eight hours in an overall period of ten hours). This daily contract is covered by a minimum payment (£225 at the time of writing).

Any actor who has taken part in a BBC programme is entitled to repeats and residuals accruing from that programme. Repeat fees are based on the basic residual fee (the category fee and any extra days worked outside the category period) and are paid at 80 per cent of that fee for repeat transmissions within two and a half years of the original transmission. Programmes repeated after that period ('out of time') attract a bigger percentage on a scale rising to 800 per cent for programmes made between 1963 and 1967. If, however, the repeat is made in an 'off-peak' period, defined as before 4.00 p.m. and after 10.30 p.m. on BBC 1, and before 6.00 p.m. and after 10.30 p.m. on BBC 2 on weekdays and after 11.00 p.m. at weekends or public holidays, then the repeat fee will be 50 per cent of the 'out of time' repeat fee.

Residuals arise from the sale of programmes to foreign countries, airlines, 'trapped audiences' (in prisons and on oil-rigs), and cable and satellite channels (non-terrestrial broadcasting). The Multi-Media Royalty Agreement changed the basis on which foreign residuals were paid by the BBC. Previously, residuals were based on a set percentage defined by the country to which the programme had been sold and roughly reflecting the number of television sets per head of its population (rather than the country's size or total population). Television sales executives felt that this was affecting their ability to sell programmes, because the fixed cost made the programme too expensive for some countries to afford. They wanted to be free to negotiate a price appropriate to each individual case. Consequently it was agreed (though a period of monitoring the results was part of the agreement) that residuals should be based on a percentage of sales or monies received. In this way it was hoped that more British television would be sold abroad and therefore a net increase in residuals payable to actors would result. So far the monitoring period has proved this to be the case: actors have received more money overall under the new regime.

The agreement also includes sales of video cassettes. Actors receive a royalty on these too, calculated as a percentage after the distribution and other costs have been taken into account.

UK Gold, the satellite station broadcasting BBC and Thames Television repeats, became a recent subject of dispute because it claimed that its programmes should come under the Multi-Media Agreement, a claim strongly resisted by Equity. Eventually a new agreement was reached to cover UK Gold transmissions of BBC programmes, giving actors a 10 per cent residual of their original fee for two transmissions over two years, or 15 per cent for four transmissions over five years, with a minimum £10 payment, and increases in the percentages paid for older, 'out of time' programmes.

At the time of writing the agreement for the transmission of Thames Television programmes on this satellite has still to be concluded, though Thames have started making payments on a notional agreement on the understanding it will make up any difference once eventual agreement is reached.

Independent Television Contractors

The agreement for television productions made by holders of an Independent Television franchise is much more straightforward than the BBC agreement. This agreement has no 'categories', and offers a lump-sum payment for all the work involved plus a payment (non-negotiable) for every rehearsal day and every studio or filming day actually worked. The fee offered will be a reflection of the length of the contract period which will, in turn, inevitably reflect the size of the part on offer. The contract will state the date at which the actor must be available to work (though this may not be the actual day work begins) and the date on which the production company no longer has a call on the actor's services. As these productions are mostly studio based, rehearsing first and then recording in the studio for one or two days at the end, the element of unpredictability is very limited.

The fee, called the programme fee, is expressed in the contract as being for up to 25 per cent of the UK transmission area. Each franchise holder has been attributed a percentage of the national television audience as follows:

Anglia	7%
Border	1%
LWT/Carlton	19%
Central	15%
Channel	1%
Granada	12%
HTV	8%
Meridian	9%
Scottish	6%
Tyne Tees	5%
Ulster	2%
West Country	3%
Yorkshire	10%

If the programme is to be transmitted across regions totalling between 26 and 50 per cent, then an amount equal to two programme fees must be paid. If the total is between 51 and 75 per cent, then three programme fees are due, and if between 76 and 100 per cent, four fees must be paid. In effect, most contracts are issued for a full 100 per cent transmission across the network, so the programme fee is arrived at by dividing the offer by four (e.g. £1500 gives a programme fee of £375) rather than starting with the programme fee and working up.

As with the BBC, the programme fee will be negotiated either for a series or for a one-off programme. Sometimes, if the schedule is a particularly complicated one, say for a series over some months with filming on location plus rehearsals and studio days, the company will be prepared to guarantee a sum of money for the standard rehearsal and studio/filming day payments, which will be expressed in the contract as, for instance, an episode fee of £1000 plus a guarantee of not less than £1500 per programme, meaning that the actor will collect no less than an additional £500 in rehearsal and studio fees. If this additional amount is not in fact earned during the rehearsal and studio/filming period, then the company will nevertheless be obliged to make up the difference to the guaranteed amount.

All ITV contracts attract repeats and residuals. The repeat fee structure for ITV is however a great deal more complicated than the BBC agreement, basically because the ITV network is made up of regions for transmission purposes, whereas BBC programmes are generally networked across the whole of the UK. Each ITV region has a different percentage rate for repeat fees, based on the number of television sets in that region, according to BARB figures: these are the percentages that appear opposite. A repeat can be made in any number of regions. If it is made across the whole network it will attract a 100 per cent repeat fee; if across only one or two, the fee will be a great deal less, though there is a minimum of 25 per cent on any repeat in any area.

As with the BBC, there is a system for off-peak repeats and for 'out-of-time' repeats, which came into effect on 1 May 1993. Networked peak programme transmission times attract 100 per cent of whatever repeat fee is due. Off-peak daytime transmissions attract 50 per cent and off-peak night-time repeats (which the BBC agreement does not allow for, since the BBC do not have all-night broadcasting) attract 25 per cent of the repeat fee.

'Out-of-time' repeats attract a bigger percentage the longer ago the original programme was made. But unlike the BBC, the interval is not calculated from when the programme was first transmitted, but from when the actor was first engaged. The percentage structure for 'out-of-time' repeats is currently under negotiation.

Overseas residuals are paid on the same basis as for the BBC: i.e. under the Multi-Media royalty agreement, which provides for the actor to receive a percentage of the actual money received for a sale of the programme.

Channel Four, Satellite and Cable

Since Channel Four and the satellite and cable companies do not make their own programmes, they have no production agreements with Equity. All their programmes are made by independent television companies under commission, and are therefore covered by that Equity/PACT agreement.

Independent Television Production Companies

After long negotiation an agreement between PACT and Equity is being concluded at the time of writing. With 45 per cent of BBC drama now made by independent producers and an ever increasing amount on ITV, it is likely, in the future, that this agreement will become the most important in the employment of actors on television.

The basic minimum terms will be £360 for the first day in any seven-day period, plus £40 for each day worked after the first day, with the guarantee that the producer will pre-purchase world rights for 35 per cent of the fees paid (bringing the minimum to a total of £486). UK repeats will be at 55 per cent of the total fees paid, with off-peak times at half this rate. World rights exclude video, theatrical and USA uses for which the Multi-Media agreement will operate. Overtime, meal breaks, special skills and other supplementary payments are currently being finalised.

Since this agreement also covers productions commissioned by the BBC, it can have an adverse effect on an actor's earnings when the BBC decides that a programme it was originally making 'in-house' is to become 'independent'. *Alas Smith and Jones* is an example of this: at first made under the BBC contract, the production was then farmed out to Talkback Productions, and actors were offered contracts under the Equity/PACT agreement. Though the amounts earned in fees would have been roughly the same, the repeat structure under the later arrangement was far less generous.

TELEVISION COMMERCIALS

Most TV commercials are made in one or two days, and the agreement reflects this. A basic studio fee (BSF) is paid which usually represents one day's work. If a second day is required it is paid at the same rate as the basic studio fee, but is not included in calculations for residuals, which are based on the basic studio fee alone.

The most important element of the contract is the structure for residual payments, since this is where an actor can expect to make most of the money from a TV commercial. All residual payments are based on the BSF and no distinction is made between an actor engaged for a voice-over only, or one appearing in vision.

At the end of each month the number of transmissions of the commercial across each region and television station (i.e. Channel Four, Breakfast TV (GMTV), plus the ITV regions) is calculated and a figure arrived at which represents the total number of individual viewings the commercial may have had. This total is expressed as a percentage of the total available UK television audience and this percentage is called the TVR (Total Viewing Rating). The number of transmissions determines the band of TVR (of which there are four) and in turn the percentage payable of the BSF.

Number of transmissions	% of BSF payable per transmission
0–200	7.41%
200–400	3.68%
400–800	2.42%
over 800	1.64%

A commercial shown 550 times across all channels would accrue payments as follows:

200 networked transmissions × 7.41% (1482%) plus
200 networked transmissions × 3.68% (736%) plus
150 networked transmissions × 2.42% (363%)
= 2581% of BSF (if £200 this = £5162)

BARB (the Broadcasting Audience Research Boards), who are responsible for producing the figures on TVRs, also 'consolidate' or add in transmissions later watched on video recorders following the same formula used to establish TV ratings.

The life of a commercial is deemed to be three years, and further use after that period must be re-negotiated. The agreement also provides for a payment, after the first transmission, of a sum equivalent to the BSF as a non-returnable advance against repeats.

In 1992 the basis for overseas use of a television commercial was changed. Now each country is classed in one of six categories, depending on the number of 'TV homes' it is regarded as having. The residual rates of the basic studio fee are as follows:

Number of TV homes in country

up to 50,000	15% residual
50,000–250,000	25%
250,000–1 million	50%
1–5 million	100%
5–10 million (ex. Canada)	275%
over 10 million (ex. USA)	400%

Canada and the USA are paid according to the local prevailing rates; i.e. the payments must be the same as if they were under contracts issued to actors resident in that country. Payment of these fees entitles the company to one year's use of the commercial. No distinction is made between the various signal delivery systems, i.e. cable, terrestrial transmission or satellite.

There has been a great deal of concern among actors that commercials are used in foreign countries without their permission, and it is necessary for the advertiser to get the actor to consent to overseas use. However, there have been many cases of an actor travelling abroad and seeing his commercial on a foreign television station for which he has not been paid. Similarly special uses of the commercial, in shops on video equipment, have been spotted, which should also attract further payments but have not done so.

The problem here is that the advertising agency makes a commercial for the manufacturer of a product or service. It is the manufacturer who pays the bill, and when they turn round to the advertiser and ask for the commercial to be delivered to them the advertiser has little choice but to comply. The manufacturer – and this may be a multi-national company – then has the finished commercial in its hands, possibly with little idea of the copyright obligations entailed in transmission. It ships the tape out to its various worldwide subsidiaries who use it indiscriminately. A few years ago, for instance, a major international credit card organisation made a commercial through its advertising agency. One of the actors in the commercial was visiting his local post office which had just set up video screens showing advertisements to the waiting customers. He saw himself in the credit card commercial, and immediately complained as he had not been paid for any such usage. The card company, he was told, had not been aware that they had any obligations to pay additional money (the Equity contract does not cover such use, and a separate negotiation should have taken place to establish a fee structure). Apparently they were still not aware when the practice continued a second and third time. Similarly an actress visiting Dubai saw herself in a washing-up liquid commercial, for which again no payment had been made prior to transmission.

NON-BROADCAST TELEVISION AND VIDEO

There is no Equity-negotiated contract governing work in non-broadcast television and video productions. Usually you will be offered a sum of money on a daily basis which will be paid for every day you actually work, but sometimes a lump sum is offered which amounts to the same thing. The written agreement may consist simply of a letter which states the fee and the number of days involved, including the start and stop date, but little else. It *should* state categorically that the end use will be restricted to non-broadcast reproduction. With many engagements of this sort, even a basic letter is slow to arrive.

The arrangements and terms tend not to be closely defined, and care should therefore be taken. As no Equity agreement exists, the union cannot offer legal protection and if there is some breach of the terms and conditions that you or your agent have agreed, such as non-payment of the fee, or some industrial injury complaint, you may be on difficult ground. If you are working for a large and respectable company like Barclays Bank or Marks & Spencer, even though you will be actually employed on their behalf by a video production company, you at least have the option, if something does go wrong, of appealing to the originator, who will probably be unhappy to see their name associated with misconduct. Even if they are not, you can threaten them with the fact that, if you were not paid, they do not have the right to use your performance in their film.

If however, the production company and the company for whom they are making the film are unknown to you – in the case of a foreign company, for instance – there can be a risk of non-payment, and it is better to try to get at least a proportion of the fee paid before you start work, or alternatively have the whole fee paid into escrow (held by lawyers or some other reliable third party). If the job involves travelling abroad (and this applies to *any* job abroad), never agree to travel unless you are given a valid return ticket. Even if everything collapses, then you will at least be able to get home.

RADIO

The BBC radio agreement provides for a basic fee plus payment of a number of additional days at a standard rate (currently £80 per day). A contract will be for UK domestic use and World Service and will include the right to two transmissions. The minimum fee at the time of writing is £136.

For the third transmission on the UK domestic network, you will receive 33⅓ per cent of the total original payment (fee plus additional days), if transmission is made within three years of the first repeat. On World Service, 23 per cent is payable if the transmission is within seven days of the first repeat; otherwise 13 per cent is payable.

As with other media, radio carries residuals for sales abroad (which in BBC jargon is called 'transcription'). Transcription can be either full (for the rest of the world) or limited, or cable. Full transcription attracts payment of 80 per cent of all fees paid, limited 66 per cent, and cable 40 per cent. There is also the option to buy out rights country by country at differing percentages.

The negotiation of the basic fee depends, perhaps more than in any other media, on your experience in radio itself. The radio bookers are notoriously unimpressed when told that you have starred in a television series or a film. They will base their calculation on the last time you appeared on radio and what sort of part you had. Starring in a major feature film will definitely not be as effective in enhancing your fee as having starred in a radio adaptation of a Dickens classic!

RADIO COMMERCIALS

Like television commercials, commercials made for radio use have fees divided into only two parts: the basic studio fee (in radio called a 'session' fee) and repeats (or 'use' fees). A session is either of one hour or one-and-a-half hours: five commercials or ten 'tags' can be recorded within a one-hour session, and seven commercials or fourteen 'tags' in a one-and-a-half hour period. A 'tag' is defined as a 'change of information relating only to time or place within the same station area and/or relating to dealer information'. Tags are used, for instance, to advertise the extension of a special offer or the introduction of a new price.

A radio commercial may be used for one year, but can be renewed by re-negotiation. During the first year it will attract use fees for each three-month period on the following scale: first frequency ILR stations London/Manchester/Glasgow/Liverpool/Birmingham, £30 per station; other individual first frequency ILR stations, £23 per station; use on split frequency channels of above stations, 50 per cent of first frequency use; ILR network first frequency only, £650; ILR full network (including split frequency), £975; Classic FM full network (including split frequency), £350; Radio Manx, £30; Classic FM England and Wales only, £300;

Classic FM Scotland and N. Ireland only, £200; Newslink Network, £650.

Tags, as opposed to full radio commercials, attract a use fee of 50 per cent of all the above rates.

At the time of writing, Equity is re-negotiating the radio contract, and although it is unlikely the basic principles will change, some of the details undoubtedly will.

THEATRE

TIE and Children's Theatre

The contract governing a TIE or SCYPT engagement can be either a specialised contract covering one particular company; an Equity Small-Scale Theatre contract; part of the Provincial Theatre TMA (Theatre Managers' Association) contract – sessional appendix; or a normal repertory theatre agreement if the company involved is attached to a repertory theatre. All these contracts provide for basic terms and conditions of employment and a disputes procedure in the event of disagreements. Salary is paid on a weekly basis, and there is a provision for overtime – although this may not materialise in practice, due both to company members' enthusiasm and employer's lack of funds. With many companies it is specified that all members are receiving the same salary.

Subsidised Regional Repertory

An Equity TMA contract covers terms and conditions in repertory theatres, as well as rates for overtime and additional performances, with the basic salary covering an eight-performance week (i.e. six evening performances and up to two matinees). There are provisions for minimum weekly salaries in four ranges (middle-range salary levels or MRSLs), determined by experience. (At the time of writing the four minimum levels are £219.50, £192.50, £177.50 and £165.00.) A standard weekly subsistence allowance will be paid on top of this salary to each actor, regardless of experience.

Usually when joining a repertory theatre an actor will be offered a rehearsal salary for the period of rehearsal which will then be increased once the play has opened to the public. However, the contract is based, perhaps anachronistically now, on the assumption that a company will be rehearsing in the day and performing at night. Under the contract, unless the actor works more than 48 hours in a week, or does more than eight performances in a week, he will be paid only his performance salary. If the actor does work overtime, payment is due at one-and-a-half times the hourly rate for the additional hours worked (see p. 96).

National Subsidised Companies

Each of the three companies in this area (the Royal National Theatre, the Royal Shakespeare Company and the Royal Court) has a separate agreement with Equity, with different provisions according to their special circumstances. All these agreements cover subsistence allowances, travelling expenses and dispute procedures. At the Royal Court and the RSC the contract provides for a basic salary (a rehearsal salary followed by a playing salary) which entitles the company to 48 hours per week, as with the standard repertory contract.

The National Theatre has a different arrangement, however, which reflects the many changes of productions it makes in the course of a week. An actor is paid a rehearsal salary in the normal way and then a playing salary *plus* a fee for every performance. Both the playing salary and the performance fee are negotiable, though the rehearsal salary is often a set figure for all members of the company.

This introduces an important additional element into the negotiation. It may be that due to the scheduling of the plays, an actor may not perform for several weeks at a time. It is important, therefore, that the basic weekly salary is sufficient to cover these periods. If, on the other hand, the play is very successful in its first booking period, it may well be scheduled for a greater number of performances during the next booking period, and the actor will earn considerably more in performance fees than was originally envisaged. Usually the casting director will be able to tell you the schedule for the first booking period and the anticipated outline for the second, so it is possible to work out approximately what your earnings per week will be. Clearly if the play is not going to have many performances, it is better to stick out for a high weekly salary; on the other hand, if the play is going to be performed a great deal, especially over a short period of time, it is better to try and get as high a performance fee as possible.

All theatres in this group operate a maximum wage policy – that is, they will not pay an actor over a certain figure. The expression 'that's our maximum' is common. However, experience shows that maximums tend to vary and what is quoted as the absolute maximum available can be tempered by what was once described by a casting director as the 'Vanessa Redgrave maximum'.

Commercial Theatre Outside the West End

Once again all tours and pantomime engagements are covered, as to terms and conditions, overtime and expenses, by an Equity contract, this time negotiated with the TMA (Theatre Managers' Association).

Salary is divided into rehearsal salary (usually the same amount paid to all performers in the company) and playing salary, as with the other theatre contracts. For tours, rehearsals are often in London, thus saving the cost of expenses (for London-based actors, at least) but once the show goes out on the road expenses become payable at a rate negotiated every year between Equity and the TMA. Generally all actors receive the same expenses, which are far from generous. For leading actors in a production a percentage of the box-office gross, less VAT and library discounts (the discounts given to ticket agencies buying tickets in bulk), is also negotiated. This can range from anything between 1 and 10 per cent, but is rarely higher.

A touring management is obliged to deposit a sum of money equivalent to two weeks' salary for the cast and stage management with Equity prior to the tour. This system was instituted some years ago because of the increasing number of tours going out without financial backing and subsequently collapsing, leaving their casts out of pocket. This arrangement means actors are assured of payment, if not for the whole of the period they were originally promised, at least for part of it, in the event that the management's money runs out.

West End Theatre

The contract between Equity and SWET (the Society of West End Theatres) governs the terms and conditions of all plays produced in the West End. (Confusingly, SWET has now, from 1 January 1994, become SOLT – the Society of London Theatre – to reflect the fact that its membership includes organisations outside the West End. The name change does not affect any agreements.) As with other theatrical productions, the salary for rehearsals is paid at one rate – usually the same for all members of the cast – and for the playing weeks at a higher rate.

The playing salary is a matter of intense negotiation. If the part in the play justifies it, then the salary will be expressed as a non-returnable advance against a percentage of gross box-office receipts less VAT and library discounts. This percentage can range from 1 per cent to as much, in rare cases, as 12½ per cent. The size of the percentage will often be determined by how many other people in the cast feel they are entitled to a 'piece of the action'.

In working out what is a reasonable salary it is not difficult to estimate what a West End production is likely to cost in terms of its 'get out' figure (the money it has to make in order to break even) and the amount that can be taken at the box office depending on the capacity of the theatre and the seat prices. Some deals include a provision for the salary to increase after twelve weeks or the break-even point, whichever is the sooner. ('Break even' means the point at which the production has recovered its capital costs.)

A West End contract is either for 'the run of the play' – which means your engagement will last for as long as the play, with two weeks' notice that the play is to close – or for a limited season specified in the contract, or for a set period, usually six or nine months. In the case of the last, a clause in the contract gives you the option, after the passage of a defined period of time after the opening night (the press night, not the first preview), to give notice to the management of your intention to leave the production. However, any time during this period the management can also give *you* notice that the production is going to close and your services are no longer required.

Holiday Pay and Overtime

Although during long West End runs some stars may have short holidays, generally speaking it is unlikely that an actor working in the theatre will find time to have a holiday. There is therefore a provision in all the agreements for money to be paid in lieu of holiday. The terms can be summarised as follows:

Subsidised regional theatres: Two days' holiday entitlement for every four weeks worked. Each day's entitlement paid at one twelfth of weekly salary.

Commercial theatre outside West End: Half a day's holiday for each week worked. One twelfth of weekly salary for each half-day due.

West End: Half a day's holiday for each complete week worked. One sixth of weekly salary or one sixth of £540 (whichever is the less) for each day due.

Provision is also made as follows for overtime:

Subsidised regional theatres: Standard 48-hour week. Overtime paid at 1½ times hourly rate, calculated at 1/48th of weekly salary.

Commercial theatre outside West End: Standard 48-hour week. Overtime paid at 1½ times hourly rate, calculated at 1/48th weekly salary.

West End: Standard 45-hour week. Overtime paid at 1/45th of weekly salary or 1/40th of £234 (whichever is less).

Extra performances in all theatres are paid at the rate of one eighth of weekly salary where the contract is for once-nightly performances. There is, understandably, no such provision for extra performances on a 'twice nightly' contract!

NEGOTIATIONS

Whether you have an agent or not, you will be involved in negotiating salaries and fees for yourself throughout your career. Agents are employed for their experience in knowing the market, gauging what a producer will pay, and what they won't: they also have experience in dealing with other clients in similar situations. But it is worth remembering that, even with an agent, in the end it is entirely up to you what you will or will not accept as a suitable fee. You pay an agent for advice, but it is your decision as to whether or not you accept it. An agent is only a proxy for you in any negotiation and you are – and should be – as much a part of the decision-making process as the agent or employer.

It is important to remember this. Agents who accept a deal without consulting their clients are not doing their job properly. Equally importantly, an agent should tell his client of each and every offer received, and not turn anything down without talking first to the client, however insignificant the job may be. An agent who does not do this – who for instance turns down a job at Perth Rep because he or she feels it would be better for you to remain in London – is not doing the job properly. It may be the right decision in the context of your career at that particular moment, but in the end the decision must always be yours. Similarly an agent should not turn down a fee on the grounds that it is not enough without consulting you.

An agent's responsibility is to get the best deal that is available and then present it to the client with a recommendation as to whether it should be accepted or rejected. For instance, a West End producer may categorically refuse to pay a percentage as well as a salary. Once the agent firmly believes that this is the case, that no more arguments can be advanced to change the producer's mind, and that he has negotiated the largest salary possible, the facts should be presented to the client, together with the agent's opinion that this is the most that can be got. In addition the agent should offer a recommendation as to what, in their judgement, you should do – either accept the offer as it stands or refuse it. In either case the ultimate decision must be yours.

Of course, having an agent does add another dynamic to the equation. There is a tendency to look on the agent as an employer (see Chapter Eight) and therefore to feel somehow obliged to accept what is on offer. Inevitably your relationship with your agent will affect your decision. You may feel that your agent is keen for you to accept a particular offer because they want to earn the commission and that, if you turn it down, your agent will subsequently view you in a different light and not work as hard on your behalf. In a perfect world you could simply weigh up the pros and cons of the offer. But it is not a perfect world, and you will probably have to take some of these other factors into account.

Negotiating without an agent can pose different problems. Once again when it comes to negotiations on fees and salaries, the comparison with other professions is striking. Whereas most people will talk about their pay and conditions perhaps twenty or thirty times during their entire career, an actor may have to deal with such matters perhaps as many times every year.

One of the main reasons for employing an agent is the embarrassment many people feel in talking about their own value in monetary terms. Without an intermediary it is tempting to accept the first offer that is made and end the conversation there. But if you do not have an agent, it is worth at least trying to negotiate. Remember that in most cases a producer or casting director will be expecting to have to increase their offer, even if only marginally, and if they are dealing with you direct they will almost certainly make a lower offer than if they were dealing with an agent.

Having formally issued an offer, the casting director is preparing to enter a legally binding agreement. If you ask for more they will either tell you there is no more money available and you must take it or leave it (though they will undoubtedly use more subtle language), or they may say that they will go away and think about it or consult their producer. The latter is a good sign. They will probably come back after an hour or so and split the difference between their original offer and what you have asked for, or make some other concession, however small.

If you reject the offer then clearly no agreement exists. But once you have accepted the offer, a legally binding contract exists between both parties: even though no written contract has been signed, any breach of your verbal contract is actionable in law. That is why a casting director will be so precise as to the form of words used. An 'availability' is merely a check on whether you are available over a particular set of dates. You may be sent a script but even this does not constitute an offer unless the word itself is used. It is only when the word 'offer' is mentioned that the contract process begins, and only when you accept that offer does a contract exist.

A contract implies obligations on both sides. The verbal contract with a casting director obliges the company to pay you for your work on the agreed dates at the agreed price. But it also obliges you to turn up for work on those dates. If you do not, you can be sued for breach of contract and for damages. Though it is unlikely such a case would ever be brought if you failed to honour the verbal contract, you can be sure, unless there were very special circumstances, that the casting community would be very reluctant to give you another job.

In order, therefore, to avoid misunderstandings, it is a good idea if you are doing the negotiation yourself to write down on a dated piece of paper what is said during the various conversations leading to the agreement. You will usually receive written confirmation a day or two after the conversation and you should then check it against your understanding of what the deal was. If any misunderstanding has arisen ring the casting director immediately.

Some negotiations will be comparatively easy, others extremely difficult. Positions on both sides can become entrenched and sometimes, though hopefully only occasionally, acrimony can creep in. As far as possible this should be avoided, especially if you are negotiating for yourself. Never allow your frustration over being offered what you feel is too little to spill over into rudeness. It will do you no good whatsoever. The offer a casting director makes is subject to the budget they are given and is not a question of personality. You are much more likely to get an increase by using charm than anger.

Whether you are negotiating for yourself or you have an agent to advise you, some negotiations will inevitably come to a crunch where you will feel you are not being offered enough money and that you should consequently turn the job down. This is a decision that should only be taken with the most careful thought. As has been said many times in this book, work leads to work. A job lost is an opportunity lost too. In a highly competitive world – possibly the most competitive when it comes to employment – there is always someone waiting to step into your shoes, someone who will accept the lower offer. That is simply a fact of life in the business you have chosen.

There may well be occasions when you would be justified in turning down a job because the money is inadequate, particularly later in your career when you feel you have an established value to the production and that value is being under-rated. But for a young actor, though it is obviously important to be paid as much as possible, this has to be weighed against the importance of seizing the opportunities that every new job offers and not standing on principles based on a perhaps unrealistic assessment of what you should be paid. You may feel you are being exploited. Well, maybe you are. But with the number of out-of-work actors chasing the few available jobs, it is inevitable that salaries will be lower than if actors were in shorter supply. One definition of inflation is too much money chasing too few goods: the market for actors is the opposite, with too many actors chasing too few jobs, and the effect is to drive prices not higher, but lower.

PERKS

If you are in a strong bargaining position (i.e. the producer really wants you for the production), there are a few perks that can be negotiated in addition to the salary. In the theatre it is possible to negotiate for the sole use of a dressing room and even for a particular dressing room – the convention that the leading lady had first choice has all but disappeared. You can also request that a certain number of 'house' seats are kept for you every night with the proviso that you tell the box office by midday whether they are required or not. Approval of any photographs used 'front of house' and of the wording of the biography used in the programme are also 'add ons'.

In films the main perk is expenses and travel costs which are all negotiable. *Per diem* payments on location, especially abroad, can be generous and it is possible to specify at what level travel expenses will be paid, i.e. first class, club or economy for flying, and first or second class on the train. The use of a car is also included in negotiation. At the top of the range a car is provided for 'exclusive' use at all times, which means that the car will be there solely for you whenever you are required to go to the studio or location. On the other hand a shared car may be made available to take you to work; that is, it may be used to pick up other members of the cast and crew too. Part of the contract can also be the provision of a caravan (usually a Winnebago) on location and again this can be exclusive or shared. For actors playing the leading roles other provisions are made, including payment of travelling expenses for partner and family as well as, in more extreme cases, for stand-ins (some actors like always to work with the same stand-in, who acts as a sort of personal valet), hairdressers, dog-minders, and various assorted offspring.

Television has the fewest perks. Sometimes the leading actors are provided with a car to and from the studio or location but other than that there is very little outside the contract fee and expenses. As with films, expenses and travelling costs can sometimes be negotiated upwards. The only other discernible 'perk' is that the company may often be prepared to give you a video tape of the programme in advance of transmission.

Television, film and (to a lesser extent) theatre all share a common perk, however. During the wardrobe calls you will often trail round the shops looking for suitable clothes for your character with a costume supervisor or designer. These clothes, which can sometimes be extremely expensive, will be bought by the production company. At the end of the shoot or run of the play, these clothes can usually be bought at a fraction of the original cost. This can often prove to be a bargain.

5 How Should I Be Billed?

ILLING IS THE generic name given to all the various ways in which an actor's name is advertised in connection with the production in which he is appearing, as opposed to its use in the cast list or in publicity material handed out by the production company. Billing is, of course, negotiable and forms part of the contract for your employment, though there are many productions, for instance in repertory theatre, where there is no billing at all. Television, too, occasionally has productions in which the actors will not be billed but merely included in the cast list at the end of the programme. But if billing is given, even if it is only alphabetical, this should be stated in the contract and a breach of the terms is as actionable in law as non-payment of fees (though the amount of damages in financial terms would be extremely difficult to calculate).

In the theatre the basis of all the billing is the poster which will be produced by the theatrical management to advertise the production. This poster will be reproduced in different sizes to fit the various advertising sites throughout London or the region concerned – on buses, the underground, flyposting, and on all the normal poster sites, including outside the theatre.

The billing on posters is divided into two types: above the title and below the title. Sometimes, very rarely, a particular name may be boxed (that is the name surrounded by a rectangular box) for emphasis, or what is called 'full bottom' may be offered, a term used in the old variety posters which featured a well-known artiste, not quite well enough known to appear above the title, but meriting special attention and so billed right across the bottom of the poster (sometimes boxed as well), using wording like: 'with ANDY GARCIA as Pastor Manders'.

Differences in billing can be seen in this arrangement for a non-existent production:

IAN SHAW   HELEN MIRREN

in

GHOSTS

by
Henrik Ibsen

ANDY GARCIA   ALAN SLATER   DANIELLE NEALE

With poster billing, everything has to be spelled out in the contract. It is specified that all names will be in the 'same style and type', to prevent one name being made more prominent by use of a distinctive typeface. The size of the lettering is negotiable: if the production has a major international star, his or her name will undoubtedly be in the largest type, and this will be expressed as a percentage of the size of the type being used for the title. For instance, taking the title as 100 per cent, the star's name above the title may be expressed as being '130 per cent of the size used for the title'. Equally actors appearing below the title will have the size of their name expressed in the same terms, e.g. '80 per cent of the size used for the title'.

The position of the name in relation to other names also has to be sorted out. The position to the left is always regarded as being the first position. In our example, the contract for Ian Shaw would read 'to be billed above the title in 100 per cent of the size of the title in the same style and type and with no other name to the left'.

Helen Mirren's contract for our example would be the same, except it would state 'with one name to the left'. It would also state whether the name on the left or right would be higher or lower or 'on the same line'. The diagram overleaf represents another possible way of emphasising the importance of a star:

IAN SHAW

HELEN MIRREN

in

GHOSTS

The same applies to actors billed below the line. The position has to be stated as does everything else. Alan Slater's contract would read 'to be billed below the title in 80 per cent of the size of the title in the same style and type to the right of Andy Garcia and to the left of Danielle Neale and on the same line.' Again in billing below the title the position in relation to lines can vary. For instance a way of emphasising Alan Slater's pre-eminence would be:

GHOSTS

by

Henrik Ibsen

ALAN SLATER

ANDY GARCIA   DANIELLE NEALE

Naturally all the performers on the poster have to agree to the position of everyone else. Billing is, in the end, a question of perceived status, which can be the trickiest area of negotiation and can take a great deal of time and effort to complete to everyone's satisfaction. In the example above, Andy Garcia might feel he was just as important to the production in terms of his role and just as experienced professionally as Alan Slater, and therefore object to Slater's elevated position on the poster. In order to forestall such arguments, especially if there are six or seven actors to be billed below the title, a producer may opt for alphabetical billing though, once again, the success of this ploy depends on everyone's agreement to it. The complications of the position above the title can be just as labyrinthine, though there are usually fewer names to juggle with.

The billing and design of the poster are generally used on the cover of the theatre programme and for what are called 'display' advertisements in the newspapers (as quarter, half or even full pages). Again this should be stated in the contract – that is, that your billing will be reproduced in all advertising. The contract will usually exclude small ads, however. As the number of lines used in a small ad determines its cost, and as the cost of advertising in what is deemed to be the necessary newspapers is very expensive, producers are reluctant to be contractually bound to feature particular names. But sometimes the exclusion can be lifted, and producers may agree to a formula which states that, in the event of one person's name being mentioned in small ads, all the names above the title, say, will be mentioned.

Theatres (some of them, at least) have a unique form of billing which in the UK is known as 'front-of-house' and in the USA as 'marquee'. This involves the way the front of the theatre itself is set out. Usually following the pattern of the poster, the names above the title (and sometimes the names below) will be repeated on the 'neon' above the canopy in the same position and size as agreed for the poster. A neon is especially made for each show. There is also billing around the edge of the canopy and on any surface underneath it, and all this can be negotiated. Other front-of-house advertising will feature blown-up photographs of the production taken during the final dress rehearsal, the first preview or a special 'photo call'. Some contracts even specify that an actor will have approval not only of the photographs used but also of the number of times his or her likeness will appear in these displays.

In television there is no poster billing. Occasionally a television programme is advertised on posters on the London Underground or on billboards (especially during a franchise auction, when companies are vying against each other for public awareness), but these posters are not billing in the proper sense. They are technically called 'teasers' and are exempt from the billing clause in television contracts unless, of course, the exemption is negotiated away and the company is forced to include a particular actor's name. Generally, however, billing on television is restricted to the billing that appears on the screen. The format follows the same principles as in the theatre with the same expressions used. Leading actors are billed above the title either one to a 'card' or sharing a card with another actor in an agreed position, though it is rare to define the size and style of type in screen billing. After the title has appeared on screen there are then other actors to be billed. Sometimes these are preceded by the words 'starring' (even though there have been 'star' names above the title) or 'also starring' or 'guest stars'. Again names can appear individually on cards or with four or five names on the same card and obviously the position of the actor's name is again a matter of careful negotiation.

With many television programmes, especially serials and series, a style of billing has been established which is the same for every episode, and, indeed, there may be no billing for actors at all. If an actor wishes to appear in the programme he will have to accept that he is not going to be billed, his name appearing only in the cast list. Similarly many television programmes have no billing above the title, actors' names appearing only after the main credits. Other programmes insist on alphabetical billing, sometimes preceded by the words 'in alphabetical order'. Another common device is to add the words 'cast in order of appearance' when there may be many well-known actors vying for position and unable to come to agreement. The words 'special guest star' usually denote the presence of a well-known actor in a rather small part.

Whatever option has been agreed should be spelt out in plain language in the contract and should be as binding as any other part of that document.

Television has another special feature and that is billing in the *Radio Times* or *TV Times*. Billing, reflecting the billing negotiated for use on the screen in these magazines can be included in a television contract but as they are both independent organisations and not legally party to the contract, they may not be bound by the formula agreed, so the phrase 'the producer will use his best endeavours to see this billing is reproduced' is often used to exclude possible contractual breaches. Whether the magazines are independent or not has been the cause of much heated debate over the years between producers and agents when clients expecting magazine billing have been let down. One famous case involved the actor Rupert Davies (then playing Inspector Maigret) who claimed he had been contractually promised the cover of the *Radio Times*. Since 1992, with the abolition of exclusive copyright on television schedules and the fact that both magazines now carry all TV programming (including satellite), there is less room for billing though no less argument about the degree to which the magazines are controlled by the BBC and ITV respectively when billing has been agreed.

Film billing is perhaps the most complex of all, covering the poster, display advertising in newspapers, small ads, teasers and billboards as well as screen credits.

The composition of the poster follows the same lines as for theatre billing, with all the same concerns over size of type, position and style. There is also the question of 'likeness'. An actor may receive billing above the title but may not be given the right to equal 'likeness' in the design of the poster. In the case of *The Sting*, for instance, although Robert Shaw was billed above the title with Paul Newman and Robert Redford, Universal Pictures did not feel he was a big enough star to justify 'likeness' billing, so the poster was dominated by the images of Redford and Newman.

Once the position on the poster has been agreed this will be reflected in the paid advertising. But the contract will spell out a number of exclusions where the contractual billing does not have to be used. One of these is 'teasers', posters which tease the public into wondering what is going to happen or what a particular programme is. These can be in the underground, in the papers, or on billboards or buses. Other exclusions cover the size of a display advertisement in a newspaper (normally specified by a number of column inches – eight or four) which does not have to include the actors' names, and what is called unpaid advertising and publicity material, which involves all the press handouts and stories distributed to the press by the film company's press officer.

Screen billing will define the position of the actor in relation to the title, whether the name appears on a single or a shared card, and sometimes even how long the card has to remain on the screen in seconds. It will again define the size of type used in relation to the title for the star actors, whether they appear above or below the title. There is another form of billing on screen in films, called 'featured' billing. After the name of the stars there is frequently a list of actors, usually on one or two cards with perhaps as many as ten or twelve names. As with all billing, the position in this list is negotiable, though it is often alphabetical.

Radio billing follows the same format as all other billing. Some programmes have no billing at all and include only a cast list at the end of the programme. Others, mostly plays, bill above the title: 'Saturday Night Theatre. Maureen O'Brien and Martin Jarvis star in *Ghosts* by Henrik Ibsen . . .' And there is usually below the title too: '. . . with Patrick Connell and George Baker.' With the same provisos that apply to television, this billing will be what appears in the *Radio Times*.

6 Money, Tax, NI and VAT

NYBODY WHO WORKS on a freelance basis has to face a particular problem over money.

A person in a regular job gets a regular salary and can balance expenditure against weekly or monthly income with a reasonable, though sadly no longer absolute, certainty that his salary will continue to be paid. A freelance does not have this luxury. It is impossible to know what lies ahead, so it is extremely difficult to make rational judgements about how much of one's income should be spent and how much saved against a rainy day or as a hedge against tax.

The income tax system allows one year's profit to be set against another year's loss, but that does not properly take into account the wild fluctuations of income to which an actor in particular may be liable. Actors in the immensely successful RSC production of *Nicholas Nickleby*, whose previous earnings might have been as low as £5000 per annum, would have had at least two years of income at the level of £35,000 for playing even quite small parts, due to the show's long West End run, the LWT 'South Bank Show' version, the Broadway run and the production for Channel Four which was seen on that Channel's opening night. Their income after that, however, could well have returned to the lower level. Similarly; an actress in a Yorkshire Television situation comedy was taken to Los Angeles for the American version of the show. Her income rose from £15,000 a year to well over £80,000 a year for two years, until the show was dropped by the network. In both cases tax was paid at a high level for the profitable years, without regard to the lower levels of income that might well prevail for some time.

But it is not only the tax system that causes difficulty. Wild fluctuations of income make financial planning of any sort extremely difficult.

What is certain is that as soon as you achieve a reasonable level of income you should employ an accountant. On Schedule D an accountant's fees are tax deductible, and unless you are particularly good at keeping accounts and doing figures and understanding the various provisions of tax law that affect you as a freelance, your accountant will save you money. Your accountant should also advise you on the most tax-efficient way of saving money and making provision for pensions and other financial matters with the intention of optimising your income and minimising your tax bill.

Some actors have also employed financial advisers. A word of caution should be issued here. If you are offered an investment scheme or tax shelter or any other kind of financial deal which involves you parting with money, always seek independent advice – from your accountant or bank manager – before you sign anything and especially before you write a cheque. *Never* write a cheque out to an individual. Always check out any company name you are given with FIMBRA (the Financial Intermediaries' and Marketing Brokers' Regulation Authority), but remember that, even if they are registered with that agency, it does not mean your money is necessarily safe.

If you are lucky enough to have a windfall early on in your career, a house or flat of your own is an obvious investment. But caution should be exercised here, too. Don't go for a huge mortgage on the basis of a couple of years' good earnings. One of the most important reasons for not stretching yourself too much financially is to do with your career: if you are having trouble meeting mortgage payments and the like, you may not have the financial flexibility to accept a really good leading role in a repertory theatre which pays very little, and an opportunity may be missed.

NATIONAL INSURANCE

If you are earning more than £57 per week as an actor you will, like everyone else in the UK between the ages of 16 and 65, have to make National Insurance (NI) contributions. In relation to NI, actors enjoy a unique status. For tax purposes actors are treated as 'self-employed', but for the purposes of NI they are classed as 'employees', which means that when under contract to a company, whether in film, television or theatre, Class 1 contributions should be deducted at source. This means that actors are entitled to claim Unemployment Benefit, which is not available to other self-employed people, for instance those running their own businesses.

As Unemployment Benefit is payable on the basis of your 'contribution record' (that is, the number of NI contributions and their amounts), it is important to make sure that any employer you work for makes an appropriate deduction. They are obliged to make the deduction by law and if they do not you must inform the local Department of Social Security (DSS) office, who will contact the employer direct. Also, if you have any reason to believe that the deductions made from your salary by a company are not being sent on to the DSS, you should contact the local office as soon as possible. Do not leave it till after the job is over – the company may disappear. If they have made deductions and not passed them on, it is you who will suffer by not having an amount deducted from your salary credited to your account with the DSS. A fourteen-week contract with a touring company deducting NI every week amounts to a considerable sum of money and you must ensure it is being dealt with properly.

In addition to Class 1 contributions, you may receive an assessment from the DSS for Class 4 contributions, which is designed as a 'top up' for people who are self-employed. Confused? You may well be. You pay Class 1 contributions as an 'employee', but for Class 4 you are being regarded as 'self-employed'. Class 4 contributions are payable on annual profits between £6490 and £22,360, with normal business expenses deducted before calculation of the qualifying amount. But you will only receive an assessment for Class 4 if you have not paid sufficient Class 1 contributions; that is to say Class 1 is offset against Class 4 – they are not two separate sets of contributions. Only if your Class 1 contributions are not sufficient to cover what you should be paying under Class 4 will you have to pay more. But of course, if you have no profits above the £6490 level then you have no Class 4 contribution to make and will no receive a Class 4 assessment.

Class 4 contributions can be deferred until the end of the tax year. As actors are rarely sure of what their 'profits' in any one year will be, and will also be unable to calculate the number of Class 1 contributions they are liable to make, deferring is obviously a good idea if it is at all likely you will exceed £6490 in profits. Deferment application forms are available from the DSS; alternatively, this is something that your accountant could handle on your behalf.

Class 2 and Class 3 contributions also exist. Class 2 are contributions made by wholly self-employed people (i.e. those who are never classed as 'employees' for NI purposes), and are not counted in respect of a contribution record for Unemployment Benefit. Class 3 contributions are made at a flat rate when other contributions throughout the year have been insufficient for the year to count towards entitlement to a full state pension upon reaching retirement age.

Your NI contributions will be credited without your having to pay them when you are out of work, but only if you are 'signing on' for Unemployment Benefit or Income Support.

UNEMPLOYMENT BENEFIT

If you have made sufficient NI contributions, when you are out of work you will be entitled to claim Unemployment Benefit (£45.45 per week for a single person). To qualify there are two conditions:

1 In one of the last two complete tax years (i.e. 6 April to 5 April inclusive) before the benefit year in which you first claim (the benefit year begins on the first Sunday in January) you must have paid contributions on earnings equivalent to 25 times the lower earnings limit, i.e. currently $25 \times £57$ (£1425).
2 In each of the last two complete tax years, Class 1 contributions must have been paid or credited on earnings equivalent to 50 times the lower earnings limit, i.e. currently $50 \times £57$ (£2850).

If you meet these conditions you should claim on the first day out of work, though benefit is not due for the first three days of your claim. The benefit is payable for a period of up to one year. To receive benefit for longer than this, you will have to re-qualify. This is done by working for 13 weeks for not less than 16 hours a week. It does not matter for how many employers, or whether the weeks are consecutive, but the 13 weeks must fall within a 26-week period, between the date of the last claim and the date of the new claim. If you get a job for a period of less than eight consecutive weeks, and sign on again afterwards, the last and the new claim are 'linked' and treated as one claim. You do not thus lose three days' benefit, as you would if your new claim were to be treated as a fresh claim.

Earnings received from residuals or royalties or repeats while claiming unemployment benefit do not affect the benefit. Nor does one or more day's work, though the DSS office should be told of the work done.

It is a condition of the benefit that you are 'actively seeking work'. This may be proved in a variety of ways by the methods this book is designed to encourage. Claimants are given a period of between one and thirteen weeks when they can restrict the type of work they seek to their 'usual occupation'. At the end of this period claimants may be asked to accept work of a different sort.

After six months on the Unemployment Register a claimant will be automatically called in for a Restart interview, when prospects of employment are reviewed and possible retraining considered. Refusal to co-operate either with seeking work outside the 'usual occupation' or with suggestions for retraining may result in loss of benefit. Restart interviews are compulsory.

INCOME SUPPORT

If your entitlement to Unemployment Benefit runs out you may be entitled to Income Support. This is a means-tested payment made on two conditions:

1 You do not have enough money to live on in the view of the DSS.
2 You do not have savings above a figure of £8000.

The basic single person's weekly allowance is currently £36.15 but this may be supplemented by premiums for families, disabled children, etc., and by payment of housing costs.

INCOME TAX

Every resident of the UK is liable to pay income tax unless their income falls below the tax-free allowance. This allowance varies according to an individual's circumstances; for instance, the figure for a single person is £3445 in the 1994–5 tax year. Tax is then payable on any income above the allowance. Currently tax rates are 20 per cent on the first £3000 of taxable income, 25 per cent on the next £20,700 and 40 per cent on anything above that.

What has become crucial to actors, however, is the question of whether they are treated as 'self-employed' in relation to income tax or as 'employees'. The anomalies in relation to this and NI have already been noted, but for tax purposes it is a considerable advantage to be self-employed, as you will then be placed on the 'Reserved Schedule D Status'. Effectively this means that tax is not deducted from your wages before you are paid (though NI is and should be). Tax liability is instead calculated at the end of the year and can be subject to the deduction of legitimate expenses, of which there can be quite a few:

1 Agent's/manager's fees and commission
2 Secretarial services for keeping books and records, answering fan mail and dealing with enquiries
3 Travelling and subsistence on tour if supporting a permanent home at the same time
4 Make-up
5 Hairdressing
6 Wardrobe and props necessary for professional engagements
7 Laundry and cleaning of wardrobe and props
8 Renewal, replacement and repair of wardrobe and props
9 Travelling and expenses incurred in attending interviews and auditions

10 Gratuities to dressers, doorkeepers, make-up staff
11 Postage for business letters, fan mail
12 Business stationery
13 Tuition and coaching for dancing, singing, speech and any other professionally related skills
14 Professional publications, e.g. *Radio Times*, *The Stage*, *PCR*, *Broadcast*, etc.
15 Records, cassettes, scripts, videos and sheet music
16 Cinema and theatre tickets
17 Equity subscriptions
18 Accountant's fees
19 Legal charges for debt recovery, contract disputes
20 Photographic sittings and reproduction
21 Advertising, e.g. *Spotlight*
22 Maintenance of instruments and their insurance

In addition to this you should decide what proportion of the following is used for business purposes and claim that too:

1 Telephone and fax costs
2 Hire of television and video; licence payment
3 Motor car expenses including petrol, servicing, insurance and road fund tax

The Inland Revenue have also accepted cases on an individual basis for deduction of fees for physiotherapy, chiropody, cosmetic dentistry and trichology treatments. They will also consider claims for a capital allowance for certain items related to business purposes. A 25 per cent rate is allowed on the cost of items like a motor car, answerphone, office furniture, television and video equipment and musical instruments.

As you can see, Schedule D status is well worth having. Unfortunately, for reasons best known to themselves, the Inland Revenue have decided that actors working in the theatre are not entitled to Schedule D status and are not self-employed. They will therefore be classed as Schedule E and liable to PAYE, and theatres have been instructed to deduct tax from these actors' wages at source. Only actors who had already paid tax under Schedule D for three years prior to 1990 were exempt from this draconian measure, which came into effect on 6 April that year.

How the Inland Revenue can claim that a contract, even a long contract in the theatre, represents regular employment and is not part of the normal course of an actor's career, which is patently self-employed, is hard to comprehend. But the decision represents considerable hardship for a young actor. An actor engaged on a ten-week contract at £220 per week will have NI and income tax totalling approximately £80 deducted at source, despite the fact that at the end of the contract there may be no other job to go to. An actor may earn less in a year than the personal allowance for a single person but still have the tax deducted. If this is the case, the tax will be refunded at the end of the tax year, but in the meantime the actor is left desperate for money.

This ruling has now been successfully challenged by Equity. In October 1993, the Special Commissioners of the Inland Revenue ruled favourably in an appeal brought by the union on behalf of two actors. After hearing evidence that there was essentially no difference between work in the theatre, television or films and that actors conducted their professional life as a business, the Commissioners agreed that these actors' income from theatre should be assessed under Schedule D and not be subject to PAYE. It is to be hoped that the Inland Revenue will not seek leave to appeal against this decision.

At the time of writing, the Inland Revenue has not changed its rules, though, so you cannot expect to avoid paying PAYE on earnings in the theatre for the time being – unless, of course, you are fortunate enough to be one of those who already qualifies for Schedule D. Hopefully, this will not be the case for much longer.

Employment on Schedule E also means that a person is entitled to make only very limited deductions against tax. Allowances are made for agent's commission, make-up, dancewear, stage clothing, sheet music, scripts, records, and cassettes which have to be bought for a specific part, but that is all. Moreover, relief for these items is not made until the end of the tax year and comes in the form of a tax refund – though if you are on a very long contract of over a year, it is worth applying for a tax code re-adjustment, which will mean a reduction in the tax deducted from your salary.

One area of confusion when considering tax has been over expenses, the *per diems* given on films or in television, or the subsistence allowances given on tour or at a regional repertory theatre. Expenses should be entered on your income tax form as income. Any actual costs in relation to travelling expenses and hotels will then be deducted, but if there is a surplus this is treated as income. Remember too that all film, television and theatre companies are required by law to make a return to the Inland Revenue of all payments made to each employee. The BBC sends you a copy of this return at the end of the tax year. Other companies don't, but that does not mean they don't make a return. The amount included in this return is the total of all income and expenses.

WITHHOLDING TAX

If you go to work abroad for a foreign company you may find your salary is subject to withholding tax, usually at 25 or 30 per cent. This will only be done if that country has a Double Taxation Treaty with the UK (the USA, for instance, has such a treaty). These treaties were introduced as part of an effort to thwart international tax avoidance schemes. Tax deducted in one country can be set against your liability to pay tax in the UK, so in other words it is like a pre-payment of UK tax. Unfortunately if you have no tax liability in the UK it is difficult to reclaim the tax from the withholding country.

Work done in a country without a Double Taxation Treaty will not be subject to withholding tax. But remember that as long as you are resident in the UK all foreign earnings are taxable in full.

VAT

In the event that you earn more than £45,000 in any one year (this is the 1994–5 figure, but like all other figures in this chapter is subject to change in every budget) and are taxed under Schedule D as being self-employed, you are liable to register for Value Added Tax. Every quarter you must fill out a return to the Customs and

Excise, who administer VAT, which will state your 'output' tax, the tax you are obliged to charge on all your services (except services that are exported, i.e. work done abroad), currently at 17.5 per cent and, on the other hand, your 'input' tax, which is the tax you have had to pay on items or services purchased as part of normal business expenses. The output tax is collected by you and sent off to the Customs and Excise, less the deduction of whatever input tax you have incurred. Items that can be deducted roughly follow the pattern of deductions as allowable expenses against income tax.

The Customs and Excise have extensive powers to examine your records and even to enter your house without a search warrant. You are obliged, once registered, to keep accurate and up-to-date records. There are also powers to fine for late payment and non-payment and for inaccurate and false accounting.

KEEPING RECORDS

It is not only for VAT that it is vitally important to keep detailed records of all your income and expenses and the dates when you are in and out of work. Keeping a note of such things is not something that most people enjoy but it is essential to ensure that you do not pay too much tax or fail to get the Unemployment Benefit or Income Support to which you may be entitled. This cannot be over-emphasised. The Inland Revenue and DSS are not known for their kind and understanding nature.

An actor's life is difficult enough without having to spend time and money and, most importantly, energy, dealing with endless problems caused by disputes with government departments. Clear and precise documentation will solve most queries quickly and easily, leaving you more time for the business of getting a job.

Information in this chapter is provided as a guide only. All figures and conditions are based on 1994/5 rates, but are subject to change, and the latest position should be checked with the Inland Revenue, the DSS or the Customs and Excise as appropriate. Alternatively Equity may also give up-to-date guidance on tax, National Insurance, benefits and other rights, and they regularly publish an excellent Advice and Rights Guide *covering all these points.*

7 Working Abroad

EFORE THE INTRODUCTION of the 1973 Employment Agencies Act, theatrical agents in London were licensed by Westminster City Council. The Council's prime motivation in setting up controls on employment agencies was an increasing number of complaints and press reports about agencies shipping out dancers ostensibly to work in cabaret in Paris or Rome, but whose real destination was allegedly the kasbahs of the Middle and Far East where they would be sold, in the newspaper jargon of the day, and probably with a good deal of exaggeration, as 'white slaves'. Officially therefore, up to 1973 even respected theatrical agents like Fraser and Dunlop were supposed to inform Westminster City Council of any offer of employment received for a female (not male) 'artiste' to work abroad, and obtain the appropriate permission. If, for instance, Dame Peggy Ashcroft was asked to appear in a film in Rome, or Vanessa Redgrave in New York, an application should have been made to Westminster City Council.

The Employment Agencies Act fortunately swept all such apparatus away, but working abroad, desirable as it is, can still be fraught with problems. Basically work abroad can be divided into two types: work for a foreign company, either in the company's home country or in other foreign countries, or work for a UK company that happens to take place abroad.

The latter is the easiest to deal with. If you are offered work by a UK company abroad – anywhere in the world – it is up to them to get all the necessary clearances and consents, visas and work permits, and anything else that is required. You will be paid your expenses abroad, but your salary will be paid in England and the contract governed by English law. Not only that, but in the event of a breach of contract the employing company, being resident in the UK, can be sued in this country, where it presumably has assets which would be subject to the court's jurisdiction. The company is also vulnerable to being put on the Equity blacklist for non-payment.

None of this applies to a foreign company. A foreign company will usually offer employment on condition that you can obtain the necessary papers (though they may help you with the formalities); you will be paid in foreign currency from a foreign bank (and therefore fluctuations in the exchange rate will affect your earnings); it is difficult to know whether the company that has made the offer is reputable; and it will be even more difficult, in the event that the contract is breached, to sue for recovery of fees owed or damages.

In addition there is a danger that the product of your work may be less subject to regulation in terms of copyright than in the UK. A commercial made abroad for a foreign company may be used all over the world for years without your earning a further penny.

To make sure you are paid, the best advice is to ask the company to pay the fee into escrow (i.e. into the hands of a reliable third party, such as a firm of lawyers) before you leave England. Then at least you know they have the money in the first place. And you should of course insist on a return air or rail fare. If they refuse, you may still wish to go, but at least you are aware of the risk. Don't, incidentally, think that these precautions need not apply to American companies. They can be just as difficult in the event of problems. Obviously if it is a big company like Warner Brothers their reputation should be enough, but sometimes, especially in films, though the distributor may be Warner Brothers, the contract for the film is made with some offshore company whose only asset is the contract with Warners to make the film. In the event that the contractor and Warners fall out, the contract for your employment would be worthless. In this case it is common practice to get Warner Brothers to guarantee (what is called giving an 'indemnity') that they will honour the contract directly.

Many UK actors work every day for companies producing films, commercials and theatre (the English Speaking Theatre in Vienna is an example of the latter) throughout the world with no difficulty. However there are regulations governing employment of 'aliens' in various countries which have to be overcome. Generally, for the purposes of work permits, the world is divided into three: EC countries, the USA and the rest of the world.

The Treaty of Rome established free movement of labour throughout the member states of the European Community (at the time of writing, Belgium, Denmark, France, Germany, Ireland, Italy, Luxembourg, Portugal, Spain, Greece and the UK). It is an obligation on all these countries not to put up any barrier to employment of a national of a member state. In effect, as far as actors are concerned at least, the natural barrier of language prevents a large-scale invasion of these other European nations: similarly, there are few European actors working in the UK.

A British actor wishing to work in the USA must first have an offer of employment, and second, a 'green card' work permit. Any actor applying for a green card to the State Department will automatically be referred to the American Actor's Equity Association, which will oppose the granting of a permit unless the actor or the company wishing to employ the actor can prove he or she has 'star' status, or is in some way uniquely qualified for the job, or is part of the British–American Equity exchange agreement by which British actors are allowed to appear in American theatres, while American actors are allowed to appear in British – there were eleven exchanges of this kind in 1992.

The criteria for star status or uniqueness are extremely tough and claims to either will be fought tooth and nail by American Equity – just as British Equity will fight applications from American actors. But of course many British actors, both the famous and not-so-famous, do manage to establish themselves either in New York or, more commonly, in Los Angeles, appearing regularly in American films and television series.

There appears to be little reason why one actor is accepted and another rejected, which makes it especially frustrating if you are refused a work permit. Generally, it seems to depend on how far the company making the offer is prepared to go to support you, and how good the lawyer is who has to be hired to deal with the application.

The rest of the world varies from country to country. There are obviously opportunities for British actors in Australia and Canada, where language is not a barrier, but both adopt a protectionist stance in relation to their own talent, and it is unlikely that they will accept a non-star actor for film or television work. Other countries, particularly those with limited numbers of actors, have a more *laissez-faire* attitude, but of course work in these countries may be correspondingly limited.

Overall, working abroad should be regarded as a bonus rather than a career goal. If you particularly want to work in the USA, which for a lot of actors represents an ambition they would like to fulfil, you will almost certainly need to establish a reputation in this country first. Obviously work done here but seen in America – a film made by an American company in the UK, or a West End play transferring to Broadway – is the best way to begin the long process of achieving recognition from prospective American employers.

8 Agents

Despite the fact that agents are categorically not employers they are included at this point because they act as a bridge, a conduit between employers and actors.

FINDING AN AGENT is perhaps one of the major concerns in every actor's life and one of the areas most fraught with difficulty. Attitudes to agents vary from total contempt to outright fear, frequently based on mis-information, gossip, supposition and rumour.

But getting an agent is only part of the problem. Once having got yourself on to an agency's list, it is just as important to build and develop a productive relationship that will be a positive benefit to your career. This relationship cannot be taken for granted. If it is not given careful consideration and worked on constructively then it can soon wither and die, necessitating another search for another agent. Changing agents is often as taxing as getting one in the first place.

I have said before that an agent must not be seen as the be-all and end-all of an actor's efforts to get himself work. There is a tendency for actors cheerfully to hand over all responsibility for that side of their professional life to their agent and sit back to wait for the phone to ring. This is a mistake.

A theatrical agency is, first and foremost, a business. It makes money from charging its clients commission on their professional income. The commissions coming in are used to defray expenses – rent, salaries, telephone bills, etc – and if they exceed the costs then the agency will be in profit. This may be stating the obvious, but it is important to realise that however friendly an agency may seem, the bottom line is that unless they make a profit they cannot and will not survive.

Because an agency represents a number of clients it is possible to balance the costs of one against the profits from another. The cost to the agency of an unemployed actor may not appear to be great but from a business point of view, taking into account telephone calls, secretarial time, postage and stationery costs, it soon mounts up. An agency therefore needs clients who are successful, who are making money, in order to support the ones who are not.

This is where the first problem arises. Inevitably the clients who are making the agency money will receive and expect more attention than those who are not. There are some very good and caring agents who will nurture clients over a number of years through a sequence of hard times, but continued, persistent unemployment, though it may not lead to disenchantment, can dull the initial edge of enthusiasm that was generated when the actor was first taken on.

As being taken on by an agent is very much an exercise in sales – selling oneself – the initial 'pitch', the letter and subsequent interview, will properly create a feeling in the agency that you are an actor who is interesting, talented, well-connected and going somewhere, and who will therefore earn the agency money. If this promise, over a period of time, fails to materialise then it is quite natural that the initial excitement may wane.

But isn't it up to the agent to develop the connections and deliver on the promise? Isn't that why you wanted and were prepared to pay an agent in the first place? The answer is obviously yes. However, unless you have actually been employed you will have paid nothing and the longer this situation goes on, the more strains are placed on the relationship.

This makes it sound as if the only thing agents are concerned with is money. That is not true. There are some very conscientious individuals who work hard for their clients regardless of their earning capacity, taking the long-term view that talent will eventually be rewarded. Some actors form a bond of mutual trust with their agent that lasts a lifetime. But frequently such relationships are formed with clients whose financial circumstances are secure, who regularly earn the agency more or less substantial amounts

of commission. In the end, however strong the friendship or conscientious the agent, difficulties may arise if the client continues not
to make money for the agency over the medium term. And naturally enough an actor in such a situation will also be feeling
discontent with his lack of employment.

So it is important to be realistic about the actor–agent relationship, which can all too easily assume mythic proportions in the
mind of an actor. One of the main factors in this relationship will
be the type of agency you are represented by or wish to be represented by.

TYPES OF AGENCY

There are many different types of agency but basically they fall into
five broad categories:

1 A small business run by one (usually) or two individuals with
  the help of assistants and/or secretaries, who have a long-term
  relationship with one or two 'star' clients on whom they rely for
  their profits. Overall their client list will be small, sometimes no
  more than thirty. They occasionally take on non-star clients but
  only seldom. Often they deal exclusively with actors, i.e. not
  directors, producers, writers or other personnel.
2 A business run by one or two individuals, sometimes without
  secretarial assistance, with a very large client list composed almost exclusively of actors, few or none of whom are well-
  known or star actors. The business profits, often meagre, are
  generated by a large volume of relatively small commissions.
3 A large business run by a large group of individuals who have
  many clients in a number of fields – directors, producers,
  writers, etc – as well as actors and star actors. In some of these
  businesses the actors are still the most important element, but in
  others the acting side of the agency is subsidiary, in terms of
  profits, to the money generated from other clients. In general the
  client lists of these companies are extremely long.
      A sub-section of this group consist of agencies which are
  American owned, and, though having English directors, ulti-

mately American run. These companies are multi-million-pound businesses with offices in many of the entertainment capitals of the world.

4 Cooperatives. These are agencies formed by groups of actors who band together to share the operating costs and man their offices on a rota. Their client lists are necessarily small and everyone on them works, part time, in the office.

5 Specialist agencies which represent clients only in one field of activity, usually either for commercials and corporate videos, or (the largest number) for voice-overs on commercials.

You may have formed an idea of the type of agency which you would like to join. A lot of actors feel that being accepted by an agency in the third group would be the best of all possible worlds. But it might not be as advantageous as is first supposed.

The temptation for a young or less than well-known actor to join a large 'powerful' agency with its massed ranks of star clients is obviously strong. Being able to say that you are represented by such a company bestows status and kudos, it speaks of quality. An agency of this sort has, at least in theory, a great deal of vestigial power. It will have access to scripts, know a great deal of the future plans and projects of many employers and be able to call people, on a one-to-one basis, who are controlling or initiating productions across a whole range of media. Indeed producers and directors will themselves be wooing the agents from such a company, trying to persuade them that their star client should put his name to a script. In this situation a *quid pro quo* might be exacted. There will be cases where one client is unavailable, allowing the agent to put forward another. There will be cases where a project actually begins life in the agency, is 'packaged' with writer, director and star, and sold to a film or television company or theatrical management. Here too it might be thought there are opportunities to introduce less well-known clients.

The extent to which this power is exercised varies with each agency. Undoubtedly there are instances of such manoeuvring having significant effects on an actor's career. But they are far rarer than is imagined, and when, for instance, one star client is unavailable and another is suggested, the latter will often be another well-known face. Persuading a star client to become involved with a project in return for asking the director to take on a new talent in one of the smaller roles may seem like a good idea from the point of view of the agency, but in reality it is fraught with difficulties.

The occasions when a search is launched for a new talent to play a particular role (Scarlett O'Hara in *Gone With the Wind*, Natasha in *War and Peace*, a new James Bond) may well give the big agency an inside track, in that the director or producer may be on their client list and therefore easily accessible, but that does not mean their particular suggestion for the role will necessarily carry any more weight. It is conceivable, even, that it will carry less.

Against this background the problems of being a less than exalted client of a big agency are obvious. It is easy to be over-looked. Day-to-day attention to your problems and prospects cannot be guaranteed, as time and energy will all too readily be diverted to the clients who are earning the agency money. As a principle, contrary to what might be imagined, the bigger the agency the more concerned they are with profits. Many companies operate performance-related pay schemes for their executives, who will therefore look carefully at how they spend their time in rela-tion to how quickly it can produce increased commissions. Overheads – a West End office, a large non-executive staff, etc. – are high and money needs to be generated to pay for them. Often this leads to a short-term view in assessing an actor's potential earnings. Indeed sometimes financial targets are set for each client and failure to reach them has led to actors reporting receipt of letters saying that they can no longer be represented as their earn-ings are insufficient.

The experience of a number of actors is that a big agency can be completely satisfactory if success is achieved within the first year to eighteen months of joining. After that, if things have not gone well, it has often been the case that actors no longer feel they are on the 'active' list, and the number of calls they receive from their agent is severely reduced.

If you are lucky enough to be offered representation by one of the agencies in the first group, then many of these problems are mitigated. The agent has more time and is under less pressure. It is possible to deal with clients' problems on a more individual basis, while at the same time having a certain amount of clout due to representation of one or two star names. Unfortunately there are few agencies in this group and they take on clients very rarely.

The problems with joining an agency in the second group are of an entirely different sort. The main one is competition. Generally the agents in these companies work very hard. They have to, in order to keep their heads above water against a background of ever-increasing overheads. In addition to the work they do themselves to find out what is being cast, they will receive a fair number of calls from casting directors looking for a particular type. When talking to a casting director they will inevitably have four or five (or more) actors to fit the bill, and will suggest them all. It is a scatter-gun approach. Hopefully one of the number will get the job.

Clearly, with some agencies in the second group, having a hundred to a hundred and fifty clients divided between one or two agents and a secretary or assistant, the agent's knowledge of and concern about each individual client will necessarily be limited. There is no time to develop a meaningful relationship with the clients, and for the actor the experience of being with an agent of this sort can be frustrating and is often contemplated as a last resort. But these agencies do have one distinct advantage. They have a great deal of day-to-day contact with casting directors and will often know a great deal about what is going on.

This is in contrast to the agencies in the first group. With a small client list it is unlikely they will have more than one client to fit any particular role, if they have anyone at all. Clearly this means they will push for that client strongly because if he or she doesn't get the part no one in the agency will. The ideal situation, you may think. But even this has drawbacks. Because the agency is known for having only a few clients it will not get as many calls as the larger agencies from casting directors and directors looking for a particular type. If a casting director is looking for a middle-aged fat man for a small role, he or she will call the bigger agencies first, knowing they will be able to provide a wide choice. Only if this trawl does not produce results will they bother with the smaller agencies.

Cooperatives also have good and bad points. Among the good

is the fact that, firstly, they represent a positive step for an actor trying to do something about his career. If a cooperative is run efficiently and consists of a group of people who get on well together and who are prepared to work hard for each other in ferreting out information and making suggestions to casting directors, it can be successful in obtaining employment for their members.

The down side of this is that some cooperatives are subject to clashes of personalities, have members who do not wish to commit themselves to the necessary office work, and, of course, are subject to fluctuations in staff and efficiency due to members getting jobs and not being available to help run the agency. In the day-to-day running, too, the actors manning the phone have to be scrupulous as to who they suggest for any particular part, especially if the part is one that could be played by themselves. A cooperative can also be unbalanced when one of its members becomes successful, leaving the other, less fortunate members to do all the work.

It has to be said, also, that casting directors and directors can be chary of calling cooperatives and are much happier dealing with traditional agencies. They feel awkward talking to an agent who is really an actor. There is an element of honesty between an agent and a casting director which is built up over the years, and respected by both parties, which enables them to talk of actors with a degree of realism and ease. This is not going to happen with a cooperative. Neither will the personnel have the same experience in negotiating salaries, contracts and billing as a traditional agent.

It is worth mentioning here the specialist agencies of the fifth group. Is it worth trying to join them? Firstly, if you have an existing agent they may not be happy with the idea of your going to another agency for, say, voice-overs; indeed, if you have signed an agency contract this may be specifically forbidden. Voice-over work is very lucrative and your agent may feel you are depriving them of part of their rightful income. But if your agent agrees, or if you don't have another agent, is it worth trying to get the interest of one of these companies? For voice-overs the answer is probably not, unless you have a particularly distinctive and effective voice. The market is dominated more and more by star names and specialists, who can deliver what the advertising agency wants quickly and efficiently. They are known quantities to the company whose product is being advertised, and can, in the case of the star names, also deliver a certain glamour and kudos to the brand.

The realistic chances of breaking into the voice-over market are therefore very small.

Agencies specialising in commercials and industrial and corporate videos may be of some benefit if they are prepared to take you on. They deal in areas that mainstream casting directors and agents may not be aware of, particularly when foreign companies wish to make commercials or videos with English actors and crew. The money will be unspectacular, but probably worthwhile.

But specialist agencies are not going to make a significant impact on your overall career. They may provide much-needed finance, but it is a mistake to spend too much time on peripheral diversions such as this.

ACTORS' REGISTERS

There have been in the past, and may well be again, companies that have offered actors the chance to enter their names on a register holding names and CVs. Such a register is supposed to be circulated to casting directors and other employers, and a sum of money is demanded for this registration. These companies have proved in the past to be fraudulent and have been investigated by the police. *Never* get involved with an agent who asks you for any sort of registration fee or, indeed, money for anything apart from photographs. Operations of this kind are not part of the normal casting process.

CONTRACTS AND COMMISSIONS

All agencies, in whatever group, charge commission and some ask you to sign an agency contract before they will agree to take you on. The contract usually states that you will be represented *exclusively* by that agency, meaning that no other agency will represent you, and on a worldwide basis. If, say, an American agency approached you to represent you in the USA, you would have to refer the enquiry to your existing agent, who would negotiate with the Americans, usually agreeing to split the commission on any American work they might get for you. This is a common practice.

The contract will be for a specific period of time, perhaps two years, with options for further periods at the discretion of both parties. If, therefore, during the two-year period you become dissatisfied with your agent, you cannot just walk away. You must state your dissatisfaction, preferably in writing, and provide good reasons as to what precisely is wrong, reasons which must involve demonstrably unprofessional conduct. Usually an agency will then agree to release you – a release you should, once again, be sure to have in writing. If the matter is not resolved amicably in this way, remember the agency may be entitled to whatever their commission is on your gross income for the remaining period of the contract. They will have to sue you to get it and obviously if the amount involved is small they won't bother: but if you were to make a great deal of money they would undoubtedly do so, particularly if they felt you could not prove that they had acted in a manner which breached their contractual obligations.

Commissions vary from agency to agency and there are many different formulae. Some agencies take a basic rate on everything you earn (rarely, these days, the legendary 10 per cent; it is more likely to be 12½ or 15 per cent), while others charge different rates for different things (7½ per cent for repertory theatres and radio, 15 per cent for films and television, 12½ per cent for West End theatre, 17½ per cent for commercials, etc.). These rates are invariably non-negotiable, but you should certainly find out what they are, especially if you are choosing between one agency and another.

The actual process of collecting commissions should be noted too. When you sign a contract for employment with a production company of whatever sort, there will be an 'all monies' clause, which states that the fee for the engagement will be paid to the agent and that 'receipt by same will be due discharge'; in other words, once the money is paid to the agent you have no recourse to the employer to complain that you have not been paid. The agent will bank the cheque and send you an 'advice note' showing the amount received and deductions for commission and VAT on commission (if the agent is registered for VAT – most are), plus a cheque for the amount due. This is normal procedure.

However, there are two problems that can arise. Under the Employment Agencies Act which now regulates *all* employment agencies, the money received should be paid out within ten working days. Despite this requirement, agencies can suffer cash-flow problems and be slow to pay out. If these cash-flow difficulties develop into something more serious and the agency goes into liquidation, you will have effectively lost whatever money is due to you. Be sure, therefore, to insist you are paid promptly, as is your right.

The 'all monies' clause also means that the agent will be sent all residuals and royalties due under the contract and will take commission on them. When you leave an agent they will continue to receive these residuals unless you specifically write to *all* the companies you have worked with who pay residuals (i.e. television and film companies and advertising agencies), requesting that monies are sent to you direct. This is something you may wish to do, but many agents regard the commission on residuals as part of their entitlement for getting you the job and negotiating the contract, and they may be right. If, for instance, an agency was instrumental in your landing a large part in a long-running television series and negotiating a complicated contract for it, and you left that agency after a few months, instructing monies to be sent to you direct, the agency might well feel justified in claiming commission on your continuing fees and on all residuals. Such a claim might run into a large sum of money and might be sympathetically treated by the courts if the matter could not be settled amicably.

LEVELS OF EXPECTATION

The relationship between actor and agent can therefore be unsatisfactory and difficult. It can also be useful and productive, but the experience of most out-of-work actors is of the former kind.

One of the main reasons for this is the level of expectation, and how agents are perceived by actors. Actors appear to fear, revere and despise agents all in the same breath. Such contradictory attitudes based on extensive disinformation can lead to extreme dissatisfaction when faced with the reality of the situation. The fact is, *agents do not employ actors*. They cannot give an actor a job. The power an agent has is severely limited, and even an agent with important clients, even an agent who has an extensive network of contacts and friends who do employ actors, cannot *guarantee* to get an actor work. An agent can, and the better ones do, persuade and cajole, wheedle, wine and dine, beg and plead for one of his clients to be given work, but in the final analysis that is all he can do.

This may be stating the obvious, but it is surprising how many actors feel (rather than think) that, in some magical way, an agent is actually responsible for their employment. It is an attitude that may be a hangover from the days before the Second World War when agents were actually employed by the theatres and not by the actors.

Before the Second World War, agents acted as a sort of casting director for the big theatrical companies and for the numerous musical halls, auditioning and selecting actors and arranging their contracts. With the arrival of film in the twenties and thirties however, and its creation of 'star' actors with considerable power (Charlie Chaplin and Mary Pickford, for instance, forming United Artists), more and more actors saw the need for separate representation, and soon their power was exercised through managers, at that time usually ex-lawyers. In this country personal managers – this title was used to distinguish them from agents working for the theatres – grew up as part of this movement, usually as off-shoots of literary agents (Christopher Mann) or Americans who came to start up businesses over here (Al Parker).

With the enormous and sudden decline of music hall and theatre during and after the war, and the creation of casting directors for film and television, the old agents disappeared. Now the term personal manager and agent are virtually synonymous.

WHAT AN AGENT DOES

Generally speaking an agent has a great deal less to do with getting an actor work than is commonly imagined. If an agent were honestly to say how many times they have actually got a client a job – that is to say, if the agent hadn't suggested his client, the job would not have materialised at all – the answer would probably be as few as once or twice over ten or more years. That doesn't mean the agent hasn't had a hand in securing all sorts of employment, keeping his client's name in front of directors and casting directors, making numerous suggestions, selecting and sending out photographs and CVs – routine work for a good agent, but nevertheless important to ensure that his clients are constantly being thought of and discussed. But direct responsibility for securing a job is much rarer.

Of course, if a casting director rings an agent with an offer of a job out of the blue, or because the client has just been seen on television or in the theatre, it is tempting for the agent to embellish the truth a little and tell the client that the offer is the result of his own suggestion. This is a common and understandable practice, but it does not help in trying to assess realistically what effect an agent has on an actor's career.

In a sense it is when an actor is already successful that an agent has a more important role to play. He is responsible for negotiating the contract which will involve money, royalties, billing and various ancillary rights. He can also play a major part in guiding an actor into certain parts and away from others, and persuading directors that his client should be given the chance to extend his range. The amount of work a successful actor generates for an agency is staggering. There are endless calls from members of the public wanting to know whether the client is available to open fêtes and charity events, from organisations wanting shops to be opened or publicity events attended, and more significantly, from within the business a stream of requests for 'availability' (information on whether or not an actor is available over a certain set of dates), and all sorts of offers, including sometimes entirely inappropriate jobs, for instance, whether a major film star might consider playing a small part in *Coronation Street*. This is to say nothing of the demands of the personal relationship that may develop in helping the actor to cope with family and professional problems and financial and tax affairs, which can go far beyond normal business life.

There are, therefore, many demands on an agent's time. The amount of time actually spent on what is usually referred to as 'casting' (finding out information on future projects and making suggestions for them) varies from office to office. Some agencies prepare information on their clients' availabilities and send it to a list of prospective employers on a regular basis. Inevitably this list will reflect the agency's area of expertise and their own perception of where they can make money. However big the agency, their mailing will not be all-embracing. Many agents, as already noted, have felt it is better not to have their clients working in rep theatres because it means they are then unavailable for television or film work in London. It is unlikely, therefore, that such an agency would bother to write to or collect information from reps – a huge source of employment.

DO I NEED AN AGENT?

You may well be asking by now whether you should bother with an agent at all. The answer is yes – but with some significant qualifications.

At the beginning of your career, if your aim is to go into rep and build up your experience, then you do not need an agent. An agent may have an association over the years with one or two reps built on the basis of clients appearing there regularly (or perhaps on representing the artistic director), but will not have a general knowledge of all of them. Nor will they be very interested in writing round to them on your behalf. The salaries involved are too small.

So if this is your plan you will do better on your own. You can cover all the reps, and all the TIE companies and even summer seasons and pantos. In addition, reps are used to receiving letters direct from actors (unlike television companies who prefer suggestions to come through the filter of an agency).

It is when your career develops to the point where you want to try television, film and West End theatre that you will actually need an agent. Casting directors have to sift through enormous numbers of letters, and the fact that your name is attached to a reputable agency helps: at least, they reason, your work has already been seen and approved of. And there are occasions when suggestions will be accepted, and information on casting given, only through an agency.

This is the prime reason you *need* an agent – not as someone who is magically going to get you a job.

HOW DO I GET AN AGENT?

The next question that needs to be addressed is: how do you go about getting an agent? Like so much that faces an actor, it is not easy. Agents, like casting directors, are deluged with requests. It is important to try and be realistic. If your entire experience in the business is a two-year engagement with a TIE company, it is unlikely that a powerful and high-profile agency like ICM is going to be interested in representing you. Nor would it be the right agency for you, for reasons that are now, hopefully, obvious.

Firstly you need to get a list of agents. A list is provided in the information section of this book. There is also a list published by the Spotlight organisation in *Contacts*, and another list in *The Knowledge*, but the list published in Part Three of this book has been edited to try – as far as possible – to include only those agents that are active and worth your while to approach.

Despite this, the list should only be regarded as a working document. It needs further research by you. The next stage is to find out what clients an agency represents and roughly how many they have on their books. This is a relatively simple matter. The *Screen International Yearbook* will give you a guide to who represents the better-known actors (who sometimes no longer bother to advertise in *Spotlight*) and *Spotlight* will allow you to go through its latest editions at its offices. A couple of hours spent on these directories will give you an accurate idea of which group an agency falls into, who specifically they have on their books, and a general feel for the sort of clients they handle and therefore the type of agency they are. Additionally, if you already have an agent and are thinking of changing you will be able to see who your existing agent represents, if you don't already know, and whether any other clients have left recently.

You will notice that some agencies are members of the Personal Managers' Association (PMA). Membership of this organisation is by invitation, which implies that only experienced and reputable agents are members. (However, though the Association does have a code of conduct it does not have any financial bond or insurance to indemnify its members against claims of misconduct. Nor does it have a fund to reimburse actors if their fees are caught up in an agency liquidation.)

From the research you have done you should begin to get a picture of the agencies you feel would ideally be right for you. But you will need to make a list, and quite a long one, in order of preference. It is unlikely you will be taken on by your first choice.

While you have been going through *Spotlight* you will probably have noticed several faces who are going to be your competition: the same age, type, appearance. There is a theory that it pays to be with an agent who represents a successful rival of this sort, the theory being, that when the other actor is busy the agent can suggest you in his or her stead. The theory is occasionally valid, but generally an offer for a well-known actor will involve a leading part in a production that is looking for his name and reputation to enhance it. The producer is therefore unlikely to take on an actor who does not have the same status as a replacement. The possibility of substituting one non-actor for another, however, is more likely.

Having compiled your list of agents you may wish to ring them up and ask if they are taking on any new clients. Many agencies will automatically say no. Over the phone, and because of the number of prospective clients, that is often the easiest course of action. It does not necessarily mean they are not considering new clients, unless the response is so emphatic as to leave no doubt. So, though a preliminary phone call is an idea to establish that their address is unchanged, you should not necessarily take no for an answer at this stage.

A letter is the best approach, and with it you should enclose a photograph and (always) a stamped addressed envelope. The remarks made on letters and photographs (see Chapters 9 and 12) apply. An agent receives a great number of such letters. Don't be tempted to be funny or quirky; it has all been done before. A straightforward letter with a good photograph will draw a serious response.

Timing the letter is most important. If, in a few days' time, you are due to be seen on television in a part that shows you to advantage, that is the time to write. If you are in a film that is about to be released or in a West End production, again, assuming the part merits consideration, this is a good time to send off your letter. The agent will probably be seeing the production anyway and will undoubtedly make a note of your name, and, if interested, call you.

If you are in a fringe production or a repertory production it is a different matter. There may be someone else in the cast whose agent is on your list and is coming to see them. Then, by all means, write, preferably telling the other actor what you are doing. But if you are in a production at Theatr Clwyd, or the Northcott in Exeter, or even as near central London as Brentford, do not expect that an invitation to an agent to see the production will be well received. Perhaps if you are playing King Lear, but not otherwise. The calls on an agent's time are simply too great.

The chances of an agent coming to a London fringe production are higher, especially if it is one of the better-known venues and centrally placed. Many of the younger agents visit theatres like the Soho Poly, King's Head and Orange Tree to trawl for clients, so you may well get a positive response. Once again, however, be realistic. An agent is not going to come to see an hour-long show in a room above a pub in Welwyn Garden City.

But of course if you are out of work it is a different matter. If you have a substantial CV and a video tape of your work it is certainly worth writing in. An agent may be looking for a certain type to fill a gap in his client list. The agency may already be aware of your work and be happy to see you. In addition they will be able to see your work on tape.

However if you are not in this position you are faced with a problem. An agency may be prepared to see you on the basis of your photograph and 'type', but unless they are able to see your work it is unlikely they will take you on. And of course they may not see you at all.

If this is the reaction after you have worked your way down your list of preferred choices what should you do? Most importantly, don't despair. Once again, having an agent is not the be-all and end-all of an actor's life. If you persevere and get your own work, gradually establishing yourself you will eventually get an agent. Indeed you may find, as a result of a particular role in a particular production, that agents approach you.

Meanwhile, the energy and commitment you put in to finding yourself work will probably be greater than an agent can give, especially at an early stage. And you have the advantage of knowing exactly what you have done. You will not, of course, have the psychological prop of being able to blame your agent for failure to get work, but in the end, agent or not, it is your responsibility to find yourself work. And nobody else's.

A WORKING RELATIONSHIP

Even if you have succeeded in getting an agent, it is a mistake to sit back and wait for the phone to ring. There are two points to be considered here: i) the amount of work you should continue to do for yourself and, ii) your relationship with your agent.

Getting an agent should not mean abrogating your efforts to obtain work, and instead waiting for your agent to come up with something. An agent should be regarded as an important and valuable asset in helping you get work but it is a profound mistake to rely on them entirely.

At the beginning of your association you should talk over with your agent what you are going to do for yourself and what they will be doing. Most agencies have more contacts in one area than another – for instance an agent may be particularly interested in television drama, but have few contacts in West End theatre. Another may know a great deal about what is going on in American television 'specials' (two-hour television films or 'mini-series') but have few contacts in radio. Some of the better ones will freely admit this and tell you that they have no objection to you continuing to investigate the areas where they can do less for you. They may even help by giving you access to their directories.

Some agents, it has to be said, will take a less *laissez-faire* attitude and do not wish their clients to write personal letters, even in areas where they have little or no interest (see 'Working With an Agent' in Chapter 9).

Your relationship with your agent will largely define itself. It may be extremely friendly and social, or merely businesslike and functional, or a combination of the two. Often there is a honeymoon period when you will receive many calls and be 'put up for' a welter of jobs. Then, especially if no employment results, the number of calls may diminish along with the number of interviews and/or auditions, and an actor may begin to feel that the initial enthusiasm for his cause has waned. If the honeymoon period continues and a sequence of jobs materialises, then the relationship between agent and actor strengthens, but if this is not the case, then strains can rapidly become apparent.

One of the best and most respected agents in the business used to have a rule that clients should be called once a week, regardless of whether there was anything specific to say. He felt this kept the actor in touch with what was going on and made him feel that the agency was still thinking about him. This is undoubtedly a counsel of perfection. At the other end of the spectrum, an actress recalls that she met an agent at a party who told her she was very attractive and asked her if she had an agent. 'Yes,' she replied testily; 'you!' The friend of another actress called the actress's agency because he'd lost her telephone number. Though the actress had been with the agency for two years, the switchboard operator told the friend, with apparent irritation, that he had never heard of the actress and she was not represented by them.

Horror stories like these are rife, but yet again they reinforce the point that it is your responsibility to establish a relationship with your agent and not let it drift into disuse. You should call your agent regularly every few days (once a week to once every ten days is probably ideal – more frequently may cause unnecessary annoyance). You should not let it go for weeks; weeks soon turn into months. If you feel that your calls are resented and are treated as a nuisance then that is clearly an indication of the breakdown of communications between agent and client, suggesting that the agency may not be working for you effectively. In this case you must make an effort to confront the problem, expressing your feelings politely but firmly.

LEAVING YOUR AGENT

Actors become intimidated by agents. They do not like to call to find out what is going on. They are actually frightened to do so.

They worry that, having spent a great deal of time finding an agent, they will be fired and go back to square one.

But logically, if an agent has lost his initial enthusiasm and is patently not working for you, is there any point in his continuing to represent you? If you feel that it will be difficult to get another agent, and you would prefer to have a bad agent than none at all, then the answer is yes. But in this case you must understand the situation and step up your own efforts to find work independently of your agent.

If on the other hand you feel you can find a better agent because of work you have just done, or if you feel being with a particular agent is doing you positive harm, the answer is no. It is certainly possible for an agent to harm your career, for instance by suggesting you for a line of parts that you feel totally unsuitable for and do not wish to play, and establishing you in the minds of directors and casting directors as something you are not. Then it is definitely time to make your views known and, if that results in a parting of the ways, in the end it will probably be better for your career.

When to leave an agent is one of the most vexed questions an actor faces. It is a constant topic of conversation amongst actors, though the discussion is often based on unrealistic expectations of what an agent does and is supposed to do. Before making a decision to leave there are several factors that should be weighed carefully:

1 There is undoubtedly value in continuity. As there is a long time delay in re-publishing directories like *Spotlight*, and many people have old editions anyway, the inconvenience for a busy casting director calling the old agency has to be considered. The agency also may not refer calls efficiently or at all, causing more delays and difficulties.

2 There is another advantage to continuity. Over the years an agent may be the only person who has seen the main body of your work. Not only will their opinion of your capabilities be respected by others in the business, but this knowledge will enable them to sell you more effectively than someone who has only seen your latest performance. Ideally they will be able to quote chapter and verse, remember when you played against

type, etc. Many very successful actors have remained with the same agent from student days, Glenda Jackson and Alan Bates being examples.

3 Moving from agent to agent frequently can be seen as a reflection of a restless personality.

Not on this list is any question of personal rancour. Actors do of course change agents. It is a fact of life. No prospective employer will have his or her decisions on whether they should employ a particular actor altered by the fact that the actor has just left an agent, even if it happens to be their favourite agent.

The grass is always greener on the other side of the fence. Bear that in mind. The heroic stories of other agents related by their clients may appear beguiling, but there is no guarantee the stories are true or that such deeds will apply to you.

Clearly, however, there is going to come a time when, if the agency hasn't bothered to call you for a while or you haven't been put up for jobs over a period of time, you will feel it is appropriate to change. But once again, you must be realistic. On many occasions the reason an actor gives for leaving an agent is a dearth of interviews and auditions over, say, a period of four or five months. Naturally enough an actor feels that interviews are the best chance of getting work, and without them he feels frustrated. However this should only prompt you to leave an agency if, in addition, you believe you have not been put up for jobs. After all, a casting director or director has only a limited number of slots available for interviews. Out of the sixty or seventy submissions they will have received for any particular part – including, of course, their own ideas of who would be appropriate – they may see only ten to fifteen people. If they don't feel you are right for the part on the basis of your photograph and CV (and maybe having seen your work), they are not going to meet you. It is quite possible, therefore, that despite the agent working hard on your behalf, a sequence of such failures will occur and you will not be seen for months.

If you go and discuss this with your agent and explain you are unhappy with the number of times you are being seen for jobs, he will hopefully explain to you what has been said above. He may, on the other hand, feel he should arrange some interviews to keep you happy. He will call his pet casting directors and ask them to squeeze you in to a casting or give you a general interview. But such interviews can be counter-productive, unless you have something specific to offer for the role, with the casting director feeling you have wasted time when they knew you were not suitable anyway, or, in the case of a general interview, that they were quite aware before of who you were and what you could do.

HOW SHOULD AN AGENT BE JUDGED?

So how should an agent be judged? The best test of the sort of agent who will be most useful in helping to get you employment is his knowledge of what is going on. If the agency has an efficient and continuous method by which information is gathered and acted upon – by sending out availability lists, writing specific letters on specific clients for certain roles, telephoning with suggestions where appropriate – and can therefore give you on a regular basis a list of the parts which you have been put up for, that is a good agency. If, on the other hand, you call your agent and he or she appears not to be very well informed, or is unwilling to talk to you, or never returns your calls, that is cause for concern.

In addition, as already noted, a good agent will be meticulous in keeping you informed of all offers made for your services, however small, and will be well aware of your market value so that he can negotiate effectively and obtain good terms for you. He or she will actively involve you in all decision-making processes and will not wish to take decisions without consulting you. An agent who makes decisions for you as if you were not competent to make them for yourself is to be avoided.

CONCLUSION

In conclusion, there are many good and valid reasons for having an agent if you are a successful and money-making actor. For actors not in this category, an agent can be a mixed blessing. If you are fortunate enough to have found a good one, then they will undoubtedly enhance and enable your career prospects. But a bad agent will do little more than put you on a client list and put the agency's name beside your photograph in *Spotlight*, then sit back and wait for the phone to ring, taking commission on jobs which you would almost certainly have got anyway.

Of course, having your name on even a poor agency's books does have some value, but the most important thing is not to be under the impression that an agent – good or bad – is an answer to your prayers, and that having one means you can put your feet up and wait for the job offers to roll in. You can't, and they won't.

Part Two
Actors

9 How to Get a Job

VERY DAY IN THE various media that employ actors, hundreds of roles are being cast. Repertory theatres are looking for actors to join their companies, some for a whole season, some for just one or two plays. Television companies are casting drama series and television commercials are looking for a variety of outlandish characters. Apart from reps, whose seasons do to some extent correspond, casting is not seasonal. Though television likes to make a big fuss of its new seasons, especially the autumn, television drama series and situation comedies are cast all year round and no one time is busier than another. There is a slight rise in the number of television commercials made around October for Christmas campaigns, and a slight fall in film production over the winter months to avoid bad weather, but overall the effect is marginal. Every day something is being cast somewhere.

The process of casting begins when the casting director or director sits down to discuss the script. As soon as the project is made public, the casting director (and often the director as well) will be deluged with letters and photographs and CVs. They will be called by agents who will make suggestions and at the same time will have their own ideas about who is right for the various parts, based on their experience of seeing actors in performance. The first basic step, therefore, is to see to it that your name is in that pile.

But if you didn't know the production was being cast, or your agent didn't (agents don't know everything by any means), clearly you cannot enter the race. It is therefore crucial to set up a system by which you can try to keep track of what productions are casting when and where.

COLLECTING INFORMATION

In Part Three of this book there is an information reference system designed to be a basic guide to the principal employers of actors in the UK. It is by no means complete and entries should be added and deleted as new information becomes available. Whether you are working alone or with the help of an agent, it is essential to try and spend time gleaning information for this system and keeping yourself up to date. This can be done in numerous ways, for instance by reading trade papers (see Chapter 12), by subscribing to a casting bulletin and, of course, by word of mouth – hearing from other actors what they are doing and what they have been auditioned or interviewed for. These days it is not only a question of keeping track of what new projects are being proposed but what new companies are being formed. In the comparatively new world of independent television production, new companies are formed almost every day. It is important, as they are a great source of employment, to try and keep track of them and what they are doing.

In order to facilitate this process it may be a good idea to club together with a small group of other actors to pool information and share the workload and the cost. If each member of the group specialises in one area of information – one doing rep casting, one television companies, another commercials – this should provide a much greater in-depth coverage than working alone. Your local public library may already have some of the periodicals you will need or it may agree to order them for you. If not, hunt around until you find a library that will help: it is an important resource.

Once you have found out that a production is about to be cast it is important, though sometimes extremely difficult, to try and find out what the parts in the production are likely to be. With the huge quantities of mail that casting directors receive, a letter making an entirely inappropriate suggestion represents a waste of your time and of theirs. The casting director at the Royal Exchange

Theatre in Manchester, for instance, remembers getting a letter from an agent making suggestions for their forthcoming production of *Waiting for Godot*. The letter mentioned several of his *female* clients.

If the project has been developed from a book or is a published play, you should read the book or play to get an idea of the characters. If it is an adaptation, the main characters should be more or less the same, though some of the minor parts may be dropped or expanded in this new version. If you feel you are right for one of the parts then state that in your letter. But, as always, *be realistic*. You will not be considered for a part you are ten years too old for. If the character is described as big and beefy and you are slim and small there is absolutely no point in writing. In fact it is counter-productive. A casting director getting a letter with a silly suggestion may not take your next letter seriously either, even if that is for a much more apposite character.

WORKING WITH AN AGENT

If you have an agent you will have to proceed differently. Most agents have areas where their knowledge and expertise is well developed, where they are constantly receiving calls for their clients and where, therefore, they collect a great deal of useful information. On the other hand there are areas about which they may know very little but which from your point of view ought to be covered, since it is obviously beneficial to cast your net as widely as possible.

Generally speaking, agents tend to concentrate on film and television casting, commercials and the West End and commercial theatre. Some bigger agencies assign a particular agent to cover a particular area. The majority do not bother with casting in regional rep, radio or subsidised touring companies because they feel these types of work generate less immediate commission for the agency than do the more highly paid jobs in film and television.

It is important then to talk over with your agent exactly which areas he is covering and find out where he is *not* very active so you can concentrate on those areas yourself.

Unfortunately it is not quite as simple as that. Some agents posi-tively object to their clients writing letters independently even to employers with whom the agent has no contact. There used to be an attitude among some agents that their client list should be 'held available' for the possibility of film and television work: a client taking a job at Sheffield Crucible for ten weeks will not be avail-able for, say, a television production in London (where the majority of television production takes place), which the agent feels would be more prestigious and more profitable in terms of commission.

Not only is this attitude unhelpful to an actor's career, in that working at a major rep company is just as likely to produce con-tacts and opportunities and press coverage as doing a television drama, but it is also unbusinesslike. An average-sized role for tele-vision may produce £1000 as a fee. Ten weeks at the Crucible will gross at least £2000. Of course the former may also generate pay-ment of residuals, but it is unlikely that residuals will amount to a doubling of the original fee. So unless you were lucky enough to get *two* television jobs during that ten-week period, you and your agent might well find the Crucible job more profitable.

Nevertheless the attitude persists. If it is an attitude your agent shares, it is as well to be aware of it: it is up to you whether you accept it. Most actors of course want to get into television and films, and, from a financial point of view, into television commer-cials. Large and small-screen work is seen as glamorous and well paid and it can lead to other things by virtue of the exposure it gives. It also means you get a performance on video tape. But it is not, and should not be, the exclusive focus of an actor's career. The stage is arguably important in the development of an actor's craft. But quite apart from that, it is undeniably far better, finan-cially and psychologically, to take a small part in a production of *Ghosts* at the Leicester Haymarket than to sit around at home waiting for the phone to ring. The job will provide you with an opportunity to learn but it will also give you the chance to broaden the base of your contacts. You will meet other actors who can give you more information about what is going on in general, and the chances are that, in the course of time, the director you worked with on the show (and the artistic director of the theatre, if this was a different person) may end up running a more prestigious theatre, or moving on to television. Stuart Burge and Richard Eyre both worked at Nottingham Playhouse; the former subsequently directed many successful television productions and the latter now runs the Royal National Theatre. If you establish a good working relationship then there is no telling where it will take you.

Perhaps one of the reasons for an agent being unhelpful in this area is the fear that if the client gets a job for himself, he will be unwilling to pay commission on it. To what extent this attitude is justified is usually a reflection of the relationship between agent and client: if the relationship is proving unsatisfactory an actor may well feel the agent does not deserve the commission when he has not been involved in finding the job. You may have a point, of course, but don't expect the agent to be particularly enthusiastic about furthering your career once you have refused to pay commission. Traditionally commission is paid on gross income from *all* professional engagements, regardless of who sourced the employment.

On the other hand, your agent may well take a much more positive attitude towards your involvement in getting work. There are agents who will readily agree if you offer to split the work load with them and who will actively encourage you to do so. They will allow you to use their reference books to expand your reference system and will tell you, on a regular basis, what is going on. In addition they will freely admit the areas where they have little knowledge and welcome your efforts to find out more about what is going on in, say, the regional repertories. As an ideal the relationship between an agent and an actor should be a partnership, not a competition.

WRITING A LETTER

Whether alone, or with the help of an agent, you will begin to develop a picture of what is being cast, where and when. Your picture will be incomplete, like a jigsaw, but obviously the more areas you manage to cover the more opportunities you will discover.

So what should you do if you find out that a play is being produced which has a part that is particularly suitable for you? If you have an agent then you should discuss it with him or her and ascertain if they are going to suggest you or whether they feel it would be better for you to do it yourself. If you are going to suggest yourself, then you should write a letter to the appropriate person (see Chapter 2) or your agent will tell you who to contact.

The letter should be short and polite and enclose a photograph (see Chapter 12) and CV. If possible, choose a photograph as appropriate to the role as possible – casting directors and directors are not known for having graphic imaginations. If the part is for an Edwardian gentleman try and send a picture in Edwardian costume (a drama school production is fine so long as it isn't too out-of-date in relation to your age), but *not* one taken in a white T-shirt and a leather jacket which looks like a still from *The Wild Ones*. Equally, if it is a film about marauding motorcyclists don't send the photograph of yourself in a suit and tie. Try to get as close to the part as you can.

Another essential is to make sure the letter is sent to the correct address. This is less obvious than it may seen. You may have found out, for instance, that Yorkshire Television is going to do a production of *Hamlet* cast by Rebecca Howard. You write a letter to Yorkshire Television addressed to Rebecca Howard. But which of the two listed addresses should you use, London or Leeds? If you write to the wrong one the letter will be delayed. And Rebecca Howard may in fact be working from her own office, not from Yorkshire Television at all. They will forward the letter to her but by then it may be too late. For smaller companies always check the address. Addresses given in reference books (including Part Three of this book), because of the length of time between research and publication, may well be out of date. Companies, especially independent television production companies, move frequently.

Do not write a quirky, prankish letter. Your letter should be short, typed if possible, but in any case clearly legible, and to the point. However witty you think you are, do not be tempted to indulge your proclivity in this direction. In terms of this sort of letter, it has all been done before *ad nauseam*.

Do not write:

Dear Rebecca,
I know you're looking for the next James Dean. Well here I am.

or:

Dear Rebecca,
You old rat bag, why don't you ever give me a job? If you do I promise I'll never call you a rat bag again.

or:

Dear Rebecca,
I have five starving children and a starving wife so I really need this job. Please help me, I'm desperate.

Do write something along the lines of:

Dear Rebecca,
I would like to be considered for the role of Laertes in the production of *Hamlet* you are casting. I have considerable experience in fencing and have worked in four Shakespeare productions, including one directed by Adrian Noble. My photo and CV are enclosed.

If there is anything in your career to date that particularly suits you for the part say so in the letter; for instance, as here, fencing skills and expertise in Shakespeare. It is always worth pointing up the fact that you have worked with a particularly distinguished director. If the part concerned requires, for example, an American accent, and you have recently played an American part, then that is something else that should be stressed. But if there is nothing of the sort don't be tempted to make something up. Keep the letter short and to the point.

If the part is particularly suitable – and you have to be honest with yourself here – then it might be worth making one follow-up telephone call to ask if your letter has been received. Here again, polite and concise is the rule. Don't say, 'My phone's been out of order and I wondered if you'd been trying to get me . . .' Don't say,

'I've just been offered another job so I thought I should check with you before I accepted it, as I'd much rather do your production . . .'

If you feel that this is an opportunity that is really particularly appropriate for you (but not otherwise) there is only one other thing you should do after that: try to find out who else is working on the production. There's often a crew and cast list in *Screen International* for films and television films, and sometimes the production assistant can be helpful. It may be that you've worked with someone on the production before or a friend has. Any sort of mention in passing to the director or casting director is useful. It puts your name forward. It may get them to pay attention to your letter. The name coming from two directions is more likely to register.

CURRICULUM VITAE

The question of your CV is important. If you are just starting out in your career you will not have much to put on it. The main parts you have had at drama school and anything you have done since will have to suffice. Do not be tempted to embellish the truth. If you are subsequently called to a meeting and asked about what you have done it could be a cause of embarrassment if you are unable to substantiate any of the items you have put down, or if someone else does not remember you being on a particular production. Embarrassment will not get you a job.

On the other hand, if you have been in the business for some time, your CV might need some pruning. Page after page of details of every single production you have been in, however small your part, is not impressive. It is better to confine yourself to one page, readable at a glance, setting out the most significant roles while stating you have played many more.

A CV should also mention the prominent directors you have worked with, and it does no harm to include star actors. A well-known modern writer is worth mentioning too, especially if they were involved with the production directly.

Make sure the CV is typed, neatly and logically laid out, and in chronological order. Remember that your letter is going to be one of hundreds, and that the person who reads it will almost certainly be under pressure and therefore not have time to decipher your handwriting or puzzle out a muddled CV.

Finally, make sure the CV mentions any specialist skill(s) you have, like being able to speak French fluently, or being a champion archer, or riding a horse or being licensed to drive a heavy goods vehicle.

AUDITIONS AND INTERVIEWS

In theory, at least, you and/or your agent should be writing several letters every week, as well as the telephone suggestions your agent will make when called by casting directors asking if he or she has someone suitable for a role or roles they are casting. By the law of averages, some of these letters and telephone calls are going to lead to auditions or interviews. And it is absolutely essential that an actor should be as fully prepared as possible for an audition when it comes.

In the course of an actor's professional life he or she is going to have literally hundreds of auditions or interviews. The way he handles them, the 'performance' he gives in interviews, will without doubt determine the course of his or her career, regardless of talent as an actor. It is *crucial* therefore, and this cannot be emphasised strongly enough, to practise and develop a technique for these occasions. The interview or audition is a life-line, a chance to haul yourself up, *the* chance to show what you can do. Many gifted and talented actors have never been able to get over their nervousness and unease in interview situations and have consequently not done themselves justice and not had the careers that their talent deserved.

The psychological pressure in an interview comes from need. Most actors who are sent up to an interview are hungry – hopefully not literally – for the job. They want it and need it. The bigger the job – a lead in a television series, or a West End play – the greater the pressure on them to succeed and, often, the worse they will perform.

These days psychologists are hired to help professional sportsmen and women deal with the pressure and stress of big sporting occasions. Where two competitors have equal talent, equal skill and equal competitiveness, the one most likely to win is the one who is better motivated, who believes more in himself and his ability to win, and, above all, who can use that belief to cope with the pressure in a final where everything is at stake.

The psychology of sport can be applied to the interview situation facing an actor: the pressure is often just as great. Frequently the competition for a job is between two (or more) equally talented actors whose experience may be very similar; there may be little to choose between them physically, either. What is therefore going to be the deciding factor in the director's mind? Probably the fact that one actor is more relaxed, more confident and appears more at ease: i.e. the actor who has been best able to cope with pressure. A director will be attracted to this, especially for a leading role or a substantial part, in the belief that this ease and apparent confidence will translate itself into an ease and confidence in coping with the stresses of the production itself, thus making the director's job easier. A display of nerves, on the other hand, may lead the director to believe that you will not be good at dealing with the undoubted stress you will be put under during the making of the programme or on stage.

Feeling at ease and confident in an interview is not something that comes naturally to many people. It is especially difficult at the beginning of your career, when you have little experience and feel, perhaps, that you have nothing much to contribute to any discussion. The key to taking the psychological pressure off yourself in such situations is to prepare properly. There is a list of things you can do to make yourself feel less like a spare guest at a wedding and more like someone who at least has something interesting to say:

1 Try to read the script before the meeting. Obviously if it is a classic play or one that has already been published, there is no problem about getting a copy. But if it is a new play or a film or television script, ask, or get your agent to ask, for a copy. If the production company are unwilling to send one, ask if you can go to the office an hour or so ahead of the meeting to read

it there and at least get some idea of what the director is talking about. You can also, in this way, formulate some idea of the character and how you would go about playing it. If there is anything unusual that strikes you about the character, so much the better.

2 If getting the script proves impossible, at least try to prepare for the meeting by learning as much about the circumstances of the production as possible and as much about the director and/or casting director as you can. Find out what their last production was – if you haven't seen it, try and get it on video. Talk to other actors about the director and find out what he is like. If he or she has a reputation for being frosty or sullen in interviews, at least you will be prepared and you won't assume this attitude is a reaction against you.

3 Look the part. Even if you haven't seen the script you will be told roughly what sort of part is on offer. If it is a 1950s rock 'n' roller don't go dressed in a suit and tie looking like a bank manager. Alternatively if the part is a solicitor, don't go in T-shirt and jeans.

4 Try to find out if you will be asked to read – meaning that you will be given a script and asked to read from it, with the director or someone else (a production assistant or the casting director) playing the other parts. If you are going to be asked to read, try not to let them hurry you into it. Ask for time to study the script properly. Most actors who have been asked to read under these circumstances will tell you the reading they gave was highly unsatisfactory and, had they been given a second chance, they would have performed differently, so it is a good idea to practise this situation at home with a friend, reading from a passage you do not know, and trying to produce a vivid, effective performance. It is a highly pressured situation and practice will help you cope with it. What a director can possibly tell from readings under such circumstances is a mystery. But however badly you think you have done, try not to let it phase you for the rest of the interview.

5 Always take a photograph with you (an appropriate one if possible: a selection may also be a good idea) and another copy of your CV. The director may not be able to find the one sent with your letter and it is always good to have a spare copy available.

There is, naturally, a major difference between an interview and an audition. In an interview you may occasionally be asked to read, but when you are called for an audition you know you are definitely going to have to perform, read, sing or dance.

Usually auditions are confined to theatre productions (and sometimes television commercials). For the theatre you will probably be performing on stage or in a rehearsal room, with the director and several other people in the stalls or sitting behind a desk. Usually also you will be told in advance what you are expected to do, but if there is any doubt in your mind at all, find out whether you are being auditioned or interviewed: that is, whether or not you need to have a speech, song or dance prepared. There is nothing worse than believing you are going to have an interview and discovering that you are in fact expected to audition.

The audition situation has been celebrated in so many plays and films that it has become legendary: the nervous actor stumbles on stage to be greeted by the glare of the spotlights and the blank indifference or positive hostility of his prospective employers huddled together in the stalls, only to be stopped, after a few seconds, by a peremptory 'Next!'.

Unfortunately this cliché does have an element of truth in it, especially when a call has gone out for an 'open' audition (i.e. an audition advertised in *The Stage*, for actors to turn up at a certain time and place without having to write in beforehand). The number of people being seen in one day prohibits more than a cursory glance at each, to such an extent that one wonders whether seeing so many people has any value at all. Open auditions are relatively unusual, however, and even in some of these, attempts are made by the managements involved to introduce an element of humanity into the proceedings. But it is as well to be prepared for the worst.

Whatever you are asked to do at an audition – read, perform one of your own 'audition speeches', sing or dance – it goes without saying that it is essential you work at it carefully beforehand. With a straight play, if it is a classic you will usually be told what scene is to be read, so you can study it without difficulty. If it is a new play, you may be sent the scene to look at. Even if you are not, you will almost certainly be given some time to read the scene before you are asked to perform. Giving any kind of performance with the book in your hand and a stage manager or another actor feeding you cues is certainly not an easy thing to do (though remember that everyone else has the same problem). But it is again a situation that can be prepared for by practice. With the help of a friend take a piece at random from a modern play (one you do not know) and try giving an unprepared reading from it. Do this frequently, always using a different text, not repeating the same one. Not only will this improve your ability to sight read, always a good art to practise, but it will improve your confidence in feeling that it is a situation you can cope with.

For a musical you will usually be asked to sing two contrasting numbers, an up-tempo number and a ballad. Sometimes the songs will be specified and sometimes the choice will be left to you. There are pitfalls to be wary of here. If the show is a well-known classic (a Rodgers and Hammerstein, say, or a Sondheim) you may be asked to sing one of its principal songs but if you are not, careful thought should be given to what you sing. In a series of auditions for various cockney musicals (such as *Liza of Lambeth* and *Me and My Girl*) the number of actors who chose to sing 'Roll Out the Barrel' was startling. The point here is that however much the piece demonstrates your ability, if the producers have heard it innumerable times before, the sound of the first few notes hammered out on the piano will inevitably lead to thoughts of 'not again'. This is not the initial impact you are aiming for. Unless you have a particular interpretation of a song – something original – then it is better to steer away from the more obvious choices. If you can manage to find a piece that demonstrates your ease with whatever is the main theme but at the same time is something new which the producers may not have heard before, then this has to be a good thing. A little thought and research can pay dividends.

Another pitfall in the choice of material is to find something that fits your personality. If you are, for instance, a fresh-faced and innocent looking nineteen-year-old, it is not a good idea to sing something cynical and world-weary, however well you sing it. Neither is it a good idea to ape too closely the phrasing and characteristics of one particular version of a song. If anyone on the production team has heard the version you are copying, they will not be impressed. They are looking for an original performance, not mimicry.

To score points at an audition you must aim to demonstrate your proficiency in acting, singing or dancing, or any two or all three together. But almost as important is to leave an impression in the production team's mind. In the course of a day they are seeing a large number of people. Some voices and performances will stick in their mind, but so will a particular personality.

Some years ago the producers of a major West End musical were looking for an actress to fill the title role of their production. They auditioned a huge number of women in the right age range and with the right vocal ability, but had little success finding someone with the sort of vulnerability they were looking for. Despite having phoned most agents in London for suggestions, it was one of the actors they were auditioning for another role who mentioned a woman he had worked with in another musical, who had not previously been suggested and had therefore not been seen.

As things were getting urgent the actress's agent was called and the actress arrived an hour later. She was wearing little make-up and an old tracksuit, and was carrying a plastic shopping bag when she strode on to the stage. Tipping the contents of the shopping bag on to the floor – a huge collection of sheet music – she knelt among the sheets. 'What do you want me to sing?' she asked the startled production team.

To what degree this was calculated as opposed to spontaneous as a result of the unexpectedness of her call it is impossible to know, but its impact was immediate and eventually the actress was offered the job.

This should not be taken as an excuse for planning some 'stunt' to impress the producers with your personality. That would backfire disastrously. But you should aim in an audition not only to demonstrate your competence as a performer but also to show that you have a personality which can be counted on to add an extra dimension to the production.

There are some definite dos and don'ts for interviews and auditions. They may seem obvious but it is surprising how often actors get tripped up by them:

1 *Be clean and well kempt* (even if the interview is for a tramp). There is no dress code, but dirty clothes and a scruffy appearance are not going to help you.

2 *Do not be over-familiar.* This is a form of nervousness and can leave a bad impression.
3 *Do not be over-servile* either. Don't call the director 'sir', for instance.
4 *Don't be late.* Interviews and auditions are always running late. If you are not there for your appointment it will simply be swallowed up by the over-run and you may either have to wait hours to be fitted in (which will not help your nerves) or not be seen at all.
5 *Don't lie.* The film, television and stage worlds are very small. Don't be tempted to say you have been in productions you have not. There may be people on the production team who worked on them and you will be caught out. That is definitely not the right impression to leave.

CASTING BY VIDEO

With the introduction of cheap video recorders, another sort of selection process has developed, favoured especially by Americans, and used almost exclusively in television, film and commercial casting. If the initial letter or suggestion is thought interesting, then the casting director will ask for a video tape (sometimes called a 'demo' tape) of your work. Sometimes this request will be for a video of you in a specific role in a specific production, sometimes merely for a general compilation tape.

This of course, puts young actors who have not appeared in any film or television productions at a great disadvantage. Some directors are not going to see actors for an interview unless they have first seen them on tape.

It also puts an emphasis on what your demo tape consists of. There are many video companies who specialise in cutting together performances from different productions you have appeared in. By editing them and splicing in credits they can produce a highly professional result. As always, with companies offering a specialist service, it is good to make a few enquiries among your friends before you commit yourself. These products are not cheap, but generally speaking standards are high.

The problem is not the technical standard of the tape but what you put on it. Often, because a tape is compiled from snippets from many diverse productions, in various styles of direction, period and mood, it can appear extremely disjointed and unappetising. Ideally, of course, it would be good to have a tape compiled, assuming you have the body of work to support it, to match the part under consideration – a tape of you playing a 'heavy', or a romantic lead, etc. It's unlikely that you could achieve this, but it does illustrate the point that what goes on your demo tape should be carefully considered and carefully ordered. Try to group performances into types rather than going immediately from playing a gangster to playing a light comedy role. Too much variety is off-putting and jumping from one extreme to another too quickly on a tape (where your extracts are being seen out of their dramatic context) may well provoke thoughts of shallowness: 'jack of all trades and master of none' is not a label you want.

Make sure that your best performance is at the beginning of the tape, and – a very obvious point but one often forgotten – make sure the tape is wound back to the beginning. In a busy casting office the tape will be viewed quickly and often in far from ideal circumstances. They will start wherever the tape starts and will not wind it back themselves. Remember also that the average time spent viewing your tape will be quite short.

VIDEOTAPING

While on the subject of videos, another relatively new phenomenon is taping an actor during the interview or asking the actor to perform specifically for a video camera. This is done, as already mentioned, mostly in television commercial casting, mainly because so many people are involved in the decision-making process – director, producer, advertising agency and client (the manufacturer of the product).

Again, like giving an instant reading, this type of audition can be difficult and actors often feel they have not given of their best. But it is another technique that can and should be practised. It is a good idea to watch yourself on video as frequently as possible, adjusting your technique accordingly and working out how you can achieve the maximum impact.

SCREEN TESTS

There is one final form of interview/audition that should be mentioned, and that is the screen test. A screen test is usually for a feature film but occasionally also for a large part in a television series, when there is a very small short list (of two or three actors at most) after the initial interviewing procedures. As the part in question will undoubtedly be a lead in a large production there will be a great deal of pressure. How you handle that pressure will determine whether you get the part or not.

There is no easy way to deal with the stresses of a screen test but, once again, you must try to prepare yourself as thoroughly as possible. If, for instance, you are being tested for a film and have never been in front of a full 35mm Panavision camera crew, try and arrange to go and see one beforehand so you know what to expect. The same applies if you have never been in a television studio. The more you know about what is going on, the more at ease you will feel and the less you will be distracted from your performance. You will be given the script for the scene to be shot well before the event, and obviously the more work you do on it the more confident you will be. Generally the producer and director involved will appreciate the pressure you are under and will be sympathetic. It is quite in order, if you feel you have not done well, for *you* to ask for another take.

STANDARDS OF BEHAVIOUR

With a little luck, your industry and hard work in writing letters and going for interviews will eventually result in your getting a job. Every job you succeed in getting will not only be valuable in developing your craft, and of course, financially, but should also increase your prospects for future employment. The entertainment industry is a very small one and most people working in it are freelance, moving from one job and one company to another with amazing rapidity. Knowledge and information spreads swiftly across this network, so if you make a good impression it will stand you in good stead for the future. It is equally important that you do not make a *bad* impression by the way you behave.

The third assistant director to whom you are rude one morning on set may, three years later, be sitting at the other side of a desk as a director interviewing you for a part in a television series. The production secretary whom you snapped at may well end up as a major television producer (a great number of television producers started as secretaries). Tantrums and misbehaviour will be remembered not only by the junior staff. If you are not well behaved, if you cause unwarranted trouble which in turn causes delay, or act unprofessionally, the producer and director will remember too. Not only will this mean that you are unlikely to be invited to join any other production they are on, but if they are called by anyone else to ask their opinion – which happens all the time – they may be less than fulsome in their praise. There is a corporate memory, too. Even though the particular director and producer may have moved on the company may be reluctant to employ you again.

Every job you get should be viewed as a means of making friends and influencing people with a view to getting other jobs – the stone thrown into the pond. This is not to say that you cannot argue your corner artistically if you feel you have a genuine contribution to make or need help in developing your performance in the context of the production as a whole. But especially in film, television and commercials, time is money and unnecessary arguments will not be viewed favourably. As Sydney Pollack tells Dustin Hoffman in *Tootsie*, if you are playing a tomato in a commercial, arguing that you can't sit down because tomatoes don't sit down will not improve your chances of being re-employed by anybody.

This is most important. An actor's career is made up of jobs from various individual directors. But as their careers develop, most actors find that their work comes, over and over again, from the same relatively small group of people with whom they have worked on numerous occasions. Most directors, though by no means all, develop a small coterie of actors with whom they have established a rapport, with whom they are comfortable, and who they know will respond quickly to their needs. This familiarity becomes a sort of shorthand, cutting down on the need for explanations, and thereby reducing the length of time necessary to rehearse.

For young actors it is therefore essential to try to form a good working relationship with each director by whom they are employed, at whatever level of the profession. A young director working in a studio theatre in a regional subsidised rep may gradually work his or her way up in the world until they are wielding considerable influence. If you have worked well with him or her in the past this can provide a considerable fillip to your career.

For an actor trying to re-establish himself it is a good idea to look back at all the people you have worked with or been connected with in the past. Names get forgotten. You may be pleasantly surprised to discover that a director you had worked with, but whose name you had maybe temporarily forgotten, is now in a prominent position elsewhere, and a reminder of your previous association may well prove rewarding.

10 Achieving Consistent Employment

T
HE PERPETUAL PROBLEM confronting an actor is not how to
get a job but how to get one job after another in a fairly
consistent fashion.

Most professions have a relatively defined career structure, affecting seniority, responsibility and salary levels. There is no
such structure when it comes to the profession of acting in the UK.
Seniority counts for little. An actor of thirty years' experience may
be playing smaller roles and earning less than he did when he was
twenty. There are peaks and troughs. Sometimes a peak comes
right at the beginning of a career and it is a very long time before
there is any downward movement. Sometimes there is a peak followed by a very immediate decline. Sometimes there is a gradual
upward movement, years of experience culminating finally in recognition and star status (Paul Eddington, Nigel Hawthorne,
Richard Wilson, David Jason, Arthur Lowe are all examples of this
pattern). Whatever the particular circumstances of an individual
career, only one thing is certain: no two careers are alike and there
is simply no general pattern.

Extremely experienced actors with high profiles (even with
awards and a string of rave reviews from the critics) can find themselves out of work for years and puzzled as to the reason. Is it mere
chance that there is no appropriate part, or is it something more
fundamental – that the business no longer rates their talent? The
obvious conclusion they frequently draw – usually incorrectly, but
naturally enough – is that they are no longer well thought of in the
profession. The fear may be absurd, but that does not make it any
less psychologically damaging, and it is one of the most difficult

things to cope with as a result of the vagaries of employment. For a young and inexperienced actor, being out of work for some time can easily be seen as a result of the incessant competition for parts. But for an actor with something of a reputation such reasoning is harder to accept, and it is easy to believe oneself completely valueless.

In fact the situation facing a young actor is very much the same as that facing an actor of considerable experience who has fallen on hard times: indeed it is the same for all but a tiny percentage of the 43,500-odd members of Equity. The business is volatile and unpredictable. Unlike most other professions or careers, reputation and status and experience can count for very little. There is no guarantee that a good run of parts and a string of good notices will necessarily lead to future employment. The principles addressed here are therefore important to all actors.

There is another problem older and younger actors share: not being known. Just as there is a high drop-out rate among actors there is an equally high drop-out rate among producers and directors in film, television and theatre. It is a highly stressed job and few, apparently, make it through into their fifties. Their places are taken by young men and women who may have been children when some of the actors they are going to be interviewing had their great successes in the West End or on television, or won an Emmy, SWET or BAFTA award. This is one reason for the expression 'you are only as good as your last job'.

USING ONE JOB TO FIND ANOTHER

Getting some sort of continuity and consistency in a career is a matter of hard work. Once one job is secured, that is the ideal time to start looking for the next. It is not the time to rest on your laurels.

It is much easier to get work when you are already working: there are two reasons for this. Firstly, you are constantly being fed information from other members of whatever cast you are in. Other actors are going to interviews, calling their agents, and getting all sorts of information that you can use and which should be slotted into your reference system. Secondly, when you write and go for interviews and auditions while you are working, especially in a good part, your confidence is high. It makes you sparkle in an interview, and, of course, gives you a ready answer to the question that most actors dread: 'So tell me what you've been doing recently?'

Unfortunately the reverse also applies. As you come to the end of a production and other actors are going off to other jobs you can become more and more depressed because you have nothing to go to. As stories of others' success abound, you become increasingly critical of your own abilities and of your agent, if he or she has not succeeded in getting you into one of the productions everyone else seems to be heading for. It is a time that brings out the worst in actors – but remember that, because of this, it is also a time when other actors are prone to exaggeration. Tales of what they are about to do don't always mesh with reality.

The empty period that follows, if you do not get one job immediately after another, is as difficult to cope with as rejection. But however bitter, this is a fact of an actor's life and has to be coped with.

One of the best ways of coping is by throwing yourself back into endeavouring to find work. If you have been in the run of a play or a long television series you will need to update your information reference system. Some of the productions that you learnt were not casting for some months ahead might now be in preparation, and there will undoubtedly be new productions on the horizon. It is a good time to visit your agent, if you have one, and have a chat about what is likely to be going on.

In addition, if you have been in a theatre production it is possible that casting directors, directors or producers will have come to see the show during its run, especially if it was in the West End or at a well-known fringe venue. Make sure you keep a record of their names in your reference system – don't rely on memory, which is notoriously unreliable. You may think you will never forget that Charles Sturridge or Ruth Boswell or John Hubbard came to see the play you were in, but in a year or two the names and dates will have become blurred. Keep a written note of anyone whom you know has seen your work, along with what they saw, when, where, and any other relevant details. (Had you invited them? Did they come with your agent? Did you get in touch with them afterwards?)

It doesn't matter, incidentally, if they did not come to the show specifically to see you. If in two years' time you find yourself in an interview with, say John Hubbard, you can remind him that you were in the production of *Much Ado About Nothing* he saw at the Regent's Park Open Air Theatre. It makes a good starting point for a conversation. It is also valuable in suggesting yourself for parts or getting your agent to do it for you. If Brian Farnham saw you playing Macduff in *Macbeth* and is casting a part with similar characteristics it is certainly worth reminding him.

If your last job was a television or film production it is also worth keeping a careful note of everyone involved in your reference system. It is amazing how many actors whose careers stretch over fifteen or twenty years do not keep a record of the directors and casting directors who they have worked for. In business terms this is like a salesman forgetting to make a note of the customers to whom he has sold his product! Not only is it important to keep track of their future projects in case there is something suitable for you, but it can be highly off-putting for them if you attend an interview and they remember your working together before but you do not.

You should keep a record of *all* the members of the production team, not just the director and casting director. As has already been said, the first assistant director of today is the director of tomorrow, the production assistant may become a producer, the cameraman may take up directing (think of Ernest Vincze or Nicolas Roeg). In film many directors started as editors (e.g. John Glenn, Peter Hunt). These may all be valuable contacts, not only because they may be future employers but because they can enlarge your network for other productions and other castings. You may find, for instance, that the production assistant will be around at the time of casting interviews.

For these reasons either keep the call sheet (the information provided by the production company with the names, telephone numbers and agents of all the participants in the production) or make a separate note for every production you work on.

After working on a film or a television programme you will also want to consider, when the film is released or before the programme is transmitted, writing round to selected casting directors and directors to let them know that you are in it, and the part you are playing.

But, to return to a persistent theme in this book, if you are considering doing this, *be realistic*. If you are playing a one-line part in the seventeenth series of *Casualty*, in which your sole contribution is, 'Doctor, I think this man needs urgent attention,' not only is it a waste of money – and a mailing is expensive – to write to a list of prospective employers, it is also a waste of time, both yours and theirs.

The same goes for a film. In fact, with a film you need to be extra careful, because the part you played in front of the cameras may now lie, partially or wholly, on the cutting-room floor. So never write any sort of letter about a film until you have actually seen it yourself. You may not be in it (even though your name may appear in the cast list). If it is a British production you will normally be invited to a cast showing. If it is American you may have to wait and buy a ticket like everyone else.

Make a realistic assessment of your role in the television production or film. If you are playing a leading role or an important character – particularly one that is crucial to the development of the storyline – or a character that puts special demands on an actor (such as a deaf mute, for instance), then it is certainly worth letting the casting community know.

Once again your letter should be short and to the point, naming your role, the programme or film, the channel or cinema and the date and time of transmission or screening. If there is something special about the part, mention that too and perhaps, if you appear in a comparatively short – but important – scene, where it comes in the programme. Nothing else. Do not try to embellish the letter with some witty remark based on puns on the title of the programme ('I'm another casualty in *Casualty*'). It's all been done before.

In deciding who you should include in your mailing list, consult your agent if you have one; he or she may be thinking of writing a similar letter, so you will want to avoid duplication. (Your agent may also tell some casting directors on the telephone that you are going to be on.) Generally speaking the mailing should go out to people who are currently involved in casting, although you could usefully include directors who are not casting at the moment but who you have worked with previously and got on well with. It is a good way of keeping them abreast of what you have been up to, and keeping your name fresh in their minds.

A word of warning here. *Never* write to a director's or producer's home address, unless you are a personal friend. Not only may the person concerned not be in the right mood to deal with business over breakfast, but the letter may be simply ignored and not taken to the office to be included with the other mail. Worse, a director may regard the letter as an unprofessional intrusion, and positively discriminate against you.

With a film going out on general release it is a good idea to delay the letter until after the press showing of the film. If the film gets good reviews people are more likely to go and see it anyway. It is even possible that you may have rated a mention in the reviews, which should definitely be included in the letter.

The reception of a performance in a play, television programme or film varies considerably. One performance can sometimes change the entire direction of an actor's career (as happened with Bob Peck in *Edge of Darkness*, Roger Rees in *Nicholas Nickleby* and Colin Firth in *Equus*). In fact, that is what usually catapults an actor from semi-obscurity – though he or she may be well known in the profession – into the public eye.

What is more surprising, perhaps, is that there can be many occasions when it seems you are in the right part, in the right play or television series, at the right time, but for some reason the final, indefinable ingredient is not there, and the expected success does not materialise. (Contrast, for example, the impact of Trevor Eve in *Shoestring* with that of John Mackie in *Moon and Son*, both programmes conceived, written and produced by the same man, Robert Banks Stewart.)

Time after time everything appears to be set fair: the pedigrees of the writers and director are excellent, the scripts good, the production values high, the subject or theme of the programme apposite, and even the reviews outstanding, but for some unknown reason the show does not catch the public imagination and fails to find an audience.

One of the many difficult things for an actor to cope with is this sort of failure, when the expectations of everyone involved are extremely high. Having worked hard to achieve a leading role in whatever medium, it is tempting to think that this is the end of scrambling around for minor roles and trying to make ends meet. Unfortunately this will almost certainly not be the case, especially in television. And it is as well to be prepared. Once a drama series has been made – however good it is – external factors can suddenly affect it dramatically. Another Robert Banks Stewart series (and as the creator of not only *Shoestring* but also *Bergerac* and *The Darling Buds of May*, there is no question as to his pedigree) for which there was a high expectation of success was *Charlie Endell*, based on a character from the LWT *Budgie* series. The first episode was transmitted in prime time, but then got caught up in the ITV strike. A similar fate befell a new series transmitted during the World Cup when England reached the semi-final. Transmission times and scheduling are often the cause of success or failure. The season of the year, day of the week and time of day when the show goes out (summer tends to have poor audience figures compared to the start of autumn or winter), as well as what is on the other channels, can all influence the outcome, and all are matters out of the control of an actor. The policy of ITV and the BBC to fight each other in a ratings war, instead of cooperating to give the viewer maximum choice, has often resulted in their best programmes being used as ammunition and has frequently meant that two drama series have failed rather than one or both being successful.

On the positive side, the momentum if success is achieved can be quite extraordinary. The impact of *Darling Buds of May*, one of the highest-rated programmes in recent years, certainly catapulted its stars into the public domain and instant demand. The film of *Lawrence of Arabia* made Peter O'Toole a star virtually overnight and he was flooded with offers, as was Bob Hoskins in *The Long Good Friday*, among countless examples.

But until the reviews are out and the ratings or box-office returns in, it is better not to count your chickens – whatever the hype or the portents suggest.

CREATING EMPLOYMENT

If the follow-up to your last job does not produce immediate results – and of course, with television or film work it may be months
(even years) before it is released or transmitted – and you find
yourself out of work again, then it may be time to look at other
ways of creating work for yourself in addition to the information
reference system and the letter-writing that should continue as a
matter of course.

There are two main areas where an actor can productively create work for himself: in fringe theatre and by working up a one
man/woman show.

FRINGE THEATRE

The development of what has become known as fringe theatre (the
term was originally used for the 'fringe' at the Edinburgh Festival)
began in the early 1970s in London with the Soho Poly and the
Basement Theatre. The idea of non-subsidised, 'profit-sharing' theatre in rooms adapted for the purpose, perhaps holding an
audience of no more than thirty or forty people, spread rapidly
from these two cellars in Soho to a wide variety of venues across
London. Upstairs rooms in pubs were converted as a variation on
the theme and soon 'pub theatre' was well established with names
like the Elephant and Castle and the Rose Tavern in Fulham
producing plays on a regular basis. Indeed some of these theatres
were so successful they developed into establishments supported by
the Arts Council – such as the Orange Tree in Richmond and the
Bush on Shepherd's Bush Green – and were run as full-time theatres. The King's Head in Islington is another theatre operating in
this way. A special Equity contract covers minimum conditions in
these premises.

The majority of fringe venues remain, however, in the unsub-
sidised area, and have no Equity contract covering conditions of
employment. A lot of the pub theatres are maintained by the
breweries or landlords as a means of consistently attracting audiences who will substantially increase the takings at the bar. The cost

of setting up the theatre, of providing lights, a stage of some sort and racking for the seats, is borne by the pub. The cost of each production, however, is met by the company of actors putting on the play, and only in rare circumstances will the pub make a contribution, if ever.

Before becoming involved in a fringe production it is a good idea to think about precisely why you are doing it. There are four reasons why a fringe production is worthwhile in career terms:

1 It gives you a chance to work on your talent in a live situation. Often fringe venues are small and the work environment is extremely intimate and intense. The concentration and effort required, and the experience of learning to deal with audiences, is invaluable.
2 It is another opportunity to meet and talk with other actors and to exchange information.
3 If you have been out of work for some time it can provide a psychological boost to confidence.
4 Principally it should be used as an opportunity to widen and enhance your career prospects. There is a possibility that the production will be seen by prospective employers and by the press. A London fringe show may be reviewed in *Time Out* and possibly by other papers, and any attention of this sort is a good thing. Even if the production gets bad reviews that does not necessarily mean that the press coverage has been wasted.

If you are in a fringe production at the behest of a friend and do not have a particularly good part, then you have to accept that it is an experience you are undertaking for the first three reasons and not for the fourth, but you can still make good use of the opportunity, and you should keep a careful note of people who come to see the show.

These are the positive factors, but there is a major disadvantage that has to be weighed in the balance. A fringe production is based on 'profit-sharing' and, frankly, there never is a profit. A play at the Rose Tavern, for instance, with a cast of only three and a very simple set, that played to almost capacity houses for its two-week run, left the participants (writer, director and the cast) sharing out

£400 for their four weeks' work. Had the audiences been even slightly smaller, there would have been nothing left from the takings, once the expenses of the production had been met. So the advantages of committing to a fringe show have to be weighed against the possibility of missing out on paid employment during that period.

The worst scenario is that you accept an engagement at a fringe theatre and are then offered a lucrative professional contract. You are then faced with an agonising decision as to whether to renege on the fringe commitment – and if it is late in the production schedule, probably destroying the show and everyone else's efforts in the process – or to carry on and lose the professional work and the money.

This is one of the reasons why agents are often unhappy about their clients participating in such productions. They will receive no commission for a job that may cause them a great deal of difficulty if another paid offer comes along.

The decision to join a fringe production must therefore be taken carefully on the basis of – that word again – realism. If you are currently up for one or two parts which you feel you have a good chance of getting, and there are other jobs in the offing, you should not consider taking part in what will be virtually a non-paid job. If, however, you have not been considered or interviewed for some weeks and there is nothing that you can honestly say is a likely prospect, then a fringe play should certainly be on the agenda.

It may be that in the normal course of things you are offered a part in a fringe production just like being offered any other sort of job. Despite the disadvantages of such productions, competition is often just as fierce for fringe shows as for normal jobs, and a fringe company may well hold auditions or interviews. In other companies things may be done on a more personal level and a group of actors will spontaneously get together with a writer and a director. In this case you will be approached by a friend to take part.

But there is a more direct way to become involved and that is by setting up a production yourself, even setting up a venue on your own.

If you are going to become more pro-active in your career, setting up a fringe theatre production is a good way to start. The first pre-requisite is finding a play, and it must be a piece that has at least three qualities: 1) it must have merit in itself; 2) it must provide you with an opportunity to demonstrate your talents (and if you are trying to establish a new direction for your career, it must have a part that expresses that dimension); and, 3) it must be capable of being adapted to a standing set in a comparatively small space. There is absolutely no point spending time and money setting up a production of a play which allows you and your company a wonderful opportunity to demonstrate your range of ability if the play is flawed and unexceptional and will not attract an audience.

Finding the right play can be a complex process. There will be young writers eager to work on their plays, and young and not-so-young actors looking for opportunities to act. There are a great number of writers wishing to see their work performed. How do you get in touch with them? There are advertisements for writers' workshops in various magazines and papers. These groups can be contacted to see if they have anything suitable. Most writers whose work is being done on the fringe will have other plays available, so if you particularly like a play you see elsewhere, you can ask the writer if he has anything else. And there are the writers you meet in the course of your career – writers working on TV soaps, for instance – who will often have plays tucked away which have not been performed in the normal professional venues. You may have an idea for a play which you do not feel able to write yourself, but which might interest another writer. And perhaps your writer could be persuaded to write a play with you specifically in mind.

It is worth trying to write something yourself. It should be fairly obvious, if you are honest with yourself, whether this is a talent you possess or not. Many actors have found that they have a natural, if untutored, ability to write, especially for the theatre. But in fact you do not need to be a writer to create your own show. There have been many successful shows which are compilations of other material, snippets of work from one writer or on one theme, and their merit is in the way they are edited together.

It is better, at least to begin with, to choose a play with a small cast. The chances of someone dropping out are reduced and, of course, the stage on which you will be performing will not accommodate large numbers. Having a small cast will also make organising the rehearsal period very much simpler.

Having found a play, the next item on the agenda is finding a venue in which to perform it. There are two possibilities: going to an established venue or starting one up yourself. The first should be the favoured option. An established venue usually has a regular audience, however small. It will also have a regular system of publicity too, with a house style for posters and, hopefully, periodic contact with newspapers on the basis of their past productions.

For this reason, the person who runs an existing venue will want to approve your play, and this will not merely be a matter of negotiating for available dates. The management will want to ensure the play you are offering meets the standard the theatre has set. This means that you may have to approach three or four theatres before your project is accepted.

Setting up your own venue has attractions, of course. It means you are responsible for the material and there is no one to interfere with what you want to do. If you are particularly friendly with the landlord of a local pub with a large upstairs room or a councillor in a borough which has a hall suitable for conversion, then the idea of creating a new venue may find favour. But if this is the path you are going to take, you will need to set up a more complex organisation. You will not only have to sort out all the details of getting the stage and lights and sound equipment set-up (and finding money for them from a sponsor), but you will have to organise the publicity, which is one of the most important aspects of the venture. It is absolutely no good mounting a production if no one comes to see it, and no one will if you do not publicise the venue properly.

Creating your own venue will also involve you in finding more than one production, because the venue owner will not want to spend money on conversion just for a two-week run. You may become involved in finding an eight- or ten-week season.

This can distract you from your main aim of getting on with your career as an actor. But just as the actor/writer tradition is well established in the English profession, so is the role of actor/manager. It may be a shadow of what David Garrick did, but running a venue is an attractive proposition and can be career-enhancing, though only for a tiny minority. For those not capable of doing two things at once, it is better to concentrate your efforts on the requirements of running your career as an actor – which is quite demanding enough.

However the production is set up, you will need a director. You may contemplate doing this job yourself, but once again you should be wary of letting this detract from your performance as an actor which is, and should be, the main point of the exercise. It is better to try and get someone else, either another actor who has already done some directing or a director you have worked with in the regions (or at drama school) who might welcome exposure in London. There are other possibilities too. It may come as a startling thought, but in television recently there has been an enormous expansion in the number of television directors, largely due to an inordinate increase in the trainees taken on by the BBC Television Training Course. This, in combination with the shrinkage of television production, has meant that a lot of television directors are out of work. The chance to work in the theatre, however small scale, where some of these directors may have had little or no experience, may therefore be welcome.

Having a television director on the production has many advantages. It means he or she may well invite friends – other directors and producers, perhaps – to see the show, thereby enlarging the circle of people who have seen your work. It is also an incentive to other actors to join the production. It also means you get to know at least one director extremely well; and often friendships and loyalties formed at this level can endure throughout a career.

In making all these arrangements to get your production on stage it is important to remember why you are doing it in the first place. Don't allow yourself to get so bogged down in the details of producing the event as to forget the prime reason for the undertaking – that is, to enhance your career prospects. If it is a play you have produced on your own initiative and one that offers you a real challenge in terms of performance then an all-out attempt should be made to get people to see it. And as many people as possible.

Your list of casting directors can be mailed and you should talk to your agent about who else to include in your mailing. Write an intelligent and informative letter, stating where the production is (with a map) and emphasise any selling point – perhaps that it is directed by someone better known for their television work, or written by a writer who has had notable success elsewhere. It may be a good idea to combine your mailing with all the other members of the company so expensive duplication is avoided and the coverage greater.

If you are looking for an agent or thinking of changing agents, it is also a good time to write to prospective choices. An agent is more likely to come to the Rose Tavern, the Gate in Notting Hill Gate, or the Tabard in Turnham Green than to a production at the Pitlochry Festival.

Writing to casting directors should be coordinated with approaching the press. First make sure you contact all the free listings in the various local papers and on local radio. You should certainly write to the arts editors of some papers (the local paper, *Time Out*, and *The Stage*) but to ask, for instance, the theatre critic of *The Sunday Times* to cover the show is just a waste of time (think how little space they have for reviews of all other theatre productions) unless you have what in newspaper terms is called an 'angle'. An angle can take various forms: for example an actress once extremely well-known in British films making her first stage appearance for some years (or at all); or a film star (Ben Kingsley appeared at a pub venue) among the cast; or a writer of some distinction – perhaps a novelist who has written his first play; or even an actor whose last job was with Paul Newman in Hollywood now working for a share of the profits in Notting Hill Gate. Stories like these make good copy, and good copy gives you a better chance of getting coverage.

Stories of this kind are what newspapers call features, and they will appear, usually with a picture, in the middle pages of the paper. They do not necessarily mean the same paper will review the production, but they create interest and that interest may be picked up by local radio – who trawl the papers for items – and may even catch the attention of local television news. In turn this will make it more likely that the arts editor of a paper will send a critic to review the production. Similarly, a casting director or director may have their interest aroused enough to attend. And of course this coverage may also help create an audience.

It is a good idea to remember these factors when setting up the production in the first place. A production with an angle is more likely to attract critics, prospective employers and audiences. Be aware that in fringe productions, just as in major West End presentations, these things play a crucial part.

There is also the question of advertising to consider. If you are working on a shoestring, advertising will come down to having some posters and fly-sheets designed and printed as cheaply as possible and distributing them around the immediate area of the venue (an established venue may well have established sites). It is possible that in the course of setting up the production you will have found a sponsor. If you have a little money in hand after the production costs, then money on selected advertising is well spent. But be careful here. There is little point advertising in the *Observer* for a fringe venue in Fulham. It is much better to advertise in a paper read by those who go to fringe events, so *Time Out* would be more appropriate.

If the production is a success, gets one or two good reviews and is attracting audiences, it may be worthwhile trying to take it one stage further by suggesting it as a production for radio and television. Channel Four have done a series of such plays and radio may well be interested if the play is sufficiently well written. Again, be realistic in your expectations. Do not approach anyone on this basis unless the production is definitely a success: to do so is a waste of your time and of theirs.

Of course not all productions will have an angle or attract reviews. You may have to be content with a review in the local paper and *The Stage* and the visit of one or two casting directors or agents. But the enlarged experience the production gives you, the information gained from being with other actors and the psychological boost are surely better than sitting at home waiting for the phone to ring. However small scale the production, it will undoubtedly have enlarged your circle of friends and potential employers.

THE ONE-MAN SHOW

The second area of work creation is the one-man show. The advantages of having a one-man show in your repertoire as an actor are numerous. A one-man show, by definition, is relatively cheap to stage (and when constructing it you should try to keep costs to a minimum) and easy to mount (again care should be taken to ensure that the show can be performed in a variety of venues, not only on a conventional stage). In travelling the country to play at rep theatres or on tour, you will find that venues like arts centres and studio theatres are always on the look-out for this sort of material to fill their programme of events. If you have something interesting, they will certainly offer you a chance to perform it and, better still, may offer you a guarantee, i.e. a non-returnable sum of money set against box-office returns. A one-man show can also be performed at fringe venues and, if it is good enough, even be proposed for radio or television production.

Basically there are two sorts of one-man show; the first is written for the purpose in the same way that a play is written, and the second is compiled from existing writings or extracted from a book (Alec McCowen's readings from *St Matthew*). The first is naturally dependent on finding a writer but the second is much more accessible and does not require a particular talent for writing, though some may be necessary in constructing links.

Listing the sort of areas that could be investigated in thinking about creating a one-man show may give you ideas about how to find a suitable subject:

1 Historical characters. A politician or monarch who affected the course of history. Taking excerpts from other people's accounts of their exploits or using their own words or a mixture of both in constructing a sort of live biography.
2 Creative figures. A writer, artist or musician can prove interesting territory. Try abridging letters or diaries, or an autobiography or biography.
3 Poetry. A much more difficult area but it is possible that a major epic poem could be abridged in such a way as to make a one-man show (T. S. Eliot or John Milton?), or a series of poems could be shaped into a performance structure (Shakespeare's sonnets?).
4 A novel or story. It may be possible to abridge a novel in such a way as to contain all its salient points and important characters and plot and still be contained in a two-hour show (about

the maximum for a one man show). Patrick Stewart's adaptation of *A Christmas Carol* is a good example of this type.

In all these areas be careful about copyright. If you can use material which is out of copyright and therefore not due for royalties so much the better. The worst of all possible worlds is to have to negotiate with numerous writers for numerous extracts. Some writers will not give blanket permissions for the use of their work and will have to be contacted for every single venue. Administrative nightmares of this kind are best avoided, especially as there is so much material in the public domain (i.e. fifty or more years have elapsed since the death of its author).

In thinking about the material, try to strike a balance between the visual and verbal elements. A one-man show that is merely a reading will not be so interesting as one that contains something visual too. Remember also that the main purpose of the show is to demonstrate your talents, so try to assess your own strengths and weaknesses as an actor and play to those.

Having got a show together, you need to arrange for it to be seen. There are a number of possibilities for a one-man show not available to a conventional production. For instance, if your show concerns a historical figure there may be a tourist destination which would be a natural venue (the Duke of Wellington at Apsley House), or a society devoted to your character's work or life which would welcome such a production. In addition, if the subject is of artistic or historic interest you may find a university is interested. Once you have had one 'date' on the university circuit, and if you are a success, you may well find you are introduced to others. In researching your material you may have noticed books on the subject written by American academics. A letter telling them that you have a show featuring their area of speciality might prompt an invitation on to the American circuit, where funds for such events are more readily available and more substantial. As I have already suggested civic arts centres and studio theatres may also be possible venues, especially the former, which may not have the facilities to mount a full-scale production, but which will have an auditorium with rostrum and spotlights that the management would like to use constructively.

The other possibility for a one-man show, as I have said, is that it will transfer to another medium. Radio is the natural choice since inevitably much of a one-man show will be vocal. But my comments about fringe productions transferring to television apply equally to one-man shows: good reviews are essential. The ability to interest radio or television will be largely dependent on the critical success of the project.

CREATING OTHER WORK

There is no reason why you should confine your endeavours to create work for yourself to fringe theatre and one-man shows. Many actors have been successful in creating 'packages' for television drama (*Upstairs, Downstairs, The Paradise Club*), as well as West End plays (Mark Burns and *Easy Virtue*) and films (Peter Capaldi and *Soft Top, Hard Shoulder*).

But unless your idea for, say, a television series, is extremely strong, and unless you have the involvement of a well-known and highly rated television writer and probably a director or producer too, as well as the agreement of at least one star actor to play one of the leads, the likelihood of a television company taking on your project is very slim indeed.

The same applies to film, but with theatre there is a slightly different situation. A theatre production, even a West End theatre production, can be financed by one individual. If you happen to have met or know someone who has a great deal of money and who is interested in investing in the theatre, then there is certainly no reason why you cannot create a package around their money. Most existing West End managements would listen to you very sympathetically if you proposed an idea that was already financed. Or alternatively you could set up the production yourself. On a slightly smaller scale the same applies to a commercial tour.

In general, though, while being aware of the possibilities, it is as well to spend your time on areas that are more likely to produce tangible results and are not quite so fraught with difficulties and risk.

OTHER ACTIVITIES

There are other areas of activity you should pursue during periods out of work and, in a sense, for the same reasons that you undertake fringe productions. One of the problems of being out of work – and the longer this lasts, the greater the problem becomes – is that you begin to feel you are not really an actor at all and that you are losing touch with the profession and your professionalism.

One of the many ways of coping with this is to join an organisation like the Actor's Centre or the Actor's Institute. These provide a social meeting place where you can talk to other actors, share views and problems and generally keep in touch. The information exchange, as ever, is useful too.

These organisations also provide courses on a wide range of acting-related skills and techniques, often run by experienced directors or actors. The Actor's Centre, for instance, ran a course in television technique given by several television directors. Not only was this valuable for actors who had not worked on television previously, allowing them to assimilate some of the shorthand involved and some of the argot, but it provided an opportunity to meet and work with a number of directors.

It is important to use time out of work constructively in this way. Being in a highly competitive business, it is important to develop and sustain any particular speciality that you have, any advantage that sets you aside from the rest. If, for instance, you speak French fluently, or ride a horse well, or have a qualification in fencing, or enjoy archery, or ski, you should make every effort to maintain your proficiency. The Spotlight organisation maintains a register of such skills and you should certainly make sure you are on it if there is anything at all unusual or exceptional that you are able to do. The most useful of such skills, and the one that does need constant work to develop and perfect, is the ability to sing and, to a lesser extent, to dance. Singing extends the range of parts available to you considerably. If you have any natural talent in that area it should be worked on until you are confident enough of it to be able to audition as an actor/singer. If you already have experience in this area, don't let lack of practice find your voice unprepared. The West End musical is a large employer currently and one that is capable of changing the shape of your career overnight, as Sarah Brightman and Elaine Page both discovered.

Whatever specialised gifts you have should be exploited to the full but be wary of trying to exploit gifts you do not have. In some instances horse-riding is a prerequisite for a job in film or television costume drama. A director may be about to offer you a part but if you cannot ride a horse he will look elsewhere. In such circumstances many actors have lied, said they can ride, and then gone off to take a crash course. This may sound like the ideal solution but if, once you are on the production, your inability to do more than walk the animal, let alone control it and bring it up to a shooting 'mark', leads to waste of time and money – or, worse still, you injure yourself in your attempts to try and deliver what the director wants – you may come to regret your deception. This is true of any speciality, even something as commonplace as driving a car. Assuming everyone could drive, a well-known director offered an actor the part of a policeman, not mentioning that the part required the actor to drive a police car. The actor did not mention that he couldn't drive until they got to the shot with the car, when he was forced to come clean. As they had already shot on the actor he could not be replaced, so a great deal of time and trouble was spent in rigging the car so it could be driven by a stuntman lying under the seat while the actor merely had to steer. Needless to say, despite the fact it was strictly speaking the director's fault for not checking, the actor was not popular.

CONFIDENCE

All the activities described in this chapter are ways of extending your career and your talents, enlarging the circle of people who know your work, and giving you the psychological confidence to maintain your equilibrium when you have not had paid employment for some time.

Confidence is a key element. It is no good making new contacts and honing your talents and skills, if, when you are offered an interview, you are so lacking in confidence, so nervous and depressed at the parlous state of your career, that you make a negative impression.

Similarly, when you are given the opportunity to act, you want to make sure your confidence is high and that you have been working constructively and positively in improving your natural gifts, so as to be able to give a performance which is notable.

But of course confidence is not merely a question of the work you have put in on training. It is vitally important when you are out of work to keep yourself alert and alive in other ways, to keep yourself mentally and culturally stimulated, not only to prevent yourself falling into a slough of despondency, but to maintain your ability to communicate interestingly and effectively. You joined the profession because you believed, broadly speaking, you had something to offer artistically and creatively. Not being given the opportunity to express yourself in this way should not diminish your interest in the work of others, however. Make sure you are in touch, that you are reading, going to the theatre, and generally part of the cultural milieu you have placed yourself in professionally.

The broader your frame of reference – the better-informed you are on a whole range of issues, from current affairs and social issues to history and science as well as the other arts – the richer your life, and the greater the contribution you can make to the creative process when you are working. And of course you need to keep watching television and going to the theatre and cinema. This is important in interviews as well: it gives you something to talk about and respond with if you are asked what you think of the latest production in the theatre or on film or television.

But this activity and interest is more profoundly important than simply as a source of conversation. It gives you a perspective and a cultural reference. It enables you to maintain contact with the world around you and to extend further your own ideas and beliefs about how you should develop as an artist. This, in turn, will feed back into your psychology and help you maintain a vital level of interest and enthusiasm and confidence.

MINORITY ETHNIC GROUPS

Opportunities for non-white actors in Britain have been extremely slow to develop, as slow as the development of racial integration in all aspects of British life. Parts for black actors in the fifties were extremely limited. Films actually dealing with racial issues were rare and frequently treated with suspicion by distributors – *Sapphire* in 1959 being a prime example.

Television was even less inclined to get involved with racial themes and while 'Play for Today' was dealing with problems of homelessness (*Cathy Come Home*) and post-natal depression (*Baby Blues*) there was nothing to address the racial tensions that Enoch Powell's inflammatory and notorious Wolverhampton speech aroused in 1968.

There has been some progress since then. Minority ethnic groups have become a common feature of some soaps (particularly *Eastenders* and *Grange Hill* – though there have been complaints about the lack of ethnic content in *Coronation Street*) and the intake of ethnic background students into drama schools has widened considerably.

It is estimated that five per cent of the population of Britain is from a minority ethnic group. Clearly this is not reflected in the number of parts played by minority actors. There are two particular reasons for this. One is the small proportion of parts written for characters of ethnic origin. The other is the reluctance of most producers and directors to cast, say, a black, Asian or Chinese actor in a part which is racially unspecified.

There is an innate and often unconscious racism which generally reserves ethnic casting solely for ethnic characters, whereas it would clearly be a more accurate reflection of society at large to cast more parts without reference to colour or race. In the interests of realism, a director may not wish to cast a West Indian actor as a High Court judge – but why not as a solicitor or barrister?

Even the question of realism is debatable. There is an argument which says that it would be unrealistic or incongruous to use actors of ethnic origin in productions of plays by, say, Shakespeare, Chekhov, Oscar Wilde or J. B. Priestley. If these plays are presented as historical period pieces, maybe so – but if the classics are to stay fresh and alive, should they not be a part of the world and the society in which they are performed? Some theatre companies (the Royal Shakespeare Company, for example) have addressed this issue and tentatively adopted a multi-racial stance, but it is scarcely a widely accepted principle as yet.

Just as it would better reflect the balance of society to use more women in roles where it is not specified or essential for the character to be male, casting irrespective of colour or race could do something to improve the distorted picture that films, television and theatre currently present of the racial mix in Britain today.

It is important for actors from minority ethnic groups to keep up the political pressure for change, just as it is important for women to be politicised in the same way. A change in casting policies throughout the media will only be affected by political activity in the long term.

Meanwhile, as an actor from such a minority you have to deal with the realities of the profession that confront you, inequalities and all.

It is not all bad news. You have a specific quality which you should exploit. Firstly, of course, there are a number of ethnic theatre companies, whose work deals with inter-racial issues or issues of specific interest to their racial community. The most prominent of these are mentioned in the list of theatre companies in Part Three of this book, all of whom should be approached regularly. You may also find there is distinct enthusiasm for a one-man show in arts centres which may be adopting a policy of positive discrimination. Historical figures from minority ethnic groups may prove good subjects in this connection.

Overall, though, theatre offers perhaps the fewest opportunities. Certainly commercial theatre would appear to offer few roles outside the West End musical, where shows like *Five Guys Named Mo* and *Starlight Express* are examples of the opportunity available to actors who can sing and dance and where colour is either not an issue or a positive requirement. The chances of employment in regional reps will depend on their choice of play: the more conventional the theatre's policy, the smaller the number of parts available. As we have seen, few theatres will employ ethnic actors in classics so it is a question of searching out theatres who either have a very distinct ethnic policy or are producing plays that reflect racial issues in some way.

In television there is certainly a great deal more ethnic casting and it is undoubtedly on the increase across the whole range of drama production, with Channel Four's *Desmond's* being the first all-black show.

One area that has taken minority ethnic groups very much on board is the film industry. Modern British films (notably Stephen Frears's *My Beautiful Laundrette* and *Sammy and Rosie Get Laid*) have used a high proportion of ethnic actors and have tried to reflect the impact of ethnic communities on society as a whole. Hopefully this trend will continue.

There is no doubt, however, that generally speaking the range of parts available to an actor of ethnic origin is severely limited (just as it is for a woman – see Chapter 11) and therefore it is difficult to build the same career structure as a white actor. There are very few major roles in which an ethnic actor can develop his range and hope to reach an audience and make an impact. Even the very few such actors who have gained public acceptance (Don Warrington, Hugh Quarshie, Art Malik, Norman Beaton and Saeed Jaffrey, for example) find it a great deal harder to sustain their position than they would if they were white. There are simply not enough parts available.

Essentially this is the major problem confronting the ethnic actor and it is a problem that remains intractable. That does not mean it is impossible to be a 'working actor' if you are from a minority ethnic group, but there is no use pretending it is not a great deal more difficult. And, as Josette Simon says, if you also happen to be a woman it 'just compounds an already unequal situation'.

WORKING OUTSIDE THE PROFESSION

Many actors, after long periods out of work, begin to take up other employment in order to make ends meet. This can be anything from working in a restaurant or driving a mini-cab to labouring on a building site or any other sort of casual labour, and is unlikely ever to amount to anything apart from an additional source of funds.

But there are occasions when the alternative employment becomes more of a commitment, when an actor finds that, having taken a job with, say, a catering firm or an interior design company, the work begins to take much of his time and energy.

There is nothing wrong with that, of course, but it will inevitably mean you will spend less time on thinking about your acting career, working on gathering information, letter writing and all the other hard work involved in getting a job. As you become more successful in your alternative career it will start to take over, especially if your acting vocation remains stalled. Of the two jobs, you will become more involved emotionally with the one in which you are rewarded by a feeling of satisfaction at achieving something and by the financial rewards. You may hanker after acting success, but your second career will have become your first.

That is the major problem with taking other employment that is not pure casual labour. Anything that requires your energy and commitment, your brain and intelligence, will detract from your efforts to find work. You will find it more difficult to divide your time between the two and in the end, through lack of the hard work necessary to sustain it, your acting career will inevitably dwindle to extinction.

The point here is not to discourage you from looking at other professions and avenues of employment. But be aware that it is the experience of most actors who divide their time in this way that it is usually to the detriment of their acting careers. For this reason agents are less than enthusiastic when told by clients that they are taking a job outside the profession: their experience is that divided loyalties do not advance careers.

Success in the acting profession comes through hard work and application and commitment. Anything less than total commitment will blunt the edge you need in a fiercely competitive world.

11 The Difference Between Men and Women

T**HE DIFFERENCES BETWEEN** men and women are obvious, numerous and profound. And in the profession of acting they are fundamental to career prospects. This is not merely a question of sexism, but of the realities that make the situation facing an actress completely different from that which faces an actor.

RADICAL SOLUTIONS

There have been many complaints about the lack of opportunities in theatre, television and film for racial minorities, saying that parts written for whites could and should be played by black or Asian actors with artistically valid and interesting results. Unfortunately, except in rare cases (such as *The Year of Living Dangerously*), it is not possible for women to play a role specifically written for a man without altering the entire emphasis of the production and changing the subject matter. As suggested in Chapter 10, however, there are plenty of parts which do not actually necessitate being played by a man, and which can easily – maybe fruitfully – be played by a woman. And it is possible (though only Sarah Bernhardt has done it) for a woman to play the great male roles as women – so why not a female Lear or Othello? This would alter the emphasis in a way that could reveal new aspects of the play (just as a modern dress production does) and of the character without necessarily changing the basic themes being explored.

THE NUMBER OF PARTS

Other than these experiments the truth is that a simple survey of any number of plays (Shakespeare, Restoration comedy, Victorian melodrama, farce), television drama, soap operas, films, even children's programming and radio drama will rapidly lead to one conclusion: the ratio of parts for men to parts for women is anything between ten and twenty to one. That is the basis on which the 21,600 female members of Equity compete against the 22,500 males.

There has been a number of television dramas over the last few years casting women in roles that would have previously been played by men. LWT's *Within These Walls* was about a women's prison, *Rock Follies* about a female rock group, *The Gentle Touch* about a female police inspector, its spin-off *Cats Eyes* about female private detectives, *Widows* about a gang of female robbers and, most recently, the phenomenally successful *Prime Suspect* about another police woman. But though these programmes had leading female characters, the ratio of parts within them, men to women, still maintained the same imbalance (with the possible exception of *Within These Walls*).

The predominance of leading roles for men and the lack of substantial roles for women in the theatre has long been discussed. It has led, arguably, to plays like *Hedda Gabler*, *Ghosts* and *Three Sisters* being over-rated and performed too frequently. There are, of course, few great Shakespearean, Jacobean or Restoration roles for women and, perhaps more significantly, few leading roles among the canon of modern dramatists from Osborne to Pinter to David Hare.

It is thus not just a problem to find roles in the first place, but once a position and reputation have been established, it is a struggle to find substantial enough work to sustain them. A number of writers are trying to improve the situation, but the efforts of, for example, Pam Gems, Lynda la Plante and even Dario Fo have made little impact overall.

There is also a much bigger problem in physical terms over the casting of women than of men. Not only are there fewer roles, but they tend to be minutely defined by physical type. In television commercial casting for instance, the expression 'young mum' is a current description of a type that is frequently required. Then there is the *ingénue*. And the vamp. And the dumb blonde. All four heavily dependent on appearance – that is, on stereotyped images of female glamour.

The number of parts for female bank managers, solicitors, doctors and company directors reflects precisely the dearth of women in such positions in society. What is not reflected is the range of ages and types of women in the real world. Judging from the work of many writers, one might imagine that women consisted principally of young pneumatic beauties or middle-aged wives. And even those actresses who have played the former cannot be sure they will subsequently qualify to play the latter.

Emma Thompson, in her speech at the 1993 Oscars ceremony, put this point when she pleaded for greater equality in the treatment of ordinary women's lives: 'I would just like films to tell us about the way women live their lives. When you get to forty or forty-five or after the menopause, when women are at their most powerful, that's the point when women become non-beings' – as far as the film industry is concerned. This is undoubtedly true. Most films of whatever type are about men.

Another problem that besets women more than men is that, whereas men will often be cast within quite a limited age range (that is, they will play a part which is near to their own actual age), producers and directors will often cast a successful actress in a part for which she is actually either too old (most commonly) or too young. Rather than find an unknown actress for a 21-year-old character, they will ask a 35-year-old actress with a 'name' to play it to increase the 'marquee' value of the production. There is no need to do this with men because they can find a man of the right age with a 'name'. Female stars are much thinner on the ground. The 60-year-old Joan Collins is often asked to play 45-year-old parts. Compare this with male casting: a 60-year-old man would not be asked to play a 45-year-old man. It would change the storyline. But with women this is a common practice, thus further reducing the parts available to other actresses.

Men have no need to extend their youth in order to gain employment; there are plenty of parts for senior barristers, judges, headmasters and retired professionals of all types. But for a woman, especially a comparatively famous woman, the need to prolong the appearance of youth is acute.

Bearing in mind the difficulties, it is not surprising that the drop-out rate for women is much higher than for men. With so many parts confined to bimbos and sidekicks, the chance of finding a role in which one can make a mark is extremely limited. When the time for these younger parts has passed, the number of available roles dries up even further, and it can be a long wait for the arrival of middle-age. The Welsh actress Rachel Roberts, never a conventional beauty, was fond of saying she would have to wait until she was 50 until she got another part as good as the wife in *This Sporting Life*, and then 'I'll be Lady Macbeth'.

That is not to say that a career cannot be built as an actress, but with very rare exceptions it will be peppered with long periods of unemployment. A successful actress, in comparison to a successful actor, will undoubtedly be paid less and, over a period of years, work less and have a shorter working life (facts confirmed by Dr Helen Thomas in a report sponsored by Equity). Joan Collins may appear to be in great demand at the moment but if you aggregate her career over the years from her early days in Rank films and a long period of semi-obscurity until her re-emergence in *The Stud* and *Dynasty*, her work rate will be considerably less than an equivalent male star. In England, only Vanessa Redgrave and Glenda Jackson in recent years have enjoyed more or less continuous success, compared to a long list of male actors of similar status.

In getting an agent, too, women face problems different to those of their male counterparts. Some agents are chary of taking on too many women clients claiming that there is a higher drop-out rate and greater difficulty in getting them work. The investment of time and money that an agent has to make on any client, some agents argue, has a higher chance of being recouped on a man than on a woman. Rather short-sightedly, they will often only consider an actress who has already made something of a name for herself and looks as though she is on the first rung of the mythical ladder. Alternatively they may only consider someone who fits special requirements in terms of a 'gap' in their list but this is simply their prejudice, and should not be considered typical of all agents.

A MOUNTAIN TO CLIMB

All these remarks are intended as a definition of the unnecessary mountain that an actress has to climb. Perhaps the mountain will diminish as women become more integrated into the boardrooms of public companies, drive more taxis and trains, stand on an equal footing with men in the professions, and escape their more traditional male-dominated roles. But until that change in society it is a question of the unfortunate realities that lie ahead.

The harsh truth is that, as we have seen, whereas the number of women competing for parts is roughly the same as the number of men, there are far fewer women's parts available. What this means, in effect, is that the sheer commitment and energy needed to succeed have to be that much greater. Everything a man does to forward his career a woman has to do harder, longer and more efficiently because the competition is that much fiercer.

All the activities listed so far should be undertaken with a vengeance. But there are, sadly, greater lengths to which an actress must sometimes go to have any hope of getting a job in an industry run largely by men. There are women producers and directors (and most casting directors are women) but the decision-making is dominated by men. Similarly the majority of parts that women are offered are written by men and are located in a man's world where the women behave according to male views or expectations. A very high proportion of these characters are written as attractive and sexy. Many women will be forced to spend much of their time going up for these parts (since that is where the majority of the work is), so it is deemed important to look after your physical appearance. As has already been stated, directors are not noted for their imagination when it comes to casting. If you turn up for the part of an elegant wife in jeans and a T-shirt the director will not want to make the effort to imagine what you could look like.

This is exactly the same rule as for a male actor going for a role of a prosperous solicitor in the same outfit. But sadly whereas a man may be going for a variety of different roles, an actress will have a much more limited choice.

Why on earth should a woman have to take more trouble over her appearance than a man? In an ideal world, clearly she shouldn't. If the roles of men and women were equal in society and those roles were perfectly reflected in the culture and art of that society, then there would be no imbalance and no need for special care. But they are not. The representation of women in television drama series, serials and plays, and even more so in films, is more often than not the presentation of male attitudes to women. Of course there are roles as doctors and nurses, and social workers and policewomen and all the other roles women portray which in no way 'require' a degree of male-perceived attractiveness. But because physical attractiveness *is* perceived as being an important quality, very few of these parts actually end up being played by women who do not conform to the norms of conventional attractiveness.

It is a sad fact that the interview relationship between a male director and an actress tends to be different to that between a male or female director and a (male) actor. Sexual politics being as they are it is often the attractive qualities (and often the physical ones) in an actress that a director is looking for, and these are the qualities that can determine his casting decision. As an actress, you will be aware of this, and your awareness can be used as another element of the way in which you market yourself at the interview.

For both women and men however, physical attractiveness without talent will not succeed. This has been seen often before and will undoubtedly be seen again, whenever good-looking actors are cast for their appearance but fall short on acting talent. (Many models have tried to transfer their success from one kind of camera to another, only to discover that there is more to it than looking stunning.) Conversely, and more importantly, there are actors, both male and female, who may be far from conventionally stunning, but who can become stunning in performance.

KEEP GOING

In conclusion, it's tougher for a woman. There are fewer parts, and on the whole they may be less challenging or interesting that those available to men. Again, a lot of women's parts are more stereotyped than are men's and they tend to be clustered into certain age groups – so you can repeatedly find yourself in the unfortunate position of having to go up for parts considerably younger than yourself.

And, distasteful as it may seem, there's a much higher premium on physical attractiveness for a woman – you don't have to be glamorous to be successful, of course, but it certainly helps. This creates its own pressures (maintaining youthfulness, maintaining your looks), which you may quite rightly resent, reasoning that you became an actress to act, not be a glamour queen.

These are some of the problems you have to face. But hard work at the business of acting is the answer. Everything I said elsewhere in this book applies – only more so. Maintain your skills, maintain your confidence, market yourself to the utmost of your ability, and you will give yourself the best possible chance of success.

12 Other Services Available to an Actor

THERE ARE MANY organisations and products in the marketplace designed for an actor's use and tempting you to part with your hard-earned cash and it is important to sort out which ones are useful and which are essential.

PHOTOGRAPHS

The first service you are definitely going to need is that of a photographer. In your armoury of weapons for battle to get a job, the photograph is probably the single most important item, and the one to which you should devote a great deal of attention, time and trouble. In the piles of mail that constantly accumulate on agents', casting directors' and directors' desks, it is the photograph that, above everything else, makes the biggest impact. It is also the first impact. Whatever your accompanying letter says, it will be the photograph that people automatically look at first. If you are writing to an agent, the photograph will tell them if you are in a group where they want to have additional clients or where they feel they have none; if to a director or casting director, they will have a good idea of what they are looking for and will go to the photograph to see if it matches the vague image they have in mind.

The photograph will be looked at both in terms of your being 'photogenic' (an important consideration with so much work done on camera) and quite simply to see what you look like. If a photograph arrests an agent's attention, he or she may rightly argue that it will have the same effect on someone else, especially bearing in mind that so many are seen in the course of a week. If a casting director or director notices a photograph it might help to shape their idea of what they are casting.

It is therefore essential to get the best possible set of photographs. This involves using a reputable photographer and, as a rule of thumb, the best one you can afford. Don't forget that this is a crucial decision. Take it with care. Talk to friends to see who they used. Go to The Spotlight offices and look through the *Spotlight* directory, making a note of the photographs in it you think are especially good.

A good photographer is not cheap (though it is a tax deductible expense if you are on Schedule D: see Chapter 6). The basic fee usually includes what is called a 'contact' sheet which is a printed sheet of all the photographs taken in 35 mm format (the same size as the actual film). From this you choose a certain number of images (usually six to eight) to be printed into 10 × 8-inch black-and-white photographs. These enlargements can then be used for reproductions and for your advertisement in the *Spotlight*. The latest legislation on copyright makes it essential that the photographer signs a clearance for such use. Normally he will provide this automatically with his account.

Look at the contact sheet with infinite care in colloboration with your agent if you have one or, if not, with someone else whose opinion you trust. Your own opinion of the photographs will, necessarily, be subjective. It is important to get a second opinion and, in the case of an agent, this will also be conditioned by how he or she feels you are going to be sold.

The images on the contact sheet are small. Don't try to look at them only with the naked eye. Use a magnifying glass. Look at each shot individually, masked off from the rest. Some will be quickly dismissed for obvious reasons like having one eye closed, or an awkward position of the body, or a shaft of light across your face. Usually the choice can be narrowed down to a dozen or so shots from which to choose the enlargements. If it is impossible to tell between these it may be worth paying extra for additional enlargements.

Once you have the 10 × 8s you have to choose which photograph to use in the next annual edition of *Spotlight* and which to have re-printed to be sent out with letters. You may think that being in *Spotlight* precludes the necessity for sending photographs with letters, but it does not. A letter saying you can be looked up on page so-and-so of *Spotlight Edition No* . . . (and every casting director seems to have a different edition, some of them not current at all) does not have the impact of a 10×8, unfortunately. It is up to you to decide whether losing this advantage is something you are prepared to do bearing in mind the cost of reproductions.

In deciding which photograph to choose, it is important that you reason out carefully what the photograph is for, and what you are aiming at. The photograph is a marketing tool, *the* marketing tool, reflecting the image you wish to present to the world. So far as possible you must decide what you want that image to be and make sure the photograph tallies with it. This may sound like nonsense, but it is important. It is no good trying to be all things to all men. What is going to make the biggest impact is a photograph that makes a clear, precise statement as to exactly what you are. What is going to make the least impact is a wishy-washy photograph that is neither one thing nor the other.

Once you have decided which picture is going in *Spotlight* and which is going to be reproduced to be sent out with letters, you can cover other bases by choosing one or two other photographs which present you in a contrasting style and image and which may be useful in the case of a particular part. For instance, if the main image you have decided on is of a romantic leading man, it might be a good idea to have a reproduction of a picture that shows you in a more humorous vein.

On the matter of photographs there is one final point to be made and it is an important one. A few years ago a young Irish actress arrived in London to get work and sent out her photograph to a number of agents asking for an interview with a view to representation. The photograph was simply stunning – an image of an elegant, sophisticated and extremely beautiful woman, exquisitely dressed, in her early thirties. The impact of the photograph was such that most of the agents she had written to immediately rang her up and asked her to come and see them, reasoning, no doubt, that their reaction to the photograph would be the same as that of directors and casting directors throughout the business who are constantly looking for a 'new' and exceptionally beautiful face. Subsequently the actress arrived for her appointment. She bore no discernible resemblance to the photograph. Her hair and face seemed completely different, and some agents simply refused to believe it was the same young woman. Unfortunately she was not offered representation.

The point of the story is obvious. With a combination of make-up, lighting and, above all, a clever photographer, it is possible to make yourself (man or woman) look like almost any image you care to imagine. Possible but not advisable. The world of casting is a real world and not two-dimensional. The image you have created in the photograph must be capable of being reproduced in reality. It is a mistake to create something perfect in a photograph – as the young Irish actress did – and not be able to reproduce it in an interview. By all means lean towards a basic image that you want to present and one that is in line with the sort of parts you are suited to play: but don't lean so far that your photograph and your appearance become two different things.

THE SPOTLIGHT

Second only in importance to your photograph and inextricably linked with it is The Spotlight organisation itself. Despite the development of various forms of casting including the VHS tape and CD-ROM, the *Spotlight* remains the primary source for casting directors, directors and a wide range of people all over the country engaged in casting all manner of things. A set of *Spotlight* directories (some of them considerably out-of-date) can be found in every theatre in the UK. There are copies in advertising agencies, film production companies, television companies, practically every office in the BBC drama department (even BBC radio!), every film studio and, of course, in the offices of every one of the hundred-plus casting directors. The Spotlight itself gives copies of all new editions to a wide range of prospective employers.

Every day someone opens a copy of *Spotlight* with the intention of finding the right actor for a particular role. They use it to match actors' faces to the parts they are casting, making up a list of suitable candidates and noting their agents' telephone numbers so they can call to make an availability check. Sometimes they use the directory to find the name of a face they have seen on television or in a film.

The directory is divided into separate editions for actors, actresses and children plus a special edition of New Actors and Actresses (combined) at the Conference of Drama Schools. Each edition is published annually, the actors' volumes in April and the actresses' in October. The actors' directory comprises four volumes and the actresses' three, arranged in alphabetical order. Within these volumes the directory is divided into sections for 'Leading Actors/Actresses', 'Character Actors/Actresses', 'Younger Character' and 'Young Actors/Actresses'.

There are two classes of advertisement in *Spotlight*, a half-page and a quarter-page (except in the 'New Actors and Actresses' edition which is all quarter-pages). The half-page is the norm, presenting a picture in either an upright ('portrait') or horizontal ('landscape') format, alongside or underneath which is the agent's logo if applicable. The half-pages come at the front of each section followed by the quarter-page advertisements (with photographs, in the 'upright' format only), again carrying the agent's details or the actor's own address and telephone number. It is more common, in this section, to find actors who do not have an agent and who are economising by not taking the full half-page. Though prospective employers do look at the quarter-pages, it has to be said that their attention goes first to the half-page advertisements: often if they get an adequate list from these they will only glance cursorily at the quarter-pages. Generally speaking they will be looking for faces they recognise, faces they can match to performances they have seen. They know they may not find these in the quarter-page sections.

It follows, therefore, that you should pay for a half-page advertisement if you can afford it. It is important. At the time of writing the cost of a half-page is £86 (including VAT). The cost of a quarter-page is exactly half that. In August 1993 the Spotlight offered their directory as a CD-ROM disc, starting with the actors' edition and soon to be followed by the actresses'. This was done as a service to casting directors and involved no extra charge to advertisers.

If you do not have an agent, rather than having your own address and telephone number printed, the Spotlight offer the alternative of having 'c/o *Spotlight*' printed under your picture. Enquiries are then directed to the Spotlight information service, which will give appropriate callers your telephone number. It is better to do this than having your own phone number printed. Remember that the deadline for copy is six months before publication, and though new editions are published every year, many copies stay in offices for several years. You may have gone through several addresses and changes of telephone number in that time. Even if you haven't, if you are away on tour or in repertory you may miss a vital call. Better to let the Spotlight know so calls can be transferred to the theatre where you are working. They will be more reliable than any answerphone.

Choosing the section in which you appear is another matter that requires careful consideration. The Spotlight do not exercise an editorial function. The choice is yours. The phrase used several times in this book already must be used again: be realistic. If you are not a leading man do not put yourself in the leading man section. A casting director looking for a character actor will look through that section first. If the search is for a younger character actor again they will look in that section. If you are not a leading man, however much you wish you were, being in the leading man section is not helpful and may well lose you opportunities.

There is, of course, a grey area where an actor is not obviously a character actor, but his appearance (and these matters are, to be frank, based almost entirely on appearance) is not quite one thing or the other. In this situation you have to think carefully but it may be helpful in reaching a decision to remember there are a lot more parts for character actors than for leading men. A play may have one or two leads but all the other parts will be younger character or character roles. Especially at the beginning of your career it is better to be in the section that is probably more widely used than in 'Leading Actors', if you have a choice. In addition, when casting the leads, producers and directors will mainly be looking for 'names' and may already have made up their list of possibles with barely a glance at the 'Leading Actors' section.

Do not let these remarks tempt you into putting your advertisement in 'Character' or 'Younger Character' when you should clearly be in as a leading man. That is just as mistaken. If you are obviously leading man material then there is no point confusing the issue by putting yourself in the wrong section.

All that has been said in reference to men applies equally to women and the women's edition, though the 'Leading Actresses' section is used perhaps more extensively than with men in the constant search for beautiful young *ingénues* or vamps. But the classification is based on appearance and if you do not have the physical qualities for this category it is far better to put yourself into 'Character Actresses' or 'Young Character'.

The 'Young Actors/Young Actresses' sections should really be called Young Leading Actors because that is precisely what it is. Mostly it is for actors under the age of 25 (though not exclusively by any means) who do not fit into the category of 'Younger Character' because, as they mature, they will be regarded as leading actors. In effect, though, there is very little difference between the 'Young Character' section and the 'Young Actors/Actresses'. There are many actors who should be in one and are in fact in the other. The only characteristic they share is youth. It is a perfectly natural confusion. In many cases it is difficult to know whether you will develop into a leading actor or not.

Fortunately most casting is done across both these sections, so if you choose one rather than the other it is not as damaging as the choice between the two sections for older actors. The characteristic the casting director will be looking for is youth, so do not be tempted to enter these sections unless that is a quality you definitely possess. Also if you are definitely a young character actor it is better to go into that section just in case a prospective employer does not bother to go through both. The same applies if you are obviously not a young character actor.

Strangely, perhaps, there is no rival publication to the *Spotlight*. It has a monopoly. *The Screen International Yearbook* takes advertisements in the form of photographs in various sizes but, though this may be a useful reminder to people flicking through its pages for reference purposes, it is not used as an aid to casting.

LASERCAST

There is however a rival to *Spotlight* in the computer world. *Lasercast* is a directory published on CD-ROM and heavily promoted by the BBC and approved by Equity. The problem with it is that the video image is really little better for identification purposes than a black-and-white photograph in *Spotlight*. It cannot demonstrate whether an actor can act. In addition, not only does the prospective employer have to possess extremely expensive hardware to access the programming, which is not portable in the way the *Spotlight* directories are (admittedly with a good deal of weight training), but it is much more inconvenient to have to type up all the details on a keyboard. With *Spotlight*, on the other hand, anyone can open a book. It is easy and indeed almost addictive to flick through the pages and is less tiring on the eyes than staring at a video screen. This said, casting directors do use *Lasercast* and it may be, as the hardware becomes more common, that the practice will spread.

CASTING INFORMATION SERVICES

Among the other services available to an actor (at a price) are publications which try to keep abreast of current casting in all the various media. The two main contenders in this field are *Script Breakdown Service* (SBS) and *Professional Casting Report* (PCR). The first is more specialised than the second. SBS tries to get hold of the scripts that are being produced and break them down into the roles available. It by no means covers the whole spectrum of activities though it tries to. SBS's success depends on its ability to persuade producers to show scripts early enough in the casting process for the information to be included in the weekly bulletins before all the casting is completed. In America the idea of such services is widespread and most of the major studios and television companies cooperate enthusiastically with such publications, believing that giving out information to them cuts down the number of calls to their casting departments from actors wanting to know what they are casting. In this country some producers are cooperative for the same reason, but others remain steadfastly opposed and never give their scripts out to third parties in this way.

It is difficult to estimate *SBS*'s success rate in obtaining scripts but averaged out over all the media it covers roughly a quarter of the casting that is going on at any one time. In some areas it does better (touring theatre productions for instance) and in others (television commercials and independent television productions) worse. It is equally hard to estimate what proportion of the information contained in each bulletin is out of date, in the sense that the casting has been done by the time the breakdown has been published.

Script Breakdown Service is only available to actors second hand, as the organisation will not accept subscriptions direct from actors but only from agents.

PCR, on the other hand, is freely available by subscription and is more like a newspaper. It will occasionally print a whole breakdown, like *SBS*, usually of a television series or television film, but mostly it reports on who is casting what and where. This information, xeroxed on three to four foolscap pages, is partly gleaned from casting directors and production companies and partly from newspaper and magazine reports. There are also a lot more general items concerning agents, changes of address, and people setting up businesses or retiring. *PCR* also publishes and regularly updates a list of prospective employers (called *Who's Where*) and where they can be found.

As with *SBS* the main problem with *PCR* is timing. In order for any of the information contained in it to be valuable it has to be current. The casting process can be over very quickly and any delay in the information coming to hand, then being printed and circularised can mean that it is too late to be helpful. It can also be much too soon. If *PCR* prints a story that Richard Attenborough is setting up a new project, it may be literally years before casting is likely to begin.

A word of warning. Casting directors and other employers can get extremely irritated by the spate of calls and letters that usually follows a story in *PCR*. Sometimes they are inundated and if it happens that the information on which the story is based is inaccurate in any way, then their wrath may well fall on you. So be careful, particularly in relation to the 'recap' section where some of the items mentioned can be fully cast or even finished though still appearing in the list.

If you are thinking of subscribing to *PCR* try and get hold of a copy first from an agent or a friend to judge for yourself whether it would be of value. Generally it is certainly a good supplement to your own information reference systems, providing you with new names and contacts and productions, but it is definitely not the only reference you should use.

There is one more publication in this area which is highly specialised: *Celebrity Service*. This does not provide details of what is casting but is merely a list of who is coming into town and where they are staying. If, for instance, Steven Spielberg is arriving for a premiere of his new film it will list his arrival and departure date and the hotel he is going to use. Or at least it will try to. It does not always succeed. The one person you are desperate to contact may be the one person they do not list.

Celebrity Bulletin is not particularly useful but it is certainly worth trying to get a look at a copy if there is one well-known director you are trying to track down.

TRADE PAPERS

Trade papers are an essential source of information and should be read regularly. They will be invaluable to you in keeping your information reference system up-to-date, and in alerting you to new productions, to the formation of new independent production companies and to changes of personnel within the larger television companies and the BBC.

The weekly trade paper specifically designed for actors is *The Stage and Television Today* (commonly abbreviated to *The Stage*), which represents extremely good value for money. It contains a vast array of information including the latest theatrical productions, news on changes at television companies and forthcoming television and film production, as well as comprehensive reviews. It is at its most informative in relation to the theatre in all its forms; rep, touring and West End.

Broadcast is a glossily produced weekly which is concerned exclusively with television and radio matters. Though it does have news on production its main concerns are the policies of broadcasters and matters concerning the financing and economics of television companies, both franchise holders and the independents. It is the best source of information about the changes in these companies and the deals that are done between them, for instance reporting news that an independent company has been awarded a contract to produce a drama series, or renew a previous commitment.

Screen International has the same format as *Broadcast* but deals with matters primarily connected to the British film industry. As this has shrunk away to such an extent, *Screen International* has been forced to diversify into writing about television and the production of television films, but generally speaking it is the trade paper for people whose primary concern is the making of films as opposed to the making of videos. Its 'European Production Guide' is a very useful souce of reference, telling you which stage a project has reached and who is going to direct and produce it.

The Stage, *Broadcast* and *Screen International* should be read as often as possible and studied in detail. Not only do they contain valuable information but they will help you understand the way the business works in financial terms and the way decision-making in relation to drama production is affected by external, apparently non-related matters. They often contain interviews with producers and directors whom you may meet in interviews, which will give you an insight into what these individuals want and how they think (see section on Interviews in Chapter 9). But there are also other publications that are useful to look at from time to time.

Campaign deals with the advertising world and can be useful in letting you know which agencies are handling which new advertising campaigns and, even more importantly, which commercial production shops are being used to produce the commercial. They can also give a valuable guide as to how much money is being spent on the launch of a product or on a series of commercials, which will be helpful in trying to calculate what you may earn if you are successful in an audition/interview. *International Variety*, a weekly edition of American *Variety*, is a good way to keep an eye on the way Americans do things and often has details of any American studios or television companies planning to shoot films or television shows in Europe, as well as proposals for Broadway shows to come to London. Conversely it has details of British shows heading for Broadway. It has accurate information on the ratings of shows on the American television networks and on the domestic (i.e. North American) gross box-office receipts of all current American feature film releases. *Hollywood Reporter* contains information specific to the Los Angeles film and television community and deals with plans for production in those areas.

Another useful but rather different publication is *The Guide to Selecting Plays*, published by Samuel French Ltd. This is a book intended to help amateur dramatic groups pick plays for production. It has a huge list of plays, mostly performed at one time or another in the West End, with a short synopsis of the plot and, most importantly from your point of view, a breakdown of the characters, their ages and types. If you learn, therefore, that a particular play is being done in the theatre, this little book may well help you to see if there is a suitable part for you, and save you the trouble of getting the play out of the library and breaking it down for yourself.

For the theatre, *Plays and Players* is invaluable for keeping abreast of who is directing what and where, and so is the *Theatre Record* which contains a section listing 'future London and region schedules', as well as giving credits for all current productions.

The information reference system in Part Three of this book is meant to act as the basis for your information gathering. There are many more sources of reference for names, addresses and telephone numbers, though they have not, of course, been designed specifically with the demands of a working actor in mind. The most useful is probably *Contacts* which is published by the Spotlight organisation and is comparatively cheap. It has listings for theatres, casting directors and film and television companies. Probably the most comprehensive reference book is *The Knowledge*. This is aimed at people who are setting up a film or television production. It lists technicians, agents, organisations, producers and directors. *Kay's Datebase*, *The White Book* and *Kemp's* are also reference books aimed at a similar market that might serve a limited purpose. There is even a reference book of all related publications, *The Handbook of International Film, Television and Video Magazines* which, its advertising says, is 'a comprehensive international source book to over 700 film and television and video magazines . . .'

BRITISH ACTORS' EQUITY

British Actors' Equity Association, the actors' union, was formed in 1930 and merged with the Variety Artistes' Association in 1967. In 1992 membership stood at 43,500, a very slight decline on the previous year's figure, though nearly 13,000 of those members were more than 26 weeks in arrears with subscriptions – an increase of nearly 2000 on the 1991 figure.

Before the Employment Acts of 1982 and 1988, the position over employment of actors was very different to today's. In order to get a job it was necessary to be a member of Equity and in order to become a member of Equity you had to have worked a certain number of weeks in a repertory company or satisfy other requirements to prove that you had worked as a professional actor. Recognised employers could allocate a small set number of jobs each year to non-union members, who thereby qualified for membership, but outside that arrangement it was virtually impossible to get into the union.

The 1988 legislation made the 'closed-shop' illegal and it is now not necessary for an actor to be a member of Equity in order to obtain employment, just as it is not necessary to be a member of a trade union to accept employment in any walk of life. Membership of Equity is therefore optional.

Equity membership is highly advisable, however, first and foremost because of the protection Equity offers against breach of contract and industrial compensation cases. The legal costs of pursuing a claim in both these areas may be prohibitively expensive for an individual and cause the abandonment of a perfectly good case. But with Equity's backing the case can be concluded. In recent years a settlement of £100,000 was achieved for a dancer injured in a production and the case for compensation over the death of Roy Kinnear in filming *The Three Musketeers* is still continuing at the time of writing. In fact, 119 contract claims were endorsed in 1992 and 37 involving personal injury, with £320,000 paid for the latter in respect of compensation.

Unfortunately there are many unscrupulous companies working in the entertainment industry – arguably more than in other areas – whose funding is far from secure. Not only does Equity help in the cases where such companies or individuals breach contracts, but they also publish a blacklist of employers who have failed to pay up in the past. Especially if you do not have an agent, Equity can be a valuable source of advice as to what engagements you should accept and what you would be better off rejecting. With international contacts, too, Equity can provide equally good advice about foreign contracts.

Equity is responsible for negotiating standard contracts in all the media and minimum levels of pay as well as collection of royalties and residuals due to its members from the increasingly complex world of copyright in areas like video production, cable and satellite transmission and blank tape levy payments.

Clearly, if you wish to have a voice in the way these matters are handled, Equity membership is worthwhile. It is still regarded as a badge of expertise within the industry.

You will be accepted as a member of Equity automatically if you have attended a course at one of the schools within the Conference of Drama Schools or have a contract for professional employment as an actor (but not for a single television commercial or as a walk-on). Fees range from £26 a year for a member earning less than £3,500 per year, to 1 per cent of the gross earnings of an actor earning over £10,000 a year, up to a maximum of £1200. There is a scale of charges for members in between the two extremes.

PRESS AGENTS

The importance of publicity and the press in any actor's career cannot be dismissed lightly. The old Hollywood cliché, 'the only bad publicity is no publicity' is still current, especially with tabloid newspapers still believing that gossip about television and film stars is capable of promoting their sales. Press attention can thrust an actor into the limelight and make it more likely that he or she will stay there. It makes producers and directors believe, in the best circumstances, that an actor is popular and therefore that his popularity and its accompanying press coverage will rub off on their project. It is not only the individual actors who can be affected. At the BBC, for instance, the initial launch of *Eastenders* was greeted with little enthusiasm by the viewing public. It was not until the story broke in the tabloids that one of the principal actors had once killed a man that interest peaked and the ratings soared.

At all levels of the business, therefore, publicity is something that can very definitely influence a career. But the press are unlikely to be interested in an unemployed actor, and the actor cannot get the help of the press in getting employment until he has done something. It is very much a question of seeing that any 'angle' you create in the normal course of your career is exploited in the press to the maximum advantage. There is no doubt that if it is used properly the story will encourage employment.

One of the main aims of the work you do to promote your own career is to get your name and face in front of prospective employers. Clearly the best way to do this is over the breakfast table in a newspaper. However, what will determine the coverage is the initial angle. Being cast as Evita in the musical of the same name got Elaine Page, a previously unknown actress, a great deal of coverage, as going out with Prince Andrew did for Kate Rabett. Playing the leading role in a new television series or film is a good angle, or taking over an understudy on a first night or in similarly dramatic circumstances (as in the story of Thomas Allen coming up from the audience to take over in *Cavalleria Rusticana*).

A press agent's job is to keep these stories alive and see that their client's name appears in the papers for more than a couple of days. Sometimes they will be successful and sometimes the story will just die a natural death. The career of Kenneth Branagh would seem to be a good example of this sort of coverage, where the press appear endlessly fascinated by his exploits and especially his youth.

But unless there is an angle which can realistically be exploited in this way there is no point employing a press agent. And there is no point in trying to create an angle by some mad stunt. Responsible press coverage and even sensational headlines ('Freddie Starr ate my hamster!') can be extremely good for a career but they can also be a two-edged sword, and it is not true that there is no such thing as bad publicity. After her initial affair with David Mellor, for instance, Antonia de Sanchez brought in a press agent to handle and try to exploit the press coverage to her advantage. Certainly this had the effect of making her a household name but there is no doubt it also seriously damaged her career prospects in the long term.

By no means is a press agent essential to an actor's career. What you should be aware of, though, is that if you find yourself in a situation where the press are interested in you, and are likely to continue to be interested in you, the best way to deal with this is through a press agent who can, to some extent, control who you give the story to and what is written, as well as nudging the press to feature you again in due course.

With or without a press agent, be extremely careful how you handle the representatives of the press. As many actors have found to their cost, flippancy and jokes and stunts have backfired badly. The tabloid press are quite capable of writing stories which echo and reflect the truth – though not in themselves true – and of putting you in an very unflattering light. Any enquiries from newspapers should be dealt with politely and efficiently, remembering they have more than a little power in the development of your career.

13 A Career Structure

ITH EXTREME competition at every level of the acting profession, it is difficult to develop a logical and definitive career structure that progresses smoothly, one step at a time, as would be the case in most professions where talent is rewarded by promotion and advancement on a regular basis.

Indeed, given the complexities and diversities of the entertainment industry, even if it were possible to structure a career on the same basis as, say, a doctor in his or her plans to progress from graduate of a medical school to senior consultant in a major hospital, there would probably not be a consensus as to what the appropriate steps would be for a newly graduated student of RADA to take towards becoming a highly respected and sought-after actor. The temptation for students today is to rush into television. Thirty years ago the glittering prizes appeared to be in the West End and Royal Shakespeare Company.

AN IDEAL CAREER

Charting what might be regarded as an ideal career is not only a way of discovering just how many unrelated factors influence an actor's success or failure, but of realising the extent to which numerous different options and choices can bring about the same result. It is always a good idea to have something in mind, something to aim for, however impossible and difficult it may seem actually to achieve.

So what is ideal? If you are just starting out on your career you might audition for a major regional rep company (the Royal Exchange or the Sheffield Crucible) and be picked for a season. In your contract you will be 'play as cast', but one of the parts will be a small but showy part in a new play or in a major revival which will be reviewed favourably by the national press and in which your performance will be noted and commended. This will be followed by an offer to re-join the company in their next season. In your contract this time the parts you are going to play will be listed and there will be at least one good supporting role. The production in which you have your best role will also be reviewed by the press and will attract a great deal of interest, especially among professionals who will come up to see it in substantial numbers. A further season at the theatre may follow, this time with a lead role specified in the contract.

During this period you will, on the basis of your reviews and the parts you have played, be taken on by an agent, possibly someone who already represents another older member of the company. Hopefully also you will have been seen by the casting director from the RSC or the National. In the ideal scenario you will be offered a contract at one of these companies, once again with named parts and perhaps including a tour of England or Europe which gives you the experience of working in different venues and locations.

One of your named parts at the RSC or National will be in a Shakespearean or Jacobean role, or in a new play, directed by a well-known or up-and-coming director; a part like de Flores in *The Changeling* or Prince Hal in *Henry IV*. The production will be reviewed in all the national newspapers and you will receive favourable mention.

A second contract will follow including an extremely good role in a new play at the end of the season. This production will receive excellent reviews, and play to packed houses. As it is the last production of the season there will be no impediment to a West End transfer for which you will be offered a six-month contract at a proper commercial salary with your name billed, possibly above the title.

At the end of the run (or even during it) your agent will exploit the list of television producers, directors and casting directors who have seen your performance in the West End and you will be offered a substantial part in a television film or play or a short television series. This will be followed by a spate of offers for television productions. Once again at least some of these programmes will not only be reviewed favourably but will be extremely popular with the public resulting in feature press coverage and interviews.

It is here that a career can falter. After a run of success like this, producers and directors begin to imagine that you are too busy and drop you from their calculations. But in the ideal situation this will be the time to step up to an international audience. Either the West End show you were in will transfer to Broadway or one of the television series you did will be sold to America and be successful there. American offers, either for television series of films, will follow.

An actor re-starting his career may well have experienced some of this success already. The ideal scenario in this case would be to join the RSC or the National or a West End production in a part completely different from the sort of thing you had been known for previously, both by the public and the professionals, or in a role that gave you an opportunity to display your talents in a much more aggressive way than all your previous parts. Once again the production would receive national press reviews and your performance would be praised and perhaps compared to your previous incarnations. The casting community would soon begin to see you in an entirely different light and offer you roles in television or film productions commensurate with your new beginning.

That will not be the end of the story. One of the television series you are offered will score a big hit with the public and the press. You will be much in demand for interviews and features because of the 'angle' that you have been in the business for many years and perhaps had a successful career in your twenties. The publicity will further cement your name in the mind of producers and directors.

From this point the ideal careers of the young actor and the actor who is re-launching himself coincide. They have reached the point where they are well known enough always to be on the list of casting possibilities whenever a list is made.

In reading this it is immediately clear how much of what happens depends on external factors over which an actor can have no control. Whether an actor is offered a play that is going to be successful, for instance, or attract press reviews, is not something the actor can do anything about. In a sense the only control an actor has is the right to say 'no' if he feels it is a bad play or the role is too small. Financial constraints may even mean that this option is severely restricted.

Any successful career is like a pyramid. The basic proposition for planning a successful career is not charting the upward movements but making sure the base of the pyramid is as wide as possible, that all the possible areas which can be built on are secured within the foundations. Which particular part of the base will start to rise first it is impossible to know. But if you do not do your utmost to make sure that every opportunity is explored and investigated, the smaller the base will be and the less chance there will be of significant upward growth. In terms of career planning it is establishing this wide, firm basis of contacts and experience and, of course, appreciation of your talent, that should occupy an actor's time. Dreaming of what might be, or envying the achievements of others, might be impossible completely to avoid, but it is not a constructive way to spend your time.

There is no formula for success other than hard work. There is no pattern a successful career follows. Some actors go from comparative obscurity to international stardom almost overnight (as did Richard Harris) while others toil away in minor parts for years before one role thrusts them into prominence (Michael Caine and *Zulu*). Every actor has a different story, but there is one common factor: most star actors developed through working, not through sitting at home waiting for the phone to ring. Most have accepted almost any job rather than be out of work. However small and insignificant, these jobs provided experience and, more valuably, contacts for the future. As a rule of thumb you should always think very carefully about turning down work, however small or unrewarding the part may seem. You never know where it might lead.

OTHER PATHS

It should be said that not all actors wish to climb the pyramid to success. They are quite happy to reach a plateau, to be a 'working actor' and make a living doing just that. The important thing, in any career, is personal satisfaction. Largely speaking, because of the press and media interest in stars, and success of this kind, there is a tendency to concentrate on actors who have made it in this way, who are known to the public, and to forget about or even denigrate the many actors who are perfectly happy in the profession they have chosen, having a pleasant and satisfying and immensely varied life without being a 'star'.

Nothing in this book is intended to suggest that the only aim of an actor should be to achieve 'stardom'. Far more important is achieving the status of 'working', at any rate first.

The key to personal satisfaction is in knowing what your aims are in the first place. If you actually want to become well-known, then it is perfectly possible that you can, with a great deal of dedication and hard work, do just that – if you do not reach your goals at least you will have the consolation of knowing you tried.

Similarly if your aim is to make a living as an actor, then hard-work and persistence will be necessary too, but the end is no less laudable. It is certainly a mistake to feel – as sometimes, with all the media coverage, you could be forgiven for feeling – that the only aim worth striving for is to be a star. There is an alternative.

Inevitably also, in such a public business, envy can eat away at personal satisfaction. Seeing others' success paraded in front of you on a daily basis, particularly someone whose work you may not respect, can be galling. However, this is where it is important to have your own agenda, and your own aims, and to remember the old adage of 'not believing everything you read in the newspapers'. What is important – really the *only* thing that is important – is your own personal fulfilment, not someone else's.

It is worth repeating once again: be realistic. The more carefully and realistically you examine what you want and what your aims are, the more chance you will have of achieving them.

THE REGIONS

Just as the press tend to concentrate on stars, so it appears that attention is always angled towards London. In the theatre the West

End has an almost mythic importance, despite the fact that standards of production at all levels may be as high, or higher, in the provinces.

An actor does not have to live and work in London. There are jobs and agents all over the UK, though it has to be said they are concentrated around regional centres like Leeds, Manchester, Birmingham, Glasgow and Belfast.

Not only are there repertory theatres offering employment, but the ITV franchises are regional by definition, and are obliged to have their studios in their particular area. Both theatre and television can save the cost of paying expenses by using local actors and frequently they do just that (for years *Coronation Street* was staffed by actors living exclusively in the Manchester area). Additionally pantomines and, in resort areas, summer seasons provide employment in the regions in theatres usually reserved for touring productions.

The BBC (see Chapter 2) is also required to have programming, both for radio and television, in regional centres. The most famous of these is, of course, *The Archers*, which is produced in Birmingham largely with actors living locally. But radio productions are also regularly mounted from Bristol, Belfast, Cardiff and Manchester, as well as television and radio from Birmingham and Glasgow.

Obviously living and working in the regions is limiting in some ways but, once again, it is a question of personal choice. The magnetic draw of London is resistible and if your aim is to be a working actor, living in a regional location, this can be a perfectly obtainable goal.

14 Conclusion

THE DIFFICULTIES facing an actor in maintaining a forward momentum in his career are considerable but not insurmountable. This book has been an attempt to show that, despite the shrinkage in the number of jobs that has taken place over the last twenty years, there are still numerous opportunities every day both for jobs that will help pay the rent and those which will offer prospects far beyond that.

But none of these opportunities are going to leap up and present themselves to you on a silver platter. Without consistent and regular work at the business of getting a job you will not be considered for most castings. Despite the stories you will undoubtedly have heard to the contrary, there are no short cuts.

Because of the diverse nature of the entertainment industry and the literally thousands of companies planning productions in the various media, the question of what best to do in order to get on can appear bewildering. This book attempts to give you a framework, a way of ordering the prospective employers into distinct groups. But that is all it must be. If you restrict yourself to phoning or writing letters to the companies contained in Part Three, you have missed the point. The point is that in order to become more pro-active in your career, this information reference system should be constantly updated with all sorts of information, on planned productions, new companies and people you have come into contact with.

Early on it might be a good idea to focus on a particular area, not necessarily because that is where you want to develop your career, but in order to gain as much information as possible. If, as has been suggested, you work with a friend or a group, each person can concentrate on a different area, one on film production, another on rep for instance.

The most important thing is that you do something. If you do not, or if you restrict yourself to finding an agent and then sit back and wait for the phone to ring, you will find that you put yourself under an enormous psychological strain. The longer you are out of work without doing anything the more depressed you will become and the more difficult it will be for you to hang on to the idea of yourself as an actor at all. And you can be sure it will be at that point, when your self-esteem is at its lowest, that you will be called to an interview and will do badly because of your lack of confidence.

The suggestions contained in this book involve hard work, intelligence and dedication. One of the difficulties in the business of getting a job is that while you slog away in the foothills, others appear to be mounting the peaks with seemingly effortless ease. But don't forget, appearances can be deceptive. Newspapers and magazines are not interested in telling the public of the hard grind that went into making a success: they like to present it as being almost magical. *The Daily Telegraph* magazine's feature 'Limelight', for instance, where an actor is featured every week, had a story on Debra Gillet in August 1993, quoting her as saying 'I'd just finished schlepping around England in a tour, and suddenly I was called by the country's two top theatres.' The story goes on not to examine the 'schlepping around England on tour' but the line of parts Ms Gillet is playing at the RSC, and it's all too easy to come away with the impression that her success had little to do with hard work.

There are exceptions, of course, but usually success comes through application to the business of getting a job, to cultivating and enlarging a circle of acquaintances among prospective employers, to studiously making sure that no opportunity is missed and new opportunities are sought out, to making sure that the work you do is seen – or heard about – by the maximum number of people and by the press, and to creating work for yourself when other sources dry up.

Work creates work. That is a basic fact of the profession you are in. Every job, however small, can be an opportunity to get another job. The more stones that are thrown into the pond the more waves you will create. As a principle always try to do every job you are offered, however small – unless there is a *very* good reason for not doing so.

And if you are in the happy position of being offered two jobs at the same time, never turn one down in favour of the other until you or your agent has checked out the possibility of your doing both. Even if the dates appear to clash completely you will be surprised at what can be accommodated, especially by a television production. What seems like an offer of two weeks' work on paper may in fact boil down to three afternoons and a day in the studio. As long as you are free for the studio day (and the company may even be able to specify morning or afternoon) your other offer, for instance rehearsing a play, will probably be able to release you for the other three afternoons too. If you are in a West End play the same may apply, as long as the studio day on the television finishes before the time you need to get to the theatre for the 'half'. Films and television films can be worked out too, and even if you are in regional rep you may be able to negotiate a release to enable you to get a train to the theatre in time.

There is never any harm in asking. Most successful actors cope with the exigencies of doing two or three jobs at the same time on a regular basis. Their agents become expert in whittling a job down to its absolutely basic time schedule.

This is an important principle not only because you can earn two salaries at the same time but because you never know which job is going to lead to what. Work creates work, and the more work you do, the more likely it is that other work will follow. A few years ago an actor was working at Birmingham Repertory Theatre for a short season. He was offered a job in a situation comedy at the BBC, rehearsing and recording in London. At the same time he was offered the small part of a Nazi officer in another BBC production, this time of Albert Moravio's *Two Women*. It was discovered that the sit-com was only rehearsing in the morning and its studio day was a Sunday, so commuting to Birmingham was no problem. It was written into the contract that he would be released from rehearsals by 1.00 p.m.

Two Women was more difficult, however. It was only a small part, and though the recording took place after the run of the play in Birmingham had finished, he was required for two afternoon rehearsals (fortunately not mornings). As the rehearsals were all taking place in the same building (the BBC rehearsal rooms at Acton), there was no problem getting between the sit-com and *Two Women*, but he still had to get to Birmingham in the evening. Railway timetables were consulted and it was agreed that the actor would be released by 4.30 p.m. For two afternoons he made a made dash to Euston.

Six months later a producer was casting a drama series for London Weekend Television. The producer knew the actor's work but felt that he was too 'soft' for the part he had in mind. His agent produced the tape of him playing the Nazi officer in *Two Women* and on seeing it the producer immediately offered him the role, his doubts about suitability successfully squashed. The part on offer was for a regular character in the series *Within These Walls*. The series ran for five years.

This is not just a homily on making sure you check out all the possibilities before you turn a job down because of a clash of dates. It has another moral. The actor concerned was very close to not doing the *Two Women* job because of the difficulties involved. But it was that job that led directly to a role in a television series. It is essential that you think very carefully before turning any job down. Work leads to work, and creates opportunities that cannot be imagined beforehand. Not working does nothing. It does not bolster confidence or add to the number of people you know and who know your work.

There are very good reasons for turning a job down, reasons of deeply held principle for instance (you may be against certain commercials advertising products of which you disapprove). But you must be very careful before turning a job down on the grounds that it is not a big enough part, or not in the right venue (a fringe theatre), or not enough money, or the right billing. Not only is it unwise in that you never know exactly what will happen, and how one role may affect your career, but it is easy to start a reputation for being 'difficult', both with your own agent if you have one – who will definitely look askance if you turn down a job he has worked hard to get – and with casting directors and producers.

Time and time again, unpromising jobs turn into something special. It is not only a question of what the particular role leads to in terms of future casting, but what happens to the production itself. If the success of a production could be predicted there would be a great deal more millionaire producers than there are. Success, as the Americans say, frequently comes out of left field. The producers of the first *Star Wars* film, for instance, only booked the film into one New York cinema, because they had no idea what its popular appeal would be. And *Dad's Army* was rejected at first by the BBC.

It is more likely that an experienced actor will turn down employment because the role on offer is too small than would a young actor. But the same remarks apply to both. Of course, if you have played Macbeth or a leading role in a television series it is difficult to accept that you are now only being offered fifteen-line parts in one episode of a soap opera. But unfortunately that is the way the business works. It is hard. And it is no place for someone whose pride is easily bruised.

In the last analysis, whatever divisions of status and experience you perceive there to be in the profession, and however these are reflected in salary and billing, there is in fact only one distinction that matters: the distinction between an unemployed actor and a working actor. The truth is that however exalted and fêted an actor, such success may not be permanent. The true mark of success for an actor is to become and remain a working actor.

Because of the enormous competition in the theatrical profession, being talented, having a unique ability to portray another human being, making the few words and hints provided by the author into a live, real and rounded person, and finding a rapport with an audience, either through a camera or in a theatre auditorium, is simply not enough to maintain consistent employment. It takes a great deal more. Being talented and gifted is an essential requirement, but it alone will not create work, until that talent has an opportunity of an airing – and a fairly extensive airing at that.

Perhaps more than anything else the ability to persevere is the single trait most needed by an actor. And persistence is not as easy as it sounds. It is not just a matter of surviving the early rejections, which everyone expects, but of coping with the much more difficult times later on when high hopes and expectations based on a good run of parts and considerable success do not lead to the anticipated breakthrough, and unemployment is back on the agenda. This is the most testing time. Many actors do not survive it. Many drop out, often with considerable bitterness at how the business has treated them.

It would be unrealistic to deny that some actors' careers are changed by a stroke of luck. By being in the right place at the right time, or by being seen by the right person in the right part, a role is offered which, with hindsight, appears crucial to an actor's development. But it is not possible to legislate for luck. What *is* possible is to apply yourself to the business of getting a job, and to see that you find yourself in the maximum number of right places the majority of times. To be a working actor you may need luck: but you will certainly need talent, persistence and hard work. And these are up to you.

Part Three
Information Reference System

The Information Reference System: Introduction

THIS PART OF the book is divided into six sections. The first is intended to give you a base of knowledge about the directors you may meet at interviews and auditions, as a starting point for your own research into what they have done, and so that you will be familiar with their work.

The following sections give names and addresses of people who employ actors on a regular basis, names and addresses of agents, and a list of possible venues for fringe and one-man shows. Space has been left so these sections can be worked on and updated, as all the various categories change rapidly, with new companies being formed and others going out of business. You may prefer to devise your own system of keeping information but the important thing to remember is that these sections are not, and can never be, definitive. Many of the names and addresses will change and all should be checked before use. The more work *you* do in updating and refining these sections the better.

At the end are blank pages with headings that are intended to help you develop a list of people you have met and worked with. Get into the habit of adding names to this list on a regular basis, and date each entry so you always know who you have met and worked with and when.

Directors

THERE IS SOME confusion now between 'film' and 'film for television'. Films from Screen One and Two may now be released 'theatrically' (i.e. in cinemas) despite being made initially for television. For the purposes of this section, film directors have been confined to directors of feature films with a non-television origin.

Some directors now work in all media (television, theatre and film) and where this has happened their credits are listed separately in each section, with a cross-reference to indicate that they are listed in another category. Many directors start in the theatre, then move into television and/or film and do not go back to the theatre. In this case their names are not listed in the theatre section.

Once again, remember this list is not definitive. In television particularly, new directors appear all the time, usually getting their first job working on programmes like *Grange Hill*, *Brookside* and *Emmerdale Farm* and daytime television soaps. Note their names down with their credits and add them to the list.

FILM DIRECTORS

Mike Apted
Gorky Park
Coal Miner's Daughter
Gorillas in the Mist

Richard Attenborough
Gandhi
Magic
Cry Freedom

Roy Ward Baker
Dr Jekyll & Sister Hyde
Moon Zero Two
The Anniversary

Clive Barker
Hellraiser
Nightbreed

Chris Bernard
Letter to Brezhnev

Bruce Beresford
Driving Miss Daisy
Her Alibi
Crimes of the Heart

John Boorman
Deliverance
Where the Heart Is
Emerald Forest

Kenneth Branagh
Henry V
Much Ado About Nothing

Alan Bridges
  The Hireling
  Return of the Soldier
  The Shooting Party

Peter Brook
  The Beggar's Opera
  The Lord of the Flies

Colin Bucksey
  Dealers

Simon Callow
  Ballad of the Sad Café

Michael Caton-Jones
  Memphis Belle
  Scandal

Jack Clayton
  The Lonely Passion of Judith Hearne
  The Pumpkin Eater
  The Great Gatsby

Tony Clegg
  McVicar
  Sweeney 2

Alex Cox
  Repo Man
  Sid & Nancy

Clive Donner
  The Caretaker
  What's New Pussycat?
  Alfred the Great

Peter Duffell
  England Made Me

Christina Edzard
  The Fool
  Little Dorrit

Mandy Fletcher
  Deadly Advice

Bill Forsyth
  Gregory's Girl
  Local Hero
  That Sinking Feeling

Cyril Frankel
  Don't Bother to Knock
  Tryon Factor
  Man of Africa

Stephen Frears (see TV)
  Dangerous Liaisons
  My Beautiful Laundrette
  Prick Up Your Ears
  Sammy & Rosie Get Laid

Sidney J. Furie
  The Ipcress File
  Lady Sings the Blues
  Little Fauss and Big Halsy

Lewis Gilbert
  Moonraker
  Educating Rita
  Shirley Valentine

Terry Gilliam
The Adventures of Baron Munchausen
Brazil
Jabberwocky

John Glen
For Your Eyes Only
Licence to Kill
The Living Daylights

Peter Glenville
Beckett
The Prisoner
Summer & Smoke

Jim Goddard (see TV)
Shanghai Surprise

Jack Gold
Aces High
The Reckoning
The Sailor's Return

Peter Greenaway
The Belly of an Architect
The Cook, The Thief, His Wife & Her Lover
The Draughtsman's Contract

David Green
Buster
Fine Birds

Val Guest
The Boys in Blue (Cannon & Ball)

Piers Haggard (see TV)
Summer Story
Venom

Peter Hall (see Theatre)
3 into 2 Won't Go
Akenfield
Perfect Friday

Guy Hamilton
Live & Let Die
Diamonds are Forever
Force 10 from Navarone
The Mirror Crack'd

Ken Hamman (see TV)
Summerfields
Sunday Too Far Away

David Hare
Paris By Night
Strapless
Wetherby

Mike Hodges
Get Carter
Black Rainbow
Flash Gordon

John Hough
Legend of Hell House
Watcher in the Woods
Dirty Mary Crazy Harry

Hugh Hudson
Chariots of Fire
Greystoke
Lost Angels
Revolution

Peter Hunt
  Gold
  On Her Majesty's Secret Service
  Wild Geese II

Waris Hussein
  Henry VIII & His Six Wives
  Possession of Joel Delaney

John Irvin
  Dogs of War
  Ghost Story
  Next of Kin

James Ivory
  Shakespeare Wallah
  The Bostonians
  Maurice
  A Room With a View

Derek Jarman
  Jubilee
  The Last of England
  The Tempest

Lionel Jeffries
  The Water Babies
  The Railway Children
  Baxter

Roland Joffe
  Fat Man & Little Boy
  The Killing Fields
  The Mission

Terry Jones
  Eric The Viking
  Monty Python
  Personal Services

David Jones
  Betrayed
  84 Charing Cross Road

Neil Jordan
  Angel
  The Company of Wolves
  High Spirits
  We're No Angels

Marek Kanievska
  Another Country

Bob Kellet
  Up Pompeii

Susi Kreschanamma
  Deadly Greek

Stanley Kubrick
  A Clockwork Orange
  Full Metal Jacket
  2001: A Space Odyssey
  Barry Lyndon

Simon Langton (see TV)
  The Whistle Blower

Mike Leigh (see TV)
  Bleak Moments
  High Hopes

David Leland
Wish You Were Here
The Big Man
Checking Out

Richard Lester
The Four Musketeers
A Hard Day's Night
Superman (II & III)
Royal Flash

Michael Lindsay-Hogg
Nasty Habits
The Object of Beauty

Ken Loach
Poor Cow
Hidden Agenda
Riff-Raff
Raining Stones

Richard Longraine
The Missionary

Jonathan Lynn
Nuns on the Run
Clue

John MacKenzie
The Long Good Friday
The Fourth Protocol
Last of the Finest

Peter Medak
Rules of The Game
The Krays
Zorro
The Changeling

Chris Menges
A World Apart

Malcolm Mowbray
A Private Function

Mike Newell (see TV)
The Awakening
Bad Blood
Dance with a Stranger

Pat O'Connor
The January Man
Fools of Fortune
A Month in the Country

Stuart Orme
The Wolves of Willoughby Chase

Frank Oz
Dark Crystal
Little Shop of Horrors
What About Bob?

Anthony Page (see TV)
Absolution
I Never Promised You a Rose Garden
The Lady Vanishes

Tony Palmer
Wagner
200 Motels
The Children

Alan Parker
Angel Heart
Bugsy Malone
Midnight Express
Shoot The Moon

Michael Radford
  1984
  Another Time, Another Place
  White Mischief

Karel Reisz
  The French Lieutenant's Woman
  Saturday Night & Sunday Morning
  The Gambler
  Sweet Dreams

Franc Roddam
  The Bride
  Lords of Discipline
  Quadrophenia

Nicolas Roeg
  Bad Timing
  Don't Look Now
  The Man Who Fell to Earth

Ken Russell
  Women in Love
  Billion Dollar Brain
  Lair of the White Worm
  Gothic

Ridley Scott
  Alien
  Black Rain
  Blade Runner
  Thelma & Louise

John Schlesinger
  Sunday Bloody Sunday
  Marathon Man
  Midnight Cowboy
  Yanks

Don Sharp
Hennessy
The Thirty-Nine Steps (1978)

Ian Sharp (see TV)
Who Dares Wins

Jim Sheridan
My Left Foot
The Field

Mel Smith
The Tall Guy

Charles Sturridge (see TV)
Runners
A Handful of Dust

Julien Temple
Absolute Beginners
The Secret Policeman's Other Ball
Earth Girls Are Easy

Gerald Thomas
Carry On Cleo
Carry on Doctor
etc.

Michael Tuckner
Fear is the Key
Villain
Wilt

Claude Whatham
Swallows & Amazons
Sweet William
That'll Be The Day

David Wickes (see TV)
  The Silver Dream Race
  The Sweeney

Michael Winner
  Appointment with Death
  Death Wish
  Wicked Lady
  Chorus of Disapproval
  Dirty Weekend

Peter Yates
  Bullitt
  The Dresser
  Krull

Franco Zeffirelli
  Brother Sun Sister Moon
  Romeo & Juliet
  The Champ

Fred Zinnemann
  A Man for all Seasons
  The Day of the Jackal
  Julia

TELEVISION DIRECTORS

Romey Allison
Coronation Street
Emmerdale Farm

John Amiel
Play for Today
Singing Detective
Sommersby
The Deep End

Sarah Pia Anderson
The Bill

Moira Armstrong
Shoulder to Shoulder
Testament of Youth
How Many Miles to Babylon
Freud
Bluebell
The Bill
Body & Soul

David Askey
Surgical Spirit

David Attwood
The Bill

Roger Bamford
Auf Wiedersehen Pet (Central)
Blott on the Landscape
Rumpole of the Bailey
Stolen
A Touch of Frost

Gabrielle Beaumont
  Miami Vice
  Hill Street Blues (US)
  The Bill

Charles Beeson
  Casualty
  Minder (Thames)
  Eastenders
  The Bill

Susan Belbin
  One Foot in the Grave
  Sitting Pretty

Alan Bell
  The Bill
  The Beiderbecke Connection
  Taggart

Alan J. Bell
  The Two Ronnies
  Last of the Summer Wine
  Hitch Hiker's Guide to the Galaxy

Derek Bennett
  Eastenders

Edward Bennett
  Inspector Morse
  Poirot
  Miss Marple
  Ascendancy

Lovett Bickford
  History of Mr Polly
  Dr Who
  Angels

Antonia Bird
  The Men's Room (BBC)
  A Masculine Ending (BBC)
  Inspector Morse

Les Blair
  The Nation's Health
  Law & Order

David Blair
  Strathblair

Richard Boden
  Dunrulin
  Health & Efficiency (BBC)
  2 Point 4 Children
  In Sickness & In Health

Sylvie Boden
  So Haunt Me
  Sean's Show (Ch 4)

Ben Bolt
  Bergerac
  Never Come Back
  Natural Lies
  Scarlet & Black

Danny Boyle
  Monkeys
  Not Even God Is Wise Enough
  Inspector Morse
  Mr Wroe's Virgins

Michael Bradwell
  Happy Feet (Screen One)

Richard Bramall
  Casualty
  Growing Pains
  All Creatures Great & Small
  One by One
  The Bill
  Eastenders

Bill Brayne
  The Professionals (LWT)
  Cluedo
  Lovejoy

Michael Brayshaw
  Casualty

Michael E. Briant
  A Tale of Two Cities
  Blood Money
  Dr Who
  One by One
  Howard's Way

John Bruce
  The Bill
  Tales of the Unexpected
  Bretts
  Sherlock Holmes
  Poirot
  Eastenders

Sue Bush
  Streets Apart
  Inmates
  Side by Side

Ray Butt
  Citizen Smith
  Just Good Friends
  Only Fools & Horses

Ed Bye
  Boys from the Bush
  Red Dwarf

Gilchrist Calder
  When the Boat Comes In
  The Onedin Line
  The Enigma Files

Robin Carr
  Second Thoughts
  The Piglet Files

Phillip Casson
  Eldorado

James Cellan Jones
  Oxbridge Blues
  Fortunes of War
  A Fine Romance (LWT)
  Perfect Hero
  The Gravy Train
  Maigret
  Rumpole of the Bailey
  Brighton Belles

Mark Chapman
  Root Into Europe

Les Chatfield
A Sharp Intake of Breath
Take Three Women
Bergerac
Moving
Brass
A Bit of a Do
Watching

Roger Cheveley
Airline
Supergran
Yellowthread Street
Heartbeat

Phil Chilvers
The Rory Bremner Show

Alan Clayton
The Jazz Detective

Tom Cotter
Floodtide
Strike It Rich
The Bill
Making Out
Casualty

Frank Cox
Sutherland's Law
Cat's Eyes
Eastenders

Ross Cramer
God on the Rocks
Riding High

Peter Cregeen
The Gentle Touch (ITV)
Juliet Bravo
The Bill (producer)

David Croft
Dad's Army
'Allo 'Allo
You Rang M'Lord

Mervyn Cumming
Emmerdale

Michael Darlow
The Barretts of Wimpole Street
Little Eyolf (Ibsen)

John Darnell
Casualty
The Bill
Emmerdale Farm

John Davies
Tales of the Unexpected
Why Didn't They Ask Evans?
P D James: Devices & Desires (Anglia)

Gareth Davies
The Diary of Anne Frank
Good Guys
The Darling Buds of May

Martin Dennis
The Upper Hand

Ross Devenish
  Bleak House (BBC)
  4 Play (Ch 4)
  Poirot

Mike Donner
  The Bill
  Eastenders

Alan Dosser
  Juliet Bravo
  Connie
  First & Last
  Between the Lines

Tony Dow
  Nightingales
  Only Fools & Horses
  Birds of a Feather
  Comic Asides

David Drury
  Defence of the Realm
  Children of the North
  The Secret Agent
  Prime Suspect III

Sue Dunderdale
  Eastenders
  The Bill

David Innes Edwards
  Brookside
  Eastenders

Mark Evans
  Friday On My Mind

Richard Everitt
  Strangers
  Bulman
  First Among Equals
  Lovejoy

Richard Eyre (see Theatre & Film)
  The Ploughman's Lunch
  Tumbledown

Ferdinand Fairfax
  Danger UXB (Thames)
  Winston Churchill: The Wilderness Years
  Jeeves & Wooster

Chris Fallon
  Eastenders

Julian Farino
  Coronation Street

Brian Farnham
  Rock Follies
  Hazell
  Agatha Christie
  Jemima Shore Investigates
  Campaign
  The Bill
  The Chief
  All Quiet on the Preston Front

Gordon Flemyng
  Philby, Burgess & McLean
  Bergerac Christmas Special
  Wish Me Luck
  Taggart

Vic Finch
  Chelmsford 123

Mandy Fletcher
  Blackadder

Clive Fleury
  Medics

Matt Forrest
  Spender

Giles Foster
  A Woman of No Importance
  Silas Marner
  Consuming Passions
  Adam Bede
  Hotel du Lac

Stephen Frears (see Film)
  Doris & Doreen (Alan Bennett)
  Going Gently (Play for Today)

Martyn Friend
  The Voyage of Charles Darwin
  Bartleby
  Inspector Alleyn Mysteries

Tim Fywell
  Chalkface
  A Fatal Inversion (Ruth Rendell)
  A Dark Adapted Eye
  Gallowglass

Robert Gabriel
  Waterfront Beat

Anthony Garner
Conversations with a Stranger
The Ginger Tree
Soldier, Soldier

Roger Gartland
Eastenders

Colin Gilbert
(currently Head of Comedy, BBC Scotland)
Rab C. Nesbitt

David Giles
The Mayor of Casterbridge
Mansfield Park
Television Shakespeare (BBC)
Miss Marple
Forever Green
The Darling Buds of May

Jim Goddard
Out
Nicholas Nickleby (Ch 4)
Reilly Ace of Spies
Kennedy
Free Frenchmen
Sharpe's Rifles

Steve Goldie
Casualty

Lawrence Gordon Clark
A Ghost Story
Flambards
Harry's Game
Paradise Club

John Gorrie
  Tales of the Unexpected (Anglia)
  Shades of Darkness (Granada)
  Rumpole of the Bailey (Thames)
  Talking to Strange Men (Ruth Rendell)
  The Tempest (BBC)
  Perfect Scoundrels

Roderick Graham
  Juliet Bravo
  All Creatures Great & Small
  One by One
  Now Then

David Green
  Whicker's World
  Chinese Detective

Neville Green
  Mike & Angelo (Thames Children's)

Colin Gregg
  Remembrance (Film on Four)
  To The Lighthouse
  The Guilty

Andrew Grieve
  Lorna Doone
  On the Black Hill
  Poirot

Alan Grint
  Sergeant Cribb
  Love Hurts
  Sherlock Holmes
  Chancer
  Spender

Gareth Gwenlan
To the Manor Born
Waiting for God
Only Fools & Horses
On the Up

Piers Haggard (see Film)
Waters of the Moon
Pennies from Heaven
Centrepoint

Ian Hamilton
Jasper Carrott
More Auntie's Bloomers

Terry Hand
Heartbeat

Ken Hannam
Day of the Triffids
Minder
Crossfire
Sherlock Holmes
Strathblair
Lovejoy

Charlie Hanson
Birds of a Feather
Desmond's

Graeme Harper
Space Cops
Bergerac
The New Statesman
House of Elliot

Paul Harrison
  May To December
  Growing Pains

Bill Hays
  Time After Time
  Tales of Beatrice Potter
  Death is Part of the Process
  Eastenders

John Heaton
  Emmerdale

Sarah Hellings
  Forever Green

John Henderson
  Spitting Image
  About Face
  The Big One
  Terry & Julian
  The Borrowers
  Bonjour la Classe

James Hendrie
  The Lenny Henry Show
  All Creatures Great & Small

Jim Hill
  Play for Today – England's Green & Pleasant Land
  Minder
  Casualty
  Lovejoy

Bob Hird
  Hunting Tower (BBC Children's)
  Emmerdale Farm
  The Bill

John B. Hobbs
  Bread

Ken Holm
  Brookside

John Howard Davis
  The Good Life
  Mr Bean (Rowan Atkinson)

Jane Howell
  The Dybbuk
  Saint Joan
  Esther Waters
  TV Shakespeare
  Amongst Barbarians
  Class Act

Metin Huseyin
  The Alexei Sayle Show
  Harry Enfield

Jo Johnson
  Brookside

Sandy Johnson
  Inspector Wexford (Ruth Rendell)
  Put on By Cunning (Ruth Rendell)

Chris Johnston
  Eldorado
  Emmerdale Farm

Peter Frazer Jones
  Tommy Cooper
  George & Mildred
  Never The Twain
  Fresh Fields
  After Henry
  Land of Hope & Gloria

David Jones
The Voysey Inheritance
TV Shakespeare
Betrayal
Trial: Screen Two

Marek Kanieviska
Hazell (Thames)
Shoestring
Another Country (Goldcrest)

Beeban Kidron
Oranges Are Not the Only Fruit
Antonia & Jane
Used People (film)

John Kilby
It Ain't Half Hot, Mum
Alas Smith & Jones
May To December
Colin's Sandwich
KYTV

Terry Kinane
Birds of a Feather

Christopher King
Forever Green

Margy Kinmonth
Eastenders
Casualty

Alex Kirby
Chronicles of Narnia (Children's)

Robert Knights
The Voysey Inheritance
The History Man
Glittering Prizes
Rumpole of the Bailey

Patrick Lau
The Bill

Simon Langton
Thérèse Raquin
Smiley's People
Poirot

Nick Laughland
The Bill

Diarmuid Lawrence
Grange Hill
Juliet Bravo
August Saturday (Screenplay)
Anglo-Saxon Attitudes

Mike Leigh (see Film & Theatre)
Abigail's Party
Nuts in May

Derek Lister
The Big Deal
Rockcliffe's Babies
The Bill

Sydney Lotterby
Up the Chastity Belt
Porridge
Some Mothers Do 'Ave 'Em
As Time Goes By

Bruce MacDonald
Resnick

Douglas MacKinnon
The Bill

Alan Macmillan
Taggart

John Madden
Sherlock Holmes
Poppyland: Screen Two
Inspector Morse
The Widowmaker (Central)

Juliet May
The Jack Dee Show

Charles McDougall
Casualty
99 to 1

Mary McMurray
Christmas Cluedo
A Guilty Thing Surprised (Ruth Rendell)
The Bill
Spender

Frances Megahy
The Great Riviera Bank Raid (ITC)
Minder (Thames)

Chris Menaul
Play for Today
Tales of Sherwood Forest
Minder (Thames)
Prime Suspect

Raymond Menmuir
The Professionals
Who Dares Wins

Gavin Millar
The Weather in the Streets
Dreamchild
A Murder of Quality

Laurence Moody
Shoestring
Bergerac
Taggart
Boon
Chancer

Christopher Morahan
Talking to a Stranger
The Jewel in the Crown (Granada)

Michael Owen Morris
Casualty

Marcus Mortimer
The Mary Whitehouse Experience

Silvio Narizzano
Come Back Little Sheba
Miss Marple
Artists in Crime (An Alleyn Mystery)

Jeff Naylor
Brookside

Mike Newell (see film)
Budgie (LWT)
When You Are Ready Mac McGill
Blood Feud

Jim O'Brien
  The Jewel in the Crown (Granada)
  The Monocled Mutineer
  Young Indiana Jones (US)

Liddy Oldroyd
  Desmond's
  Drop the Dead Donkey

Anthony Page
  Middlemarch (BBC)

Brian Parker
  Willie's Last Stand
  Lytton's Diary
  The Beiderbecke Tapes
  The Bill
  Strathblair

Geoff Parker
  The Victoria Wood Show

Kay Patrick
  Brookside
  In Suspicious Circumstances

David Penn
  Coronation Street

Nic Phillips
  Birds of a Feather

John Michael Phillips
  Gawain & The Green Knight (Thames Children's)

Lesley Pitt
  Hot Dog (Thames Children's)

Angela Pope
  Shift Work: Screenplay
  Sweet As You Are: Screen Two
  Mr Wakefield's Crusade

Tristram Powell
  Happy Days (with Billie Whitelaw)
  American Friends
  Selected Exits

Udayan Prasad
  The Bill

Anthony Quinn
  The Chief

Alvin Rakoff
  In Praise of Love
  A Voyage Around My Father (Thames)
  Haunting Harmony
  Paradise Postponed
  Sam Saturday

Alastair Reid
  Dr Jekyll & Mr Hyde (BBC/ABC Timelife)
  South Riding
  Shades of Greene
  Selling Hitler
  Tales of the City

David Reynolds
  When the Boat Comes In
  Bergerac
  The Beiderbecke Affair
  A Bit of a Do (YTV)
  Home to Roost
  The New Statesman
  Stay Lucky

Dave Richards
  Coronation Street

Pennant Roberts
  Dr Who
  Juliet Bravo
  Tenko
  Dramarama

Michael Rolfe
  Bergerac
  Birds of Prey

Renny Rye
  Casualty
  Poirot
  A Ghost in Winter (Ruth Rendell)
  The Other Side of Paradise
  Lipstick on Your Collar

Gwennan Sage
  Eastenders

Peter Sasdy
  Minder (Thames)
  House of Hanover (ITC)

Philip Saville
  Gangsters (BBC)
  The Lives & Loves of a She Devil (BBC)
  Boys from the Blackstuff (BBC)
  Angels

Geoff Sax
  The Dave Allen Show
  Lovejoy Christmas Special
  The New Statesman (YTV)
  Sleepers

Paul Seed
  Wynne & Penkovsky
  Capital City
  House of Cards
  To Play the King

Ian Sharp
  The Professionals
  Robin of Sherwood
  Codename Kyril
  Secret Weapon

Adrian Shergold
  Juliet Bravo
  Christabel
  Hold the Back Page
  Inspector Morse
  The Life & Times of Henry Pratt

Richard Signy
  In Suspicious Circumstances

Laura Sims
  The Bill

Anthony Simmons
  The Professionals (LWT)
  Supergran
  Van der Valk
  A Touch of Frost

Michael Simpson
  Driving Ambition
  An Inspector Calls
  Growing Pains

William Slater
  Tales of the Unexpected (Anglia)
  Who Pays the Ferryman
  Eastenders

Noella Smith
  The Hummingbird Tree

John Smith
  Billy Webb's Amazing Story (Children's)

Peter Smith
  Bergerac
  The Price (Ch 4)
  A Perfect Spy
  Resnick
  Between The Lines

Paul Smith
  Jasper Carrott

Harold Snoad
  The Dick Emery Show
  The Further Adventures of Lucky Jim
  Keeping Up Appearances (BBC)
  Don't Tell Father

Richard Spence
  You Me & Mandy: Screenplay
  Poirot
  Making Out
  El C.I.D. (Granada)

Bob Spiers
  French & Saunders (BBC)
  Fawlty Towers
  Comic Strip
  Press Gang
  Absolutely Fabulous

Richard Standeman
  Between The Lines (BBC)
  Medics

Mike Stephens
  The Brittas Empire
  Screaming (Carla Lane)

Norman Stone
  Miss Marple – The Mirror Crack'd
  The Justice Game

John Stroud
  So Haunt Me

Mark Stuart
  Fresh Fields
  French Fields

Charles Sturridge
  Brideshead Revisited (Granada)
  The Spoils of War

Jeremy Summers
  Tenko
  Coronation Street
  The Chinese Detective
  A Kind of Loving (Granada)

Stan Swan
  Splazt (Thames Children's)

Nadia Tass
  Stark (BBC) (Australia)

Graham Theakston
  Tripods (BBC Children's)
  The Bill
  Perfect Scoundrels

Ian Toynton
  Minder (Thames)
  Bergerac
  The Chinese Detective

Kenith Trodd
  Pennies from Heaven
  Brimstone & Treacle
  The Singing Detective
  Home & Away

Robert Tronson
  Bergerac (BBC)
  Nanny (BBC)
  Rumpole of the Bailey (Thames)
  Boon
  Jemima Shore Investigates
  The Darling Buds of May

David Tucker
  Tenko
  A Very Peculiar Practice
  The Gravy Train
  Stanley & The Women
  (A Year in Provence)

Roger Tucker
  Bergerac
  The Boy Who Won The Pools

Stuart Urban
  Bergerac
  A Pocketful of Dreams (BBC Playhouse)
  The Bill
  Good Guys

Mike Vardy
Shoestring
Minder
Northern Lights
Taggart

Nick Ward
Dakota Road (Ch 4)
Look Me In The Eye

Alan Wareing
Eastenders
Casualty

Christopher Walker
The Upper Hand

Aisling Walsh
The Bill

Paul Weiland
Keep Off The Grass
Mr Bean
Bernard & The Comic

Graham Wetherell
Emmerdale Farm
Eastenders

Ian White
Coronation Street
The Bill

David Wickes
Marlowe
Jack The Ripper
Jekyll & Hyde
Frankenstein – The Real Story

Richard Wilson
  The Remainder Man

Herbert Wise
  I Claudius
  Death of an Expert Witness
  Life After Life (LWT)

Carol Wiseman
  The Gentle Touch
  Bognor (Thames)
  A Question of Guilt
  Big Deal
  Love Hurts
  Goggle Eyes

Kathryn Wolfe
  True Crimes

John Woods
  The Bill
  Love Hurts
  Lovejoy
  Making Out
  The Inspector Alleyn Mysteries

Jonathan Wright Miller
  Spoils of War
  Coronation Street
  Eastenders

Robert Young
  The Mad Death
  Bergerac
  Robin of Sherwood
  Hostage
  Jeeves & Wooster
  GBH

THEATRE DIRECTORS

Like television directors, new directors in the theatre appear all the time, mostly beginning their careers directing in studio theatres or on the fringe. Add new names to this list as they occur and don't forget to make a note of the production.

Where a theatre is given instead of a production this is where the director concerned did a large number of productions or was artistic director for some time.

See also artistic directors listed under regional theatres.

(a.d. = artistic director)

Bill Alexander
RSC
Snowman (Birmingham Rep)

Michael Attenborough
formerly a.d. Hampstead Theatre Club
RSC co-director

Lindsay Anderson
Royal Court
The Long the Short and the Tall
David Storey plays

Alan Ayckbourn
National Theatre
Currently a.d. Stephen Joseph Theatre, Scarborough

Neil Bartlett
Lyric Hammersmith
The Game of Love and Chance (National)

Michael Blakemore
Front Page (National)
A Day in the Death of Joe Egg
Lettice & Lovage
City of Angels
Here (Donmar Warehouse)

Joe Blatchley
Hedda Gabler (Royal Exchange)

Michael Bogdanov
English Shakespeare Co
The Romans in Britain (National)
Faust (Leicester Haymarket)
Hair (Old Vic)

Kenneth Branagh
Renaissance Theatre Co Productions
(in *King Lear* with Richard Briers)

John Bromley
Tours for Newpalm Productions

Peter Brook
A Midsummer Night's Dream (RSC)
King Lear (Paul Scofield)
Now works in Paris

Bill Bryden
Currently Head of Drama B.B.C. Scotland
National Theatre
Royal Court

Jan Butlin
Numerous rep and West End productions

John Burgess
National Theatre

Stephen Butcher
Lyric Belfast

Simon Callow
Carmen Jones (Old Vic)

John Caird
Les Miserables (with Trevor Nunn)
Nicholas Nickleby (with Trevor Nunn)

Ken Campbell
Jamais Vu
The Furtive Nudist
Pigspurt

Dee Cannon
True West (New End)

Tim Carroll
Julius Caesar (Shaw Theatre)

Annie Castledine
formerly a.d. Derby Playhouse
The Choice (Mold)

Peter Coe
Churchill Theatre, Bromley

Richard Cottrell
Glyn and It (Yvonne Arnaud, Guildford)

Anthony Cornish
The Good Natured Man (Orange Tree)

Ted Craig
Currently a.d. Croydon Warehouse
Theatre Royal York

Stephen Daldry
a.d. Royal Court
An Inspector Calls (National)
Machinal (National)
The Kitchen (Royal Court)

Ron Daniels
RSC

Allan Davies
No Sex Please We're British
Sylvia's Wedding

Howard Davies
National Theatre
Les Liaisons Dangereuses

Stephen Dexter
The Ten Commandments (The Place)

Richard Digby Day
Peter Pan (Yvonne Arnaud, Guildford)

Declan Donnellan
Cheek by Jowl
Angels in America (National)
Millenium Approaches (National)
Sweeney Todd (National)

John Dove
Bingo (Royal Court)
Nottingham Playhouse
Royal Exchange

Gail Edwards
Saint Joan (Theatr Clywd)

Richard Eyre
Currently a.d. National Theatre
Edinburgh Lyceum
High Society

Peter Farago
Birmingham Rep
Don't Dress for Dinner (Duchess Theatre)

Vicky Featherstone
Brighton Rock (West Yorkshire Playhouse)

Philip Franks
Dr Faustus (Greenwich)

Bill Gaskill
Royal Court
National Theatre

David Gilmore
Nuffield Southampton
Daisy Pulls It Off
Lend Me a Tenor

Peter Gill
Royal Court
National Theatre

Kim Grant
Watford
Bromley
National tours

Peter Hall
RSC
National Theatre
Numerous West End productions
Gift of the Gorgon (Wyndham's Theatre)

Robert Hamlin
Coventry Belgrade

Terry Hands
RSC
Tamburlaine (Barbican)

Giles Havergal
Glasgow Citizens

David Hayman
Jenkin's Ear (Royal Court)

Ken Hill
Curse of the Werewolf (Theatre Royal, Stratford East)

Garry Hines
Love of the Nightingale (RSC)

Chris Honer
Library Theatre Manchester
Racing Demon (Library)

Nicholas Hytner
Royal Exchange
RSC
National Theatre
The Importance of Being Earnest (Aldwych, Maggie Smith)
The Madness of George III (National)
Miss Saigon

Peter James
Crucible Theatre Sheffield
Lyric Hammersmith

David Jones (see Film & TV)
RSC

Andy Jordan
Nuffield Southampton
Sheffield Crucible

Paul Kerryson
Currently a.d. Leicester Haymarket
Carousel (Shaftesbury Theatre)

Jonathan Kent
Joint a.d. Almeida Theatre
The School for Wives
Medea

Nicolas Kent
Currently a.d. Tricycle Theatre
Playboy of the West Indies

Barry Kyle
RSC

Robin Lefevre
Bodies (Hampstead)

David Leveaux
No Man's Land (Comedy Theatre)

Mike Leigh (see Films & TV)
It's a Great Big Shame (Theatre Royal, Stratford East)

Phyllida Lloyd
Royal Exchange
Hysteria (Royal Court)

Tim Luscombe
Easy Virtue (Garrick)
Relative Values (Savoy)
Eurovision

James MacDonald
Hammett's Apprentice (Royal Court)
Terrible Voice of Satan (Royal Court)

Sean Mathias
Uncle Vanya (National)
Ghosts (Cardiff)

James Maxwell
Currently joint a.d. Royal Exchange, Manchester
The Importance of Being Earnest

Robin Midgeley
Leicester Haymarket
Blithe Spirit (Birmingham Rep)

Sam Mendes
RSC
Cabaret (Donmar Warehouse)

Roger Michell
The Constant Couple (RSC)

Jonathan Miller
National Theatre
Greenwich
Now mostly opera productions

Elijah Moshinsky
Light Up the Sky (Globe)
Now mostly opera productions

Braham Murray
Currently joint a.d. Royal Exchange, Manchester
Smoke

Adrian Noble
Currently a.d. RSC
Travesties

Trevor Nunn
Cats
Sunset Boulevard
Les Miserables (with John Caird)

Michael Ockrent
Passion Play
Me & My Girl
Crazy for You

Richard Olivier
Time and the Conways

Harold Pinter
Man in a Glass Booth
His own plays inc. *Moonlight*

Michael Rudman
Currently a.d. Crucible Sheffield
The Real Thing
Alphabetical Order

Patrick Sandford
Yvonne Arnaud, Guildford
Currently a.d. Nuffield Southampton
Exchange (Phoenix)

Max Stafford Clark
Serious Money

David Thacker
Currently a.d. Young Vic
The Two Gentlemen of Verona (RSC)
Gellburg (Young Vic)

Di Trevis
RSC

Stewart Trotter
ex-a.d. Northcott Exeter
The Browning Version
Charlie Girl
Funny Peculiar (Mermaid)

Matthew Waehus
West Yorkshire Playhouse
Much Ado About Nothing (Queen's Theatre)

Sam Walters
Currently a.d. Orange Tree, Richmond

Deborah Warner
RSC
Coriolanus (RSC)

Peter Wood
Undiscovered Country (National)
Five Finger Exercise
The Prime of Miss Jean Brodie
Travesties

Stephen Unwin
Hamlet (Donmar Warehouse)
A Midsummer Night's Dream

Television and Radio

BBC Television
Wood Lane
London W12 7RJ   081 743 8000

BBC Enterprises
Woodlands
80 Wood Lane
London W12 0TT   081 743 5588
(Deals with all aspects of the exploitation of
programming including queries on foreign sales)
Controller BBC 1: Alan Yentob
Controller BBC 2: Michael Jackson
Head of Children's Programmes: Anna Home
Head of Drama: Charles Denton
Head of Light Entertainment: Jim Moir
Head of Comedy: Martin Fisher

Regional:

BBC Midlands and East
Broadcasting Centre
Pebble Mill Rd
Birmingham B5 7QQ   021 414 8888
Head of Drama: Vacant

BBC West
Whiteladies Rd
Bristol BS8 2LR   0272 732211
Drama Producer: Shaun MacLoughlin

BBC Scotland
Broadcasting House
Queen Margaret Drive
Glasgow G12 8DG   041 330 2345
Head of Drama: Bill Bryden
Head of Comedy: Colin Gilbert

BBC Belfast
Ormeau Avenue
Belfast BT2 8HQ   0232 244400
Head of Drama: Robert Cooper
Head of Producers: Pam Brighton

BBC Wales
Broadcasting House
Llandaff
Cardiff CF5 2YG   0222 572888
Head of Drama Wales: Ruth Caleb
TV Producers: Adrian Mourby
   Gareth Rowlands

Drama Group London

Head of Series & Serials: Michael Wearing
Head of Single Scripts: George Faber
Executive Producer Screen One: Richard Broke
Executive Producer Screen Two: Mark Shivas
Producers (in house):
   Ruth Bumgarten
   John Chapman
   Simon Curtis
   Barbara Emile

Michael Ferguson
Fiona Finlay
George Gallacio
Phillipa Giles
Emma Hayter
Peter Kendall
Louis Marks
Andree Molyneux
Geraint Morris
Peter Norris
Caroline Oulton
Chris Parr
Jacinta Peel
Ken Riddington
Hilary Salmon
David Snodin
Kenith Trodd
Leonard Lewis
Colin Ludlow
Colin Tucker
Jo Wright

Light Entertainment Group

Head of Comedy: Martin Fisher
Executive Producers:
  Kevin Bishop
  Harold Snoad
  Bill Wilson
  Gareth Gwenlan
  Peter Estall
  Mike Leggo
Producers:
  Susan Belbin
  Richard Boden
  John Burrowes
  Sue Bysh

John Hobbs
Geoff Miles
Roger Ordish
Mike Stephens
David Taylor

Children's Programmes

Head of Children's Programmes: Anna Home
Deputy Head: Roy Thompson
Producers:
Albert Barber
Greg Childs
John Comerford
Martin Hughes
Marilyn Fox
Cathy Gilbey
Christine Hewitt
Oliver McFarlane
David Mercer
Christine Secombe
Angela Sharp
Richard Simpkin
Roger Singleton Turner
John Smith
Susie Staples
Alison Stewart
Jeremy Swan
Chris Tandy
Jane Tarleton

NB: Not all producers on these lists may be working on a project and actually in the building. Some take leave of absence or are not in their offices for other reasons. NEVER send out a circular to all producers on these lists. Check first.

INDEPENDENT TELEVISION CONTRACTORS

Anglia Television
Anglia Hse
Norwich NR1 3JG   0603 615151

London:
48 Leicester Sq
London WC2H 7FB   071 321 0101
Head of Drama: Vacant
Executive Producer: Brenda Reid

Carlton Television
101 St Martin's Lane
London WC2N 4AZ   071 240 4000
Commissioning Editor Drama: Jane Trante
Commissioning Editor Children's: Michael Forte
Director of Drama: Jonathan Powell
Controller Entertainment: John Bishop
(At the time of writing Carlton have announced a
take-over of Central Television. As yet the
difference this will make to personnel and offices
is unclear.)

Central Independent Television
Central Hse
Broad St
Birmingham B1 2JP   021 643 9898

London:
35–38 and 43–45 Portman Sq
London W1H 9AH   071 486 6688
Also: 48 Charlotte St
London W1P 1LX   071 637 4602
Controller of Drama: Ted Childs
Controller Light Entertainment: Richard Holloway
Controller Young People's Programmes: Lewis Rudd

Granada Television
Granada Television Centre
Quay St
Manchester M60 9EA   061 832 7211

London:
36 Golden Square
London W1R 4AH   071 734 8080
Head of Casting: Carolyn Bartlett
Head of Drama: Sally Head
Head of Film Development: Pippa Cross
Head of Children's Programmes: Edward Pugh

HTV
Television Centre
Culverhouse Cross
Cardiff CF5 6XJ   0222 590590

London:
2nd Floor
69 New Oxford St
London WC1A 1DG   071 528 7767
Controller of Network Drama: Alan Clayton
Controller Children's & Family Programming:
Dan Maddicott

London Weekend Television
The London Television Centre
Upper Ground
London SE1 9LT   071 620 1620
Managing Director of LWT Prods: Nick Elliott
Controller of Drama: Sarah Wilson
Controller of Entertainment: John Kaye Cooper
(At the time of writing, LWT has been taken over
by Granada. As yet, the changes to personnel are
unclear)

Meridian Broadcasting
Television Centre
Southampton SO2 0TA   0703 222555

London:
48 Leicester Square
London WC2H 7LY
Controller of Drama: Colin Rogers

S4C – The Welsh Fourth Channel
Parc TY Glas Llanishen
Cardiff CF4 5DU   0222 747444
Acting Director of co-productions: Ian Jones

Scottish Television
Cowgaddens
Glasgow G2 3PR   041 332 9999

London:
200 Gray's Inn Rd
London WC1X 8XZ   071 396 6000
Controller of Drama: Robert Love
Controller of Entertainment and Drama Features:
Nigel Pickard

Yorkshire Television
The Television Centre
Leeds LS3 1JS   0532 438283

London:
Television House
31 Bedford Row
London WC1R 4HE   071 242 1666
Controller of Drama: Keith Richardson
Controller of Entertainment: David Reynolds
Controller of Children's Education Programmes:
Chris Jelley
(In 1993 Yorkshire merged with Tyne Tees
Television)

CHANNEL FOUR

Channel Four Television Co Ltd
60 Charlotte St
London W1P 2AX   071 631 4444
Chief Executive: Michael Grade
Head of Drama: David Aukin
Deputy Head of Drama: Peter Ansorge
Commissioning Editor Entertainment: Seamus
Cassidy
Commissioning Editor Youth: Bill Hilary

SATELLITE TELEVISION

British Sky Broadcasting
6 Centaurus Business Park
Grant Way
Isleworth
Middx TW7 5QD   081 705 3000

Note: Neither Channel Four or Sky produce programmes direct (see Chapter 3). Of the independent television contractors, only those producing drama and situation comedy have been listed below.

INDEPENDENT PRODUCTION COMPANIES

Alomo Productions
6 Derby St
London W1Y 7HD   071 355 2868

Amazing Productions
31 Royal Crescent
London W11 4SN   071 602 5355

Amy International Productions
2a Park Ave
Wraysbury
Middx TW19 5ET   0784 483131

Antelope Films
3 Fitzroy Sq
London W1P 5AH   071 321 0101

Ariel Productions
93 Wardour St
London W1V 3TE   071 494 2169

Artificial Eye Film Co
211 Camden High St
London NW1 7BT   071 267 6036

Arts Council Films
14 St Peter St
London SW1P 3NQ   071 973 6454

August Entertainment
10 Arminger Rd
London W12 7BB   081 742 9099

BFI Production
29 Rathbone St
London W1P 1AG   071 636 5587

Barford Productions
44 Earlham St
London WC2H 9LA   071 836 1365

Barrie Hinchcliffe Productions
Boston House
36–38 Fitzroy Sq
London W1P 5LL   071 631 1470

Big Star in a Wee Picture
The Production Centre
5 Newton Terrace Lane
Glasgow G3 7PB   041 204 3435

Blue Heaven Productions
10A Bedford Sq
London WC1B 3RA   071 637 7099

Box Clever Productions
25 Bewdley St
London N1 1HB   071 607 5766

Box Productions
4 Denmark St
London WC2H 8LP   071 240 4900

Britannia Entertainment
25 Linkfield Rd
Isleworth
Middx TW7 6QP   081 568 4023

British Lion
Pinewood Studios
Iver Heath
Bucks SL0 0NH   0753 651700

Brookside Productions
Campus Manor
Childwell Abbey Rd
Liverpool L16 0JP   051 722 9112

Burrows John Associates
4 Courtyard Hse
27 Farm St
London W1X 7RD   071 734 6505

Carnival Films
12 Raddington Rd
London W10 5TG   081 968 0968

Celador Productions
39 Long Acre
London WC2E 9JT   071 240 8101

Chameleon Television
The Magistretti Bldg
Harcourt Place
Leeds LS1 4RB   0532 438536

Channel X
Middlesex Hse
34–42 Cleveland St
London W1P 5FB   071 436 2200

Chatsworth Television
97–99 Dean St
London W1V 5RA   071 734 4302

Children's Film & Television Foundation
Elstree Studio
Borehamwood
Herts WD6 1JG   081 953 0844

Childsplay Productions
8 Lonsdale Rd
London NW6 6RD   071 328 1429

Children's Film Unit
Suite 9
Hamilton Hse
66 Upper Richmond Rd
London SW15 2RP   081 871 2006

Charisma Films
2nd Floor
Russell Chambers
London WC2   071 379 4267

Cheerleader Productions
62 Chiswick High Rd
London W4 1SY   081 995 7778

Chrysalis Television
Chrysalis Bldg
Bramely Rd
London W10 6SP   071 221 2213

Cinema Verity
Mill House
Millers Way
1a Shepherd's Bush Rd
London W6 7NA   081 749 8485

Clear Idea Television
184 Grafton Rd
London NW5   071 284 1442

Compass Film Productions
175 Wardour St
London W1V 3FB   071 734 8115

Convergence Productions
Unit 10
The Chandlery
50 Westminster Bridge Rd
London SE1 7QY   071 721 7531

Cosgrove Hall Productions
8 Albany Rd
Chorlton
Manchester M21 1BL   061 881 9211

Cuthbert Tony Productions
7A Langley St
London WC2H 9JA   071 437 8884

DBA Television
21 Ormeau Ave
Belfast
N. Ireland BT2 8HD   0232 231197

Darlow Smithson Productions
32 Percy St
London WC1X 9QR   071 278 6995

Diverse Productions
Gorleston St
London W14 8XS   071 603 4567

Domino Films
214 The Chambers
Chelsea Harbour
London SW10 0XF   071 376 3791

Double Exposure
Unit 22–23
63 Clerkenwell Rd
London EC1M 5PS   071 490 2499

The Drama House
21–25 St Anne's Court
London W1V 3AW   071 437 3689

Drumbeat Productions
17A Mercer St
London WC2H 9QJ   071 836 3710

Edge Picture Company
D'Arblay Hse
14–15 D'Arblay St
London W1V 3FP   071 734 9495

Edinburgh Film Productions
Nine Mile Burn
By Penicuik
Midlothian EH26 9LT   0968 672131

Elmgate Productions
Shepperton Studios
Studios Rd
Shepperton
Middx TW17 0QD   0932 562611

Emanco
9 Gt Russell St
London WC1B 3NH   071 323 0821

English & Pocket
Bridle Hse
36 Bridle Lane
London W1R 3HJ   071 287 1155

Endboard Productions
114A Poplar Rd
Bearwood
B66 4AP   021 429 9779

Enigma Productions
Pinewood Studios
Iver Heath
Bucks SL0 0NH   0753 630555

Eon Productions
2 South Audley St
London W1Y 6AJ   071 493 7953

Euston Films
Pinewood Studios
Iver Heath
Bucks SL0 0NH   0753 654321

Felgate Productions
455 Finchley Rd
London NW3 6HN   071 794 0909

Flashback Productions
2–3 Cowcross St
London EC1M 6DR   071 490 8996

Forum Television
11 Regent St
Clifton
Bristol BS8 4HW   0272 741490

Forge Productions
6 Auriol Rd
London W14 0RS   071 602 8658

Front Page Films
23 West Smithfield
London EC1A 9HY   071 329 6866

Fulcrum Productions
254 Goswell Rd
London EC1V 7EB   071 253 0353

Fulmar TV & Film
1 Little Argyle St
London W1R 5DB   071 437 2222

Gainsborough Productions
8 Queen St
London W1X 7PH   071 409 1925

James Garrett & Partners
25 Bruton St
London W1X 7DB   071 499 6452

The Grade Company
8 Queen St
London W1X 7PH   071 409 1925

Great Guns
28–32 Shelton St
London WC2 9HP   071 379 3338

Greenpark Productions
101 Honor Oak Park
London SE23 3LB   081 699 7234

Greenpoint Films
5A Noel St
London W1V 3RB   071 437 6492

Griffin Productions
Balfour Hse
46–54 Gt Titchfield St
London W1P 7AE   071 636 5066

Handmade Films
26 Cadogan Sq
London SW1X 0JP   071 584 8345

Hartswood Films
Teddington Studios
Broom Rd
Teddington Lock
Teddington
Middx TW11 9NT   081 977 3252

Hat Trick Productions
10 Livonia St
London W1V 3PH   071 434 2451

Havahall Pictures
125 Gloucester Rd
London SW7 4TE   071 244 8466

Hawkshead
3 Fitzroy Sq
London W1P 5AH   071 388 1234

Hiss & Boo Company
24 West Grove
Walton-on-Thames
Surrey KT12 5NX   0932 248931

Holmes Associates
17 Rathbone St
London W1P 1AF   071 637 8251

Humphrey Barclay Productions
5 Anglers Lane
London NW5 3DG   071 482 1992

Hurll Michael Services
6 Brewer St
London W1P 3SP   071 465 0103

Iambic Productions
8 Warren Mews
London W1P 5DJ   071 388 3323

Illustra Television
13–14 Bateman St
London W1V 6EB   071 437 9611

Initial Film & Television
74 Black Lion Lane
London W6 9BE   081 741 4500

Island World Productions
3rd Floor
12–14 Argyll St
London W1V 0RG   071 734 3534

Jackson Brian
39 Hanover Steps
St Georges Fields
Albion St
London W2 2YG   071 402 7543

Jam Jar Films
22 Stafford St
Edinburgh EH3 7BD   031 220 5566

Jericho Productions
29 Cholmeley Park
London N6 5EL   081 341 1834

Jim Henson Productions
1B Downshire Hill
London NW3 5EL   071 431 3737

Joll Barrie Associates
58 Frith St
London W1V 5TA   071 437 9965

Lawson Productions
2 Clarendon Cl
London W2 2NS   071 706 3111

London Film Productions
Kent Hse
14–17 Market Pl
Gt Titchfield St
London W1N 8AR   071 323 5251

Lumiere Pictures
167–9 Wardour St
London W1V 3TA   071 413 0838

Mansfield Mike Enterprises
5–7 Carnaby St
London W1P 3LH   071 494 3061

Mentorn Films
140 Wardour St
London W1V 3AU   071 287 4545

Merchant Ivory Productions
46 Lexington St
London W1P 3HL   071 437 1200

Mersham Productions
41 Montpelier Walk
London SW7 1JH   071 589 8829

Moving Picture Company
25 Noel St
London W1V 3RD   071 434 3100

New Era Productions
23 West Smithfield
London EC1A 9HY   071 236 5532

Nirvana Films
81 Berwick St
London W1V 3PF   071 439 8113

Noel Gay Television
6th Floor
76 Oxford St
London W1N 0AT   071 412 0400

North South Productions
1 Woburn Walk
London WC1H 0JJ   071 388 0351

Numo Productions
16–18 Hollen St
London W1V 3AD   071 437 2877

October Films
63–64 Camden Lock Pl
London NW1 8AS   071 916 7198

Orbit Films
7–11 Kensington High St
London W8 5NP   071 221 5548

Ovation Productions
Osprey Hse
10 Little Portland St
London W1N 5DF   071 637 8575

The Palace
8 Poland St
London W1   071 439 8241

Paravision
114 The Chambers
Chelsea Harbour
London SW10 0XF   071 351 7070

Pearl Catlin Associates
The Clockhouse
Summersbury St
Chalfont GU4 8JQ   0483 67932

Picture Palace Productions
53A Brewer St
London W1R 3FD   071 439 9882

Pola Jones Film
5 Dean St
London W1V 5RN   071 439 1165

Portman Entertainment
Pinewood Studios
Iver Heath
Bucks SL0 0NH   0753 630366

Primetime Television
Seymour Hse

Seymour Mews
London W1H 9PE   071 935 9000

Prominent Features & Television
68A Delancey St
London NW1 7RY   071 284 0242

Propaganda Films
5th Floor
1 Golden Sq
London W1R 3AB   071 287 0250

Quadrant Television
17 West Hill
London SW18 1RB   081 870 9933

Ragdoll Productions
11 Chapel St
Stratford-on-Avon
Warks CV37 6EP   0564 794076

Red Rooster Film & Television Entertainment
29 Floral St
London WC2E 9DP   071 379 7727

Redwing Film Co
1 Wedgewood Mews
12–13 Greek St
London W1V 5LW   071 734 6642

Regent Productions
The Mews
6 Putney Common
London SW15 1HL   081 789 5350

Renegade Productions
13 Arbuthnot Rd
London SE14 5LS   071 639 1688

Riverfront Pictures
Dock Cottages
Peartree Lane
London E1 9SR   071 481 2939

Roberts & Wykeham Films
7 Barb Mews
London W6 7PA   081 741 2047

Sands Films
Grice's Wharf
119 Rotherhithe St
London SE16 4NF   071 231 2209

Sankofa Film & Video
Unit K
32–34 Gordon Hse Rd
London NW5 1LP   071 485 0848

Scala Productions
39–43 Brewer St
London W1R 3FD   071 734 7060

SelecTV
3 Derby St
London W1Y 7HD   071 355 2868

Shooting Star
8 Queen St
London W1X 7PH   071 409 1925

Skreba Films
5A Noel St
London W1V 3RB   071 437 6492

Skyline Film & Television Productions
24–25 Scala St
London W1P 1LU   071 631 4649

Specific Films
25 Rathbone St
London W1P 1AG   071 580 7476

Spencer Alan Company
3–4 Bywell Place
Wells St
London W1P 3FB   071 647 7503

Taffner DL
10 Bedford Sq
London WC1B 3RA   071 631 1184

Talbot Television
57 Jamestown Rd
London NW1 7DB   071 284 0880

Talkback
33 Percy St
London W1P 9FG   071 631 3940

Teliesyn
Helwick Hse
19 David St
Cardiff CF1 2EH   0222 667546

Thin Man Films
9 Greek St
London W1V 5LE   071 734 7372

Third Eye Productions
Unit 210
Canalot Studios
222 Kensal Rd
London W10 5BN   081 969 8211

Tiger Aspects Productions
47 Dean St
London W1V 5HL   071 434 0672

Triple Vision
36A Greenwood Rd
London E8 1AB   071 388 5375

TVF
375 City Rd
London EC1V 1NA   071 837 3000

Twentieth Century Vixen
13 Aubert Park
London N5   081 672 1012

Twenty Twenty Television
10 Stucley Pl
London NW1 8NS   071 284 2020

Tyburn Productions
Pinewood Studios
Iver Heath
Bucks SL0 0NH   0753 651700

UBA
Flat 2
32 Porchester Terrace
London W2 3TP   071 402 6313

Vanson Wardle Productions
72 Chatham Rd
London SW11 6HG   071 223 1919

Video Arts
Dumbarton Hse
68 Oxford St
London W1N 9LA   071 637 7288

Wall to Wall Television
8–9 Spring Pl
London NW5 3ER   071 485 7424

Warner Brothers Productions
Warner Suite
Pinewood Studios
Iver Heath
Bucks SL0 0NH   0753 654545

Warner Sisters
21 Russell St
London WC2B 5HP   071 836 0134

Waterfront Productions
17/21 Dean St
Newcastle-upon-Tyne   091 261 0162

Wickes Company
169 Queens Gate
London SW7 5HE   071 225 1382

Witzend Productions
6 Derby St
London W1V 7HD   071 355 2868

Michael White Productions
13 Duke St
St James's
London SW1Y 6DB   071 839 3971

Wolff Productions
6A Noel St
London W1V 3RB   071 439 1838

Working Title Productions
1 Water Lane
Kentish Town Rd
London NW1 8NZ   071 911 6100

Worldwide Pictures
21–25 St Anne's Court
London W1V 1AB   071 734 3536

Yo Yo Films
173A Camberwell New Rd
London SE5 0TJ   071 735 3711

Zed Ltd
2nd Floor
29 Heddon St
London W1R 7LL   071 494 3181

Zenith Productions
(now merged with Portman Entertainments)
43–45 Dorset St
London W1H 4AB   071 224 2440

Zoom Productions
102 Dean St
London W1V 5RA   071 434 3895

NB: It is no longer possible to separate companies according to the type of production they specialise in. Most make television and film productions, some make commercials and corporate videos and documentaries. Where possible companies making factual and documentary programmes that do not employ actors have been excluded.

You will see from this list that some addresses are obviously the homes of the principal directors, which indicates a small operation. The bigger companies tend to have independent offices.

Remember this list will be subject to very rapid change. New companies will be formed and old ones disappear so make sure you keep this list up-to-date and add to it as you get new information.

RADIO

BBC Radio
Broadcasting House
London W1A 1AA   071 580 4468

Head of Drama: John Tydeman
Producer/Directors:
  John Theocaris
  Adrian Bean
  Peter Kavanagh
  Ned Chaillet
  Martin Jenkins
  Marilyn Imrie
  Claire Grove
  Cherry Cookson
  Glyn Dearman
  Jane Morgan
  Frances-Anne Solomon
  Matthew Walters
  Enyd Williams
  Richard Wortley

Head of Light Entertainment: Jonathan James-Moore
Producer/Directors:
  Andy Aliffe
  Neil Cargill
  Richard Edis
  Lissa Evans
  Armando Iannucci
  Dirks Maggs
  Jan Magnusson
  Sarah Smith
  Edward Taylor
  Sioned William

Regional

BBC Manchester
New Broadcasting Hse
Oxford Rd
Manchester M60 1SJ   061 200 2020
Drama Producers:
  Tony Cliff
  Michael Fox
  Kate Rowland
Light Entertainment Producers:
  Mike Craig
  Paul Z. Jackson

NB: Virtually no television drama is made at BBC Manchester (which is why this address is not included in the television section) but radio production is made in both drama and LE.

BBC Birmingham
Broadcasting Centre
Pebble Mill Rd
Birmingham B5 7QQ   021 414 8888

BBC West
Whiteladies Rd
Bristol BS8 2LR   0272 732211
Producers:
  Nigel Bryant
  Shaun MacLoughlin
  Philip Martin
  Sue Wilson
The Archers: Vanessa Whitburn

Plus radio production in Glasgow, Belfast, Cardiff (see BBC TV)

World Service

BBC World Service

Bush House
The Strand
London WC2B 4PH   071 240 3456
Executive Producer Drama: Gordon House

Independent Radio and Local Radio

For the purposes of this book neither BBC local radio stations nor
independent local nor national radio stations produce drama. It is
possible that this may change and any stations that start drama
production should be noted here.

Theatre

SUBSIDISED LONDON THEATRES

Royal National Theatre
Upper Ground
South Bank
London SE1 9PX   071 928 2033
Artistic Director: Richard Eyre
Casting: Serena Hill

Royal Shakespeare Co
Barbican
London EC2Y 8BQ   071 628 3351
Artistic Director: Adrian Noble

Royal Court Theatre
Sloane Square
London SW1W 8AS   071 730 5174
Artistic Director: Max Stafford Clark (Stephen Daldry)

Open Air Theatre
Regent's Park
London NW1 4NP   071 935 5884
Artistic Director: Ian Talbot

Polka Theatre for Children
240 The Broadway
London SW19 1SB   081 542 4258
Artistic Director: Vicky Ireland

Almeida Theatre
Almeida St
London N1   071 226 7432
Artistic Directors: Jonathon Kent, Ian McDiarmid

Bush Theatre Club
Shepherd's Bush Green
London W12 8QD   071 602 3703
Artistic Director: Dominic Dromgoole

Greenwich Theatre
Crooms Hill
London SE10 8ES   081 858 4477
Artistic Director: Matthew Francis

Hampstead Theatre
Swiss Cottage Centre
Avenue Rd
London NW3 3EX   071 722 9224
Artistic Directors: Jenny Topper, Richard Wakely

King's Head Theatre
115 Upper Street
London N1 1QN   071 226 8561
Artistic Director: Dan Crawford

Orange Tree
1 Clarence St
Richmond
Surrey TW9 2SA   081 940 0141
Artistic Director: Sam Walters

Theatre Royal, Stratford East
Gerry Raffles Sq
London E15 1BN   081 534 7374
Artistic Director: Philip Hedley

Tricycle Theatre
269 Kilburn High Rd
London NW6 7JR   071 372 6611
Artistic Director: Nicolas Kent

Warehouse Theatre Croydon
Dingwall Rd
Croydon CR0 2NF   081 681 1257
Artistic Director: Ted Craig

Watermans Arts Centre
40 High St
Brentford
Middx TW8 0DS   081 847 5651
Artistic Director: Mary Allen

Young Vic Theatre
66 The Cut
Waterloo Rd
London SE1 8LZ   071 968 1585
Artistic Director: David Thacker

MAINSTREAM THEATRE PRODUCERS

Ian Albery
54 Cavell St
London E1 2HP   071 790 2007

Andrew Bancroft Productions
Bala Hse
48 Mortimer St
London W1N 7DG   071 580 5839

Armand Gerrard Ltd
21 Russell St
London WC2B 5HP   071 240 5777

Baroque Theatre Co
Mezzanine Floor
Regent Hse
235 Regent St
London W1R 8AX   071 439 8401

Peter Bentley Stephens
15 Wardour Hse
110 Wardour St
London W1V 3LD   071 379 4012

Cambridge Theatre Co
25 Short St
London SE1 8LJ   071 401 9797

Centreline Productions
Ambassadors Theatre
West St
London WC2 9NH   071 379 5801

Michael Codron Ltd
Aldwych Theatre Offices
London WC2B 4DF   071 240 8291

Cooney Productions
Hollowfield Cottage
Littleton
Surrey GU3 1HN   0483 440443

Allan Davis Ltd
182 Gloucester Pl
London NW1 6DS   071 235 8814

The Drama House Ltd
12–25 St Anne's Court
London W1V 3AW   071 437 3689

Duncan C. Weldon Productions
Suite 4
Waldorf Chambers
11 Aldwych
London WC2B 4DA　　071 836 0186

E & B Productions (Paul Elliot)
Suite 3
11 Aldwych
London WC2B 4DA　　071 836 2795

English Shakespeare Co
38 Bedford Sq
London WC1B 3EG　　071 580 6505

English Stage Co
Royal Court Theatre
Sloane Sq
London SW1W 8AS　　071 730 5174

English Touring Theatre Ltd
New Century Building
Hill St
Crewe
Cheshire CW1 1BX　　0270 501800

The European Theatre Co
3 Egerton Gdns
London SW3 2BS　　071 581 2010

Harold Fielding
PO Box 1274
London W4 3PY　　081 994 4088

Vanessa Ford Productions
Upper Hse Farm
Upper Hse Lane
Shamley Green
Surrey GU5 0SX　　0483 278203

Clare Fox Associates
9 Plympton Rd
London NW6 7EH   071 372 2301

Robert Fox Ltd
6 Beauchamp Pl
London SW3 1NG   071 584 6855

Fraser Randall Productions
25 Store St
London WC1E 7BL   071 323 9328

Bill Freedman Ltd
13 New Row
London WC2N 4LF   071 497 3320

Freeshooter Productions
10 Clorane Gdns
London NW3 7PR   071 794 0414

Ian Fricker Ltd
6 Great Queen St
London WC2B 5DG   071 404 6660

John Gale
185 Walm Lane
London NW2 3AY   081 452 8086

Gero Productions
14 Old Compton St
London W1V 5PE   071 439 1628

Ginmar Productions
10 Garrick St
London WC2   071 379 6200

Derek Glynne (Australian productions)
25 Haymarket
London SW1Y 4EN   071 930 1981

Peter Hall Productions
c/o Albery Theatre
St Martins Lane
London WC2N 4AH   071 867 1123

Harley Productions
68 New Cavendish St
London W1M 7LD   071 580 3247

Josephine Hart Productions
7A Langley St
London WC2   071 713 0877

Harvey Kass Associates
156–158 Grays Inn Rd
London WC1X 8ED   071 713 0877

Thelma Holt Ltd
Waldorf Chambers
11 The Aldwych
London WC2B 4DA   071 916 1984

Hull Truck
Spring St Theatre
Spring St
Hull HU2 8RW   0482 224800

Bruce Hyman Associates
8A St Georges Mews
London NW1 8XE   071 916 1984

Imagination Entertainments
25 Store St
London WC1 3BL   071 323 3300

Richard Jackson
59 Knightsbridge
London SW1X 7RA   071 235 3671

Julian Courtenay Ltd
20 Orchards Rd
London N6 5TR   071 348 9033

Bill Kenwright Ltd
55–59 Shaftesbury Ave
London W1V 7AA   071 439 4466

David Kirk
12 Panmuir Rd
London SW20 0PZ   081 947 0130

Knightsbridge Productions
Winchmore Hse
15 Fetter Lane
London EC4A 1JJ   071 583 8687

Laurence Myers Ltd
1 Star St
London W2 1QD   071 706 7342

Lean Two Productions
18 Rutland St
London SW7 1EF   071 584 9342

Linnit Productions
Prince of Wales Theatre
Coventry St
London W1V 7FE   071 930 6677

Robert Luff Plays Ltd
294 Earl's Court Rd
London SW5 9BB   071 373 7003

Cameron MacKintosh Ltd
1 Bedford Sq
London WC1B 3RA   071 637 8866

Maybox Group
Albery Theatre
St Martin's Lane
London WC2N 4AH   071 867 1122

Lee Menzies
Playhouse Theatre
Northumberland Ave
London WC2N 4DE   071 839 9077

Millenium Productions
5–7 Carnaby St
London W1V 1PG   071 494 3059

New Shakespeare Co
Open Air Theatre
Regent's Park
London NW1 4NP   071 935 5884

Newpalm Productions
26 Cavendish Ave
London N3 3QN   081 349 0802

Northern Stage
67A Westgate Rd
Newcastle-upon-Tyne NE1 1SG   091 232 3366

Oxford Stage Co
15–19 George St
Oxford OX1 2AU   0865 723238

Pola Jones Associates
5 Dean St
London W1V 5RN   081 542 4258

David Pugh
52 Shaftesbury Ave
London W1V 7DE   071 434 9757

PW Productions
11 Goodwins Court
London WC2N 4LL   071 379 7909

The Really Useful Group
22 Tower St
London WC2H 7HE   071 240 0808

Michael Redington
10 Maunsel St
London SW1P 2QL   071 834 5119

Renaissance Theatre Co
83 Berwick St
London W1V 3PJ   071 287 6672

Peter Saunders Ltd
Vaudeville Theatre
10 Maiden Lane
London WC2E 7NA   071 240 3177

Stagestruck Productions
57 Duke St
London W1M 5DH   071 629 2334

Theatre of Comedy
Shaftesbury Theatre
210 Shaftesbury Ave
London WC2H 8DP   071 379 3345

Andrew Treagus Associates
21–23 Panton St
London SW1Y 4DR   071 839 6288

David Tudor Productions
17 St Mary's Ave
Purley-on-Thames
Berks RG8 8BJ   0734 421144

The Turnstyle Group
Duke of Yorks Theatre
St Martin's Lane
London WC2N 4BG   071 240 9891

Charles Vance Prestige Plays
83 George St
London W1H 5PL   071 486 1732

John Wallbank Associates
Ambassadors Theatre
West St
London WC2H 9ND   071 379 5665

Michael Ward Productions
39 Thames St
Windsor
Berks SL4 1PR   0753 863982

Michael White Productions
13 Duke St
St James's
London SW1Y 6DB   071 839 3971

Peter Wilson Productions
11 Goodwins Court
London WC2N 4LL   071 379 7909

NB: Many of the companies listed may only have produced one or two shows and there will be long periods when they are inactive while developing and finding the money for their next project. Others, the large companies, are in a process of more or less continuous production, not only casting new shows, but re-casting their hit productions.

The list includes touring managements and producers of West End productions.

Once again new companies come on to the scene continually and new companies should be noted down as they occur.

REGIONAL REPERTORY THEATRES

Ayr
Civic Theatre
Craigie Rd
Ayr
Ayrshire KA8 0EZ   0292 263755
Artistic Director: Victor Graham (July–mid Sept only)

Barnstaple
Orchard Theatre Co
108 Newport Rd
Barnstaple EX32 9BA   0271 71475
Artistic Director: Bill Buffery

Basingstoke
Haymarket Theatre Co
Wote St
Basingstoke RG21 1NW   0256 23073
Artistic Director: Adrian Reynolds

Belfast
Arts Theatre
41 Botanic Ave
Belfast BT7 1JG   0232 242819
Artistic Director: Paul Maurel

Lyric Theatre
55 Ridgeway St
Belfast BT9 5FB   0232 669660
Artistic Director: Patricia McBride

Birmingham
Repertory Theatre
Centenary Sq
Broad St
Birmingham B1 2EP   021 236 6771
Artistic Director: Bill Alexander

323

Birmingham Stage Co
The Old Rep Theatre
Station St
Birmingham B5 4DY   021 643 9050
Artistic Director: Karen Crouch

Bolton
Octagon Theatre
Howell Croft
South Bolton
Lancs BL1 1SB   0204 29407
Artistic Director: Lawrence Till

Bristol
Theatre Royal and New Vic Studio
King St
Bristol BS1 4ED   0272 277466
Artistic Director: Andrew Hay

Bromley
Churchill Theatre
High St
Bromley
Kent BR1 1HA   081 464 7131
Artistic Director: John Wallbank

Cardiff
Sherman Theatre & Sherman Arena
Senghennydd Rd
Cardiff CF2 4YE   0222 396844
Artistic Director: Phil Clark

Chelmsford
Civic Theatre
Fairfield Rd
Chelmsford
Essex CM1 1JH   (calls to 081 349 0802 Newpalm Prods)
Artistic Director (for Newpalm Productions): John Newman

Cheltenham
Everyman Theatre
Regent St
Cheltenham
Glos GL50 1HQ   0242 512515
Artistic Director: Martin Houghton

Chester
Gateway Theatre
Hamilton Pl
Chester
Cheshire CH1 2BH   0244 344238
Artistic Director: Jeremy Raison

Chichester
Chichester Festival Theatre & Minerva Theatre
Oaklands Park
Chichester
W. Sussex PO19 4AP   0243 784437
Artistic Director: Patrick Garland

Colchester
Mercury Theatre
Balkerne Gate
Colchester
Essex CO1 1PT   0206 577006
Artistic Director: Michael Winter

Coventry
Belgrade Theatre & Studio (TIE)
Belgrade Sq
Coventry
Warks CV1 1GS   0203 256431
Artistic Director: Robert Hamlin

Crewe
Lyceum Theatre
10 Heath St
Crewe

Cheshire CW1 2DA   0270 258818
Manager: Cliff Stansfield

Derby
Playhouse Theatre
Theatre Walk
Eagle Centre
Derby DE1 2NF   0332 363271
Artistic Director: Mark Clements

Dublin
Abbey Theatre
Lower Abbey St
Dublin 1   010 3531 8748741
Artistic Director: Garry Hynes

Dundee
Repertory Theatre
Tay Sq
Dundee DD1 1PB   0382 27684
Artistic Director: Hamish Glen

Edenbridge
Hever Lakeside Theatre
Hever Castle
Edenbridge
Kent TN8 7NG   0732 866114
Director: Richard Palmer (July–Aug only)

Edinburgh
Royal Lyceum Theatre Co
Grindlay St
Edinburgh EH3 9AX   031 229 7404
Artistic Director: Kenny Ireland

Traverse Theatre
Cambridge St
Edinburgh EH1 2ED   031 228 3223
Artistic Director: Ian Brown

Exeter
Northcott Theatre
Stocker Rd
Exeter
Devon EX4 4QB   0392 56182
Artistic Director: John Durnin

Farnham
Redgrave Theatre
Brightwells
Farnham
Surrey GU9 7SB   0252 727000
Artistic Director: Graham Watkins

Frinton
Frinton Summer Theatre
Ashlyns Rd
Frinton
Essex   0255 674443
Producer: Seymour Matthews (July–Sept only)

Glasgow
Citizens Theatre
Gorbals
Glasgow G5 9DS   041 429 5561
Artistic Director: Giles Havergal

Old Athenaeum Theatre
179 Buchanan St
Glasgow G1 2JZ   041 332 5127
Artistic Director: Mary McCluskey

Guildford
Yvonne Arnaud Theatre
Millbrook
Guildford
Surrey GU1 3UX   0483 64571
Director: James Barber

Harrogate
Harrogate Theatre (TIE)
Oxford St
Harrogate HG1 1QF   0423 502710
Artistic Director: Andrew Manley

Hornchurch
Queen's Theatre
Billet Lane
Hornchurch
Essex RM11 1QT   0708 456118
Artistic Director: Marina Caldarone

Hull
Hull Truck
Spring St Theatre
Spring St
Hull HU2 8RW   0482 224800
Artistic Director: John Godber

Ipswich
Wolsey Theatre & Studio (TIE)
Civic Drive
Ipswich
Suffolk IP1 2AS   0473 2118911
Artistic Director: Anthony Tuckey

Eastern Angles Theatre Co
Sir John Mills Theatre
Gatacre Rd
Ipswich
Suffolk IP1 2LQ   0382 27684
Artistic Director: Ivan Cutting

Keswick
The Century Theatre
Lakeside
Keswick

Cumbria CA12 5DJ   07687 72282
Artistic Director: Douglas Cook

Lancaster
The Duke's Theatre (TIE)
Moor Lane
Lancaster
Lancs LA1 1QD   0524 842134
Artistic Director: Han Duivendak

Leeds
West Yorkshire Playhouse (TIE)
Quarry Hill Mount
Leeds
W. Yorks LS9 8AW   0532 442141
Artistic Director: Jude Kelly

Leicester
Haymarket & Studio
Belgrave Gate
Leicester LE1 3YQ   0533 530021
Artistic Director: Paul Kerryson

Liverpool
Everyman Theatre
Hope St
Liverpool L1 9BH   051 708 0338
Artistic Director: Peter Rowe

Playhouse Theatre & Studio (in association with Bill Kenwright)
Williamson Sq
Liverpool L1 1EL   051 709 8478
Artistic Director: Ian Kellgren

Manchester
Contact Theatre Co
Oxford Rd
Manchester M15 6JA   061 274 3434
Artistic Director: Brigid Larmour

Library Theatre & Forum
St Peter's Sq
Manchester M2 5PD   061 234 1913
Artistic Director: Christopher Horner

Royal Exchange Theatre
St Ann's Sq
Manchester M2 7DH   061 833 9333
Artistic Directors: James Maxwell, Braham Murray, Gregory Hersov

Milford Haven
Torch Theatre
St Peter's Rd
Milford Haven
Dyfed SA73 2BU   0646 694192
Artistic Director: Vacant

Mold
Theatr Clwyd Co
Mold
Clwyd CH7 1YA   0352 756331
Artistic Director: Helena Kaut-Howson

Musselburgh
The Brunton Theatre
Ladywell Way
Musselburgh
EH21 6AA   031 665 9900
Artistic Director: Vacant

Newbury
Watermill Theatre
Bagnor
Nr Newbury
Berks RG16 8AE   0635 45834
Artistic Director: Jill Fraser

Newcastle-under-Lyme
New Victoria Theatre

Etruria Rd
Newcastle-Under-Lyme
Staffs ST5 0JG   0782 717954
Artistic Director: Peter Cheeseman

Newcastle-upon-Tyne
Northern Stage Co
67A Westgate Rd
Newcastle-upon-Tyne
NE1 1SG   091 232 3366
Artistic Director: Alan Lyddiard

Northampton
Royal Theatre & Opera House
Guildhall Rd
Northampton
Northants NN1 1EA   0604 38343
Artistic Director: Michael Napier Brown

Nottingham
Playhouse Theatre (TIE)
Wellington Circus
Nottingham NG1 5AF   0602 474361
Artistic Director: Pip Broughton

Oldham
Coliseum Theatre
Fairbottom St
Oldham
Lancs OL1 3SW   061 624 1731
Artistic Director: Warren Hooper

Perth
Perth Repertory Theatre
High St
Perth PH1 5UW   0738 38123
Artistic Director: Andrew McKinnon

Pitlochry
Festival Theatre
Pitlochry
Perthshire RH16 5DR   0796 473054
Artistic Director: Clive Perry

Plymouth
Theatre Royal & Drum Theatre
Royal Parade
Plymouth
Devon PL1 2TR   0752 668282
Artistic Director: Roger Redfarn

Reading
The Mill At Sonning
Sonning Eye
Reading RG4 0TW   0734 696039
Artistic Director: Sally Hughes

St Andrews
Byre Theatre
Abbey St
St Andrews KY16 9LA   0334 7628
Artistic Director: Maggie Kinloch

Salisbury
Playhouse & Salberg Studio
Malthouse Lane
Salisbury
Wilts SP2 7RA   0722 320117
Artistic Director: Deborah Page

Scarborough
Stephen Joseph Theatre
Valley Bridge Parade
Scarborough
N. Yorks YO11 2PL   0723 370542
Artistic Director: Alan Ayckbourn

Sheffield
Crucible Theatre & Studio
55 Norfolk St
Sheffield S1 1DA   0742 760621
Artistic Director: Michael Rudman

Sheringham
Little Theatre
2 Station Rd
Sheringham
Norfolk NR26 8RE   0263 822347
Theatre Manager: Jonathan Emery (July–Aug only)

Sidmouth
Manor Pavilion
Manor Rd
Sidmouth
Devon EX10 8RP   03955 14413
(July–Sept only)

Southampton
Nuffield
University Rd
Southampton SO2 1TR   0703 315500
Artistic Director: Patrick Sandford (Sept–July only)

Southwold
Summer Theatre
Cumberland Rd
Southwold
Suffolk IP18 6JP   071 580 2222
Director: Jill Freud (July–Sept only)

Watford
Palace Theatre
Clarendon Rd
Watford
Herts WD1 1JZ   0923 235455
Artistic Director: Lou Stein

Westcliff
Palace Theatre & Dixon Theatre
London Rd
Westcliff-on-Sea
Essex SS0 9LA   0702 347816
Artistic Director: Christopher Dunham

Windsor
Theatre Royal
Thames St
Windsor
Berks SL4 1PS   0753 863444
Artistic Director: Mark Piper

Worcester
Swan Theatre
The Moors
Worcester WR1 3EF   0905 726969
Artistic Director: Pat Trueman

York
Theatre Royal
St Leonard's Pl
York YO1 2HD   0904 658162
Artistic Director: John Doyle

SMALLER, YOUNG PEOPLE'S, COMMUNITY, ETHNIC AND ALTERNATIVE THEATRES AND THEATRE MANAGEMENTS

Action Transport Theatre Co
McGarva Way
Ellesmere Port
South Wirral   051 357 2120

Actions & Words Theatre Co
4A Downside Hill
London NW3 1NR   071 794 3979

Actors Touring Co
Alford Hse
Aveline St
London SE11 5DG   071 735 8311

African Players Theatre Co
218 Lambeth Road
London SE1 7JY   071 249 9150

Age Exchange Theatre Co
The Reminiscence Centre
11 Blackheath Village
London SE3 9LA   081 318 9105

Alien Arts Company
40 Lambhill St
Kinning Park
Glasgow GA1   041 427 5772

All Change
177 Upper St
London N1 1RG   071 359 9585

Anlau Theatre Co
46 Hart Rd
Erdington
Birmingham B24 9ES   021 384 8372

Arbela Production Co
7th Floor
15 Berkeley St
London W1X 5AE   071 499 2012

Attic Theatre Co
5 Chatsworth Ave
London SW20 8JZ   081 542 6030

Awaaz Theatre Co
4 Wyke Close
Osterley
Middx TW7 5PE   081 569 7304

Black Mime Theatre
22 Colombo St
London SE1 8DP   071 928 1311

Black Theatre Co-op
8 Bradbury St
London N16 8JN   071 249 9150

Black Theatre Forum
The Granville Centre
80 Granville Rd
London NW6 5RA   071 372 1069

Break Touring Theatre Co
George White Middle School
Silver Rd
Norwich NR3 4RG   0603 426374

Breathless Productions
The Bird's Nest Theatre
32 Deptford Church St
London SE8 4RZ   081 694 2255

Brighton Actors Theatre
6 English Passage
Lewes
Sussex   0273 475029

British Actors Theatre Co
172 Park Rd
Kingston
Surrey KT2 6DQ   081 549 8124

British Asian Theatre Co
Star Studios
1 Cornthwaite Rd
London E5 0RS   081 986 4470

Cambridge Syllabus Players
12 Guildford St
London WC1N 1DT   071 242 1046

Carib Theatre Productions
342 Kilburn High Rd
London NW6 2QJ   071 624 5860

Carnival Theatre
12 Reddington Rd
London W10 5TG   081 968 1717

Catchfavour Ltd
24 Crediton Rd
London NW10 3DU   081 960 0767

Centre for Performance Research
The Gym
Market Rd
Canton
Cardiff CF5 1QE   0222 345174

Channel Theatre Co
Granville Theatre
Victoria Parade
Ramsgate
Kent CT11 8DG   0843 588280

Cheek By Jowl
Alford Hse
Aveline St
London SE11 5DQ   071 793 0153

Cherub Theatre Co
Arch 5–6
Midland Rd
London NW1 2AD   071 388 0947

Clean Break Theatre Co
37–39 King's Terrace
London NW1 0JR   071 383 3786

Cleveland Theatre Co
Billingham Forum
Town Centre
Billingham
Cleveland TS23 2LJ   0642 363003

Combination Ltd
Albany Empire
Douglas Way
Deptford SE8 4AG   081 691 8016

Company of Cranks
62 Northfield House
Peckham Park Rd
London SE15 6TN   071 358 0571

Compass Theatre Co
The Leadmill
6–7 Leadmill Rd
Sheffield S1 4SF   0742 755328

Context
24 Attwell Park
Merry Hill
Wolverhampton WV3 7NS   0902 339745

Continental Drift
54 Peartree St
London EC1V 3SB   071 490 8623

The Crummles Co
35 The Park
London W5 5NP   081 567 8670

Cut-Cloth Theatre
41 Beresford Rd
London N2 2HR   081 359 4150

Double Edge Theatre Co
Camden United Theatre
6–8 Greenland St
London NW1 0ND   071 482 1287

Double Exposure
4 Ingatestone Rd
Woodford Green
Essex 1G8 9AL   081 504 5005

Dual Control International Theatre
Historic Dockyard
Chatham
Kent ME4 4TE   0634 819141

Durham Theatre Co
Darlington Arts Centre
Vane Terrace
Darlington
Co Durham DL3 7AX   0325 469861

Edge of the World Theatre Productions
50 Fairbridge Rd
London N19 3HZ   071 272 1131

English Chamber Theatre
410 Beatty Hse
Dolphin Sq
London SW1V 3LX   071 798 8798

European Players
Flat 3
30 Floral St
London WC2E 9DP   071 831 1553

European Stage Co
172 Gt Portland St
London W1N 5TB   071 352 5423

Field Day Theatre Co
Foyle Arts Centre
Old Foyle College
Lawrence Hill
Derry
N. Ireland BT48 7NJ   0504 360196

Forest Forge Theatre Co
Ringwood School
Parsonage Barn Lane
Ringwood
Hants BH24 1RE   0425 470188

Framework Theatre Co-op
PO Box 241
London N16 0LR   071 249 9158

Galleon Theatre Co
15 Bracewell Rd
London W10 6AE   081 969 2910

Gay Sweatshop
Holborn Centre for the Performing Arts
3 Cups Yard
Sandland St
London WC1R 4PZ   071 242 1168

Gazebo TIE Co
The Multipurpose Centre

Victoria Rd
Darlaston
W Midlands   021 526 6877

Good Co
46 Quebec St
Brighton
Sussex BN2 2UZ   0273 606652

Graeae Theatre Co
Interchange Studios
Dalby St
London NW5 3NQ   071 267 1959

Greasepaint Anonymous
4 Gallus Close
Winchmore Hill
London N21 1JR   081 886 2263

Greenwich & Lewisham Young People's Theatre
Burrage Rd
London SE18 7JZ   081 854 1316

Group 64 Youth Theatre
203B Upper Richmond Rd
London SW15 6SG   081 788 6943

Gwent TIE Co
The Drama Centre
Pen-y-Pound
Abergavenny
Gwent NP7 5UD   0873 853167

Half Moon Young People's Theatre
Dame Colet Hse
Ben Jonson Rd
London E1 3NH   071 265 8138

Heritage Theatre Co
Chester Visitor Centre
Vicars Lane
Chester CH1 1QZ   0978 823143

Humberside TIE
Humberside Cultural Enterprise Centre
Middleton St
Hull HU3 1NB   0482 24256

Inner City Theatre Co
The Print Hse
18 Ashwin St
London E8 3DL   071 249 1711

Interplay Theatre Co
Armley Ridge Rd
Leeds LS12 3LE   0532 638556

Intimate Mysteries Theatre Co
Charles Cryer Studio Theatre
39 High St
Carshalton SM5 3BB   081 770 4960

Isosceles Comedy Co
4B Grosvenor Hill
London SW19   081 946 3905

JCT Productions
22 Brookfield Mansion
Highgate West Hill
London N6 6AS   081 340 5430

Kaboodle Productions
The Unity Theatre
1 Hope Place
Liverpool L1 9BG   051 709 2818

Language Alive
Chandos J1 School
Vaughan St South
Birmingham B12 0YA   021 446 4301

Layston Productions
PO Box 64
Cirencester
Glos GLY 5YD   0285 644622

Leap Theatre Co
Leaveners Arts Base
8 Lennox Rd
London N4 3NW   071 272 5630

Live Theatre Co
7–8 Trinity Chase
Quayside
Newcastle-upon-Tyne NE1 3DF   0608 641208

London Bubble Theatre
5 Elephant Lane
London SE16 4JD   071 237 4434

London Gay Theatre Co
PO Box 778
London SW17 7HY

Lumiere and Son Theatre Co
36 Leander Rd
London SW2 2LH   081 674 7177

M6 Theatre Co
Hamer CP School
Albert Royds St
Rochdale OL16 2SU   0706 355898

Made in Wales Stage Co
Mount Stuart Hse
Mount Stuart Sq
Cardiff CF1 6DQ   0222 484017

Magic Carpet Theatre
18 Church St
Sutton-on-Hull
Hull HU7 4TS   0482 709939

Major Road Theatre Co
29 Queen's Rd
Bradford BD8 7BS   0274 480251

Masquerade Productions
Douglas Bldgs
Royal Stuart Lane
Butetown
Cardiff CF1 9BH   051 708 0877

Merseyside Young People's Theatre Co
5 Hope St
Liverpool L1 9BH   051 708 0877

Middle Ground Theatre Co
16 Hagley Rd
Halesowen
W. Midlands B63 4RG   021 501 3379

Midnight Theatre Co
103 Redston Rd
London N8 7HG   081 341 6607

Monstrous Regiment
Ground Floor
78 Luke St
London EC2A 4PY   071 613 0651

National Youth Theatre of Great Britain
443–445 Holloway Rd
London N7 6LW   071 281 3863

New Perspective Theatre Co
Mansfield Arts Centre
Leeming St
Mansfield
Notts NG18 1NG   0623 635225

Northern Black Light Theatre
The Black Light Base
Parish Rooms
Neville Terrace
York YO3 7NF   0904 651138

Northern Stage Education & Outreach
Newcastle Playhouse
Haymarket
Newcastle-upon-Tyne   091 232 3366

Northumberland Theatre Co
The Playhouse
Bondgate Without
Ainwick
Northumberland NE66 1PQ   0665 602586

Not the National Theatre
149 Eglinton Hill
London SE18 3DU   081 855 3258

Oily Cart Co
209 Welsbach Hse
The Business Village
Broomhill Rd
London SW19 4JQ   081 877 0743

Outrageous Fortune
77 Fairleigh Rd
London N16 7TD   071 241 1562

Oxfordshire Touring Theatre Co
Unit 1 John Fisher School
Sandy Lane West
Blackbird Leys
Oxford OX4 5LD   0865 778119

Paines Plough
Interchange Studios
Dalby St
London NW5 3NQ   071 284 4483

Pandemonium Theatre Co
Unit 13
Royal Stuart Workshops
Adelaide St
Cardiff CF1 6BR   0222 482821

Pascal Theatre Co
35 Flaxham Court
Flaxham Terrace
London WC1H 9AR   071 383 0920

Pentabus
The Old School
Bromfield
Ludlow
Shrops SY8 2JU   0584 77564

The People Show
St James The Great Institute
Pollard Row
London E2 6NB   071 729 1841

Pit Prop Theatre
Railway Rd
Leigh
Lancs WN7 4AF   0942 605258

Pocket Theatre
Morely St
Denton Holme
Carlisle
Cumbria CA2 5HQ   0228 512787

Praxis Theatre Co
24 Wykeham Rd
London NW4 2SU   081 202 9431

Prospectus
1 Mellor Rd
Leicester LE3 6HN   0533 857081

Proteus Theatre Co
Fairfields Arts Centre
Council Rd
Basingstoke RG21 3DH   0256 54541

Public Parts
108C Stokes Croft
Bristol BS1 3RU   0272 429608

Q20
Ivy Flea
Fyfe Lane
Baildon Shipley
W Yorks BD17 6DP   0274 591417

Quicksilver Theatre for Children
4 Enfield Rd
London N1 5AZ   071 241 2942

Red Ladder Theatre Co
Cobden Ave
Lower Wortley
Leeds LS12 5PB   0532 792228

Red Shift Theatre Co
Battersea Arts Centre
Lavender Hill
London SW11 5TF   071 223 3256

Regenerator Theatre Co
PO Box 3094
Chelmesley Wood
Birmingham B37 6PY   021 772 8667

Riding Lights Theatre Co
Marketing Hse
8 Bootham Terrace
York YO3 7DH   0904 655317

Royal Court Young People's Theatre
309 Portobello Rd
London W10 5TD   081 960 4641

Scarlet Theatre Co
Studio 8
Old Bull Arts Centre
68 High St
Barnet
Herts EN5 5SJ   081 441 9779

Scottish Youth Theatre
The Old Athenaeum
179 Buchanan St
Glasgow G1 2JZ

7:84 Theatre Co
2 Port Dundas Pl
Glasgow G2 3LB   041 331 2219

Shared Experience Theatre
The Soho Laundry
9 Dufous Pl
London W1V 1FE   071 434 9248

Sharers & Hirelings
48 Taybridge Rd
London SW11 5PT

Snap People's Theatre Trust
Unit A Caseway Business Centre
Bishops Stortford
Herts CM23 2UB   0279 504095

Sola Energy Theatre Co
31 Stirling St
London SW9 9EF   071 326 0221

Solent People's Theatre
Heathfield Centre
Valentine Ave
Sholing
Southampton SO2 8EQ   0703 443943

Spare Tyre
(Woman's Theatre)
West Greenwich Hse
141 Greenwich High Rd
London SE10 8JA   081 305 2800

Spectrum Nextage
Gordon Graig Theatre
Lytton Way
Stevenage
Herts SG1 1LZ   0438 766630

The Sphinx
(Women's Theatre Group)

Sadler's Wells
Roseberry Ave
London EC1R 4TN   071 713 0991

Spiral Theatre Co
148 Shirley Rd
Southampton SO1 3FP   0703 220485

Springboard Theatre Co
20 Lansdowne Rd
London N10 2AU   081 883 4586

Strolling Players
St Catherine's Drama Studio
26A Portsmouth Rd
Guildford GU2 5DH   0483 68788

Switch Theatre Co
13 Brundell Rd
London SW17 8DB   081 682 0423

Tag Theatre Co
Citizens Theatre
Gorbals
Glasgow G5 9DS   041 429 2877

Talawa Theatre Co
Cochrane Theatre
Southampton Row
London WC1B 4AP   071 404 5662

Tamasha Theatre Co
93 Mountview Rd
London N4 4JA   081 340 4330

Tara Arts Group
356 Garratt Lane
London SW18 4ES   081 871 1458

Theatr Powys
The Drama Centre
Tremont Rd
Llandrindod Wells
Powys LD1 5EB   0597 824444

Theatr Y Wern
Aberystwyth Arts Centre
Penglais Rd
Aberystwyth
Dyfed SY23 3DE   0970 623232

Theatre Centre Young People's Theatre Co
Hanover School
Noel Rd
London N1 8BD   071 354 0110

Theatre Factory
97 September Way
Stanmore
Middx HA7 2SF   081 954 1563

Theatre of Literature
9–15 Neal St
London WC2H 9TU   071 497 1741

Theatre Nova
1 School Rd
Padworth
Reading RG7 4JA   0734 832173

Theatre Set Up Ltd
12 Fairlawn Close
London N14 4JX   081 886 9572

Theatre Venture
Top Floor
Manor School

Richardson Rd
London E15 3BB   081 519 6678

Theatre West Glamorgan
Unit 3
Millands Rd
Industrial Estate
Neath
W. Glamorgan SA11 1NJ   0639 641771

Theatre Workshop
34 Hamilton Pl
Edinburgh EH3 5AX   031 225 7942

Tic Toc
Primrose Hill St
Coventry CV1 5LY   0203 632462

Tottering Bipeds Theatre Co
24 Newcourt
Lutton Terrace
Flask Walk
London NW3 1HD   071 794 2413

Traffic of the Stage
78B Mansfield Rd
London NW3 2HU   071 284 1171

Travelling Light Shakespeare Co
102 Plantation Rd
Amersham
Bucks HP6 6HW   0494 725186

Trestle Theatre
47–49 Wood St
Barnett
Herts EN5 4BS   081 441 0349

Triangle
5 Parrots Grove
Coventry CV2 1NQ   0203 362210

The Troupe
66 Hessel Rd
London W13 9ET   081 567 7042

Troy Theatre Co
14 Epirus Rd
London SW6 7UH   071 610 2570

Ubiquitous Theatre Co
Copyground Lane
High Wycombe
Bucks HP12 3HE   0494 520817

Umbrella Theatre
26 Lancaster Rd
Brighton BN1 5DG   0723 562090

Umoja Theatre Co
59 Bethwin Rd
London SE5 0XY   071 701 6396

Unity Theatre
6 Endsleigh St
London WC1H 0DX   071 388 1628

Vital Theatre
43 Regency Sq
Brighton BN1 2FJ   0273 727816

Wales Actors Co
2 Tai'r Fforest
Nelson Treharris
Mid Glamorgan CF46 9PP   0443 451084

Wigan Pier Actors Co
Wigan Pier
Lancs WN3 4EU   0942 323666

Winged Horse Touring Productions
The Old Athenaeum
179 Buchanan St
Glasgow G1 2JZ   021 440 4203

Women's Playhouse Trust
6 Langley St
London WC2H 9JA   071 379 9700

Yorick Theatre Co
International Theatre Ensemble
5E Pebody Buildings
Rodney Rd
London SE17 1BT   071 701 6385

Zenana Theatre Co
145 Clarence Rd
London E5 8EE   081 533 7657

Zip Theatre
Dunkley St
Wolverhampton WV1 4AN   0902 712251

NB: At the time of writing there is another round of cuts in arts funding under way, due to the lack of increase in the Arts Council grant and to rate-capping of local authorities. Many of the above companies rely wholly or partly on grants for their existence and may go out of business if these grants are withdrawn. It is always, therefore, worth ringing first before writing. If the telephone number is unobtainable it is likely the company may have become a victim of the cuts.

FRINGE AND CLUB THEATRE VENUES

Beck Theatre
Grange Rd
Hayes
Middx UB3 2UE   071 223 6557
Contact: Geraldine Collinge

Bedlam Theatre
2A Forrest Rd
Edinburgh EH1 2QN   031 225 9873

Bloomsbury Theatre
15 Gordon St
London WC1H 0AH   071 383 5976

Boulevard Theatre
Walker's Court
Off Brewer St
London W1   071 434 1238

Bridge Lane Theatre
Bridge Lane
London SW11 3AD   071 228 5185
Contact: Terry Adams

Cafe Theatre Covent Garden
45 Shelton St
London WC2H 9SB   071 240 0794

Camden Studio Theatre
Offstage Bookshop
37 Chalk Farm Rd
London NW1 8AJ   071 916 1334
Contact: John Harris

Canal Cafe Theatre
The Bridge Hse

Delamere Terrace
Little Venice
London W2 9NG   071 289 6054

Chelsea Centre Theatre
World's End Pl
King's Rd
London SW10 0DR   071 352 1967
Contact: Francis Alexander, David Micklay

Courtyard Theatre Club
10 York Way
London N1 9AA   071 833 0870
Contact: June Abbott

Doc Theatre
Duke of Cambridge
64 Lawford Rd
London NW5 2LN   071 485 4303
Contact: Tony James

Duke's Head Theatre
42 The Vineyard
Richmond
Surrey TW10 6AN   081 948 8085
Contact: David Gillies

Edinburgh Festival Fringe
180 High St
Edinburgh EH1 1QS   031 226 5257

Finborough Theatre Club
Finborough Arms
118 Finborough Rd
London SW10 9ED   071 244 7439
Contact: Mary Peate, Kathryn Horn

Freelance Theatre Co
Tabard Theatre
2 Bath Rd
London W4 1LN   081 747 8256

Gate Theatre
Prince Albert Pub
11 Pembridge Rd
London W11 3HQ   071 229 5387
Contact: Caroline Maude, Laurence Boswell

Grace Theatre
Latchmere
503 Battersea Park Rd
London SW11 3SW
Contact: Brian Croucher

Hen & Chickens Theatre
Hen & Chickens Theatre Bar
109 St Paul's Rd
London N1 2NA   071 704 2001

ICA Theatre
The Mall
London SW1Y 5AH   071 930 0493

Jackson's Lane Community Centre
269A Archway Rd
London N6 5AA   081 340 5226

La Bonne Crêpe Café Theatre
539 Battersea Park Rd
London SW11   071 228 5070
Contact: Paul Prescott

Latchmere Theatre
Battersea District Library
265 Lavender Hill

London SW11 1JB   071 223 3108
Contact: Chris Fisher

Link Theatre
Holborn Centre
Three Cups Yard
Sandland St
London WC1R 4PZ   071 405 2661

The Live Theatre
27 Broad Chare Quayside
Newcastle-upon-Tyne
NE1 3DQ   091 261 2694

Malthouse Theatre
Scotches Farmhouse
Malthouse Lane
Hassocks BN6 9JZ   0444 241047
Contact: Sandra Scriven

Man in the Moon Theatre Club
392 King's Rd
London SW3 5UZ   071 351 5701
Contact: Leigh Shine

Millfield Theatre
Silver St
London N18 1PJ   081 807 6186

The Netherbow
43–45 High St
Edinburgh EH1 1SR   031 556 9579
Contact: Donald Smith

New End Theatre
27 New End
London NW3 1JD   071 794 9963
Contact: Jon Harris

New Grove Theatre
Above Drummonds Cafe Bar
73–77 Euston Rd
London NW1 2QS   071 383 0925
Contact: Karen Gerald

Novello Theatre
2 High St
Sunninghill
Nr Ascot
Berks   0344 20881

Old Red Lion
418 St Johns St
London EC1   071 833 3053

Oval House Theatre Club
52–54 Kennington Oval
London SE11 5SW   071 582 0080

Pentameters
Three Horseshoes
28 Heath St
London NW3 6TE   071 435 3648

The Place Theatre
17 Duke's Rd
London WC1H 9AB   071 380 1268

Prince Regent Theatre
Prince Regent Hse
75 Guildford Rd East
Farnborough
Surrey GU14 6PX   0252 510859
Contact: Freddie Eldrett

Riverside Studios
Crisp Rd
London W6 9RL   081 741 2251

Rose Theatre
86 Fulham Rd
London SW3   071 225 2501

Soho Theatre Co
Cockpit Theatre
Gateforth St
London NW8 8EH   071 262 7907

South Hill Park Arts Centre
Bracknell
Berks RG12 7PA   0344 427272

South London Theatre Centre
(Bell Theatre & Prompt Corner)
2A Norwood High St
London SE27   081 670 3474

Stansted Park
The Little Theatre
Stansted Park
Rowlands Castle
Hants PO9 6DX   0705 412265

Theatre Space
(London Women's Centre)
Wesley Hse
4 Wild Court
London WC2B 5AU   071 831 6946

Theatro Technis
26 Crowndale Rd
London NW1 1TT   071 387 6617

Turrets Theatre
43 Friern Barnet Rd
London N11   081 292 7128

The Village Theatre
Production Village
110 Cricklewood Lane
London NW2   081 208 1746
Contact: Dee Hart

White Bear Theatre
138 Kennington Park Rd
London SE11 4DJ   071 493 9193

Wycombe Swan
St Mary St
High Wycombe
Bucks HP11 2XE   0494 514444

NB: This list is intended for those seeking venues for productions of their own as well as casting opportunities. A contact name has been given where possible.

There are many more venues in pubs and community centres throughout Great Britain.

A list of Arts Centres, for those looking purely for venues, is given next.

ARTS CENTRES

Aldershot 0252 21158

Andover 0264 365698   Contact: Sue Collins

Ayr 0292 281010   Contact: Edward Jackson

BAC Battersea 071 223 6557

Bampton Oxfordshire 0993 850137   Contact: Judith Warwick

Bangor 0248 351707   Contact: Dafydd Thomas

Bedhampton Havant 0705 480113   Contact: Paul Sadler

Billericay 0277 659286   Contact: Jean Taylor

Bingley 0274 566369   Contact: Ken Cusdin

Birmingham 021 440 4221   Contact: Geoff Sims

Bluith Wells 0982 553668   Contact: Julie Price

Bognor Regis 0243 865915   Contact: David Macgregor

Boston 0205 363108

Bracknell 0344 427272   Contact: Christine Bradwell

Bradford 0274 383185   Contact: Stuart Blackburn

Braintree 0376 552525 x2332   Contact: R. A. Dudman

Bridgwater 0278 422700   Contact: Nick Chapman

Brighton 0273 685447   Contact: Norma Binnie

Bristol 0272 299191   Contact: Ken Lush

Broadstairs 0843 869266   Contact: Ashley Backhouse

Bury Lancs 061 761 7107   Contact: Richard Haswell

Cannock 0543 466453   Contact: Richard Kay

Cardiff 0222 396061   Contact: Dave Clarke

Chesterfield 0246 208061   Contact: Sian Davies

Chipping Norton 0608 642349   Contact: Alison Coates

Christchurch 0202 479819   Contact: Suzette Sulley

Cirencester 0285 657181   Contact: Dan Scrivener

Colchester 0206 577301   Contact: Anthony Roberts

Coventry 0203 523734   Contact: Jodi Myers

Cumbernauld 0236 737235   Contact: Denis Clifford

Darlington 0325 483271

Dorchester 0304 266926   Contact: Ruth Harris

Dorset 0258 456533   Contact: Kate Sebag-Montefiore

Dundee 0382 201035   Contact: George Docherty

Edinburgh 031 2257942   Contact: Alan Tweedie

Epsom 0373 742226   Contact: Jan Clemitson

Evesham 0836 48883   Contact: Lauri Griffith-Jones

Exeter 0392 219741   Contact: John C. Struthers

Fareham 0329 235161   Contact: Steve Rowley

Frome 0373 461360   Contact: Simon Jutton

Gainsborough 0427 810298   Contact: David Popple

Glasgow 041 221 4526   Contact: George Cherrie

Great Torrington, Devon 0805 22552   Contact: Bob Butler

Harlech 0766 780667   Contact: Valerie Wynne-Williams

Harlow 0279 424391   Contact: Gordon Hewlett

Havant 0705 480113   Contact: Paul Sadler

Hemel Hempstead 0442 241789   Contact: Jackie Alexander

Hexham 0434 606787   Contact: Peter Cutchie

Horsham 0403 259708   Contact: Kevin Parker

Huddersfield 0484 513808   Contact: Brian Pearson

Inverness 0463 239841   Contact: Catherine Robins

Kendal 0539 725133   Contact: Anne Pierson

King's Lynn 0553 774725   Contact: Irene Macdonald

Leicester 0533 555627   Contact: Richard Haswell

Leighton Buzzard 0525 850290   Contact: Stuart Antrobus

Lichfield 0543 262233   Contact: Brian Pretty

Liverpool 051 708 8877   Contact: Chris Layhe

Llantwit Major, South Glamorgan 0446 792151   Contact: Dave
  Ambrose

London
  Chats Palace 081 986 6714   Contact: Michelle Gregory
  Drill Hall 071 631 1353   Contact: Julie Parker
  Hoxton Hall 071 739 5431   Contact: Chris Bowler
  Leaveners Arts Base 071 272 5630
  Oval House 071 582 0080   Contact: Mel Steel
  Tom Allen Centre 081 555 7289

Maidstone 0622 753922   Contact: Stephen Young

Manchester
  Forum 061 437 8211
  Green Room 061 236 1676   Contact: Bush Hartshorn

Mansfield 0623 653309

Milford Haven 0646 694192   Contact: Mike James

Newport (Isle of Wight) 0983 528825   Contact: Maggie Cook

Norwich 0603 660352   Contact: Pam Reekie

Nuneaton 0203 327359   Contact: Pat Mitchell

Oldham 061 624 5214 x2000

Plymouth 0752 660060   Contact: Bernard Samuels

Poole 0202 670521   Contact: Anthony Covell

Rotherham 0709 823641   Contact: Jeremy Blundell

Salisbury 0722 321744

Sheffield 0742 754500

Shrewsbury 0743 366993/355137   Contact: David Carter

Southport 0704 540004

Stafford 0785 53595   Contact: Nick Mowatt

Stamford 0708 63203   Contact: Celiba Frisby

Stevenage 0438 766642   Contact: R. W. Bustance

Stirling 0876 467155   Contact: Elizabeth Moran

Stockton-on-Tees 0642 611625   Contact: Frank Wilson

Swansea 0792 295438   Contact: Sybil Crouch

Swindon 0739 535534   Contact: Alan Lord

Tamworth 0827 53092   Contact: Fennah Davies

Taunton 0823 274608   Contact: Richard Bond

Totnes 0803 865864   Contact: Paul Goddard

Uley (Glos) 0453 860703   Contact: Elizabeth Swift

Ulverston 0229 582299   Contact: Denis McGeary

Wakefield 0924 810299   Contact: Clare Manning

Wallsend 091 262 4276   Contact: Mike Campbell

Washington 091 416 6440

Winchester 0962 867986   Contact: John Tellet

Windsor 0753 859421   Contact: Jenny Joyce

Wisbech 0945 585587   Contact: Ida Jones

Wolverhampton 0902 20109   Contact: C. J. Antonio

Wrexham 0978 261932

York 0904 642582   Contact: Geoffrey Mogridge

Casting Directors

Ailion Cotton Casting Associates
44 Hopton Rd
London SW16 2EN   081 769 2468
(Irene Cotton, Pippa Ailion)

Dorothy Andrew Casting
(Brookside)
Campus Manor
Childwall Abbey Rd
Childwall
Liverpool L16 0JP   051 722 9122

Keith Andrews
105 Cedar Terrace
Richmond
Surrey TW9 2JE

Jane Arnell
Flat 2
39 St Peter's Square
London W6 9NN

Tony Arnell
93 Fowlers Walk
London W5 1BQ

James Bain
Granada Television
TV Centre
Manchester M60 9EA   061 832 7211

Penny Barbour
Rosemary Cottage
Fonfridge Lane
Etchingham
E. Sussex TN19 7DD   0580 81306

Derek Barnes
26 Danbury St
London N1

Michael Barnes Casting
Suite 201
Golden Hse
29 Gt Pulteney St
London W1R 3DD   071 439 9716

Carolyn Bartlett
(Head of Casting)
Granada TV
36 Golden Square
London W1R 4AH   071 734 8080

Maureen Bewick
104a Dartmouth Rd
London NW2 4HB

Boulting Casting Associates
Twickenham Film Studios
The Barons
St Margarets
Middx TW1 2AW   081 892 4477
(Lucy Boulting)

Siobhan Bracke
Garden Flat
12 Cambridge Park
E. Twickenham TW1 2PF

Broadcasting
31C St Lukes Mews
London W11 1DS   071 229 8500

Susie Bruffin
c/o Cinema Verity
The Old Mill
Millers Way
1A Shepherd's Bush Road
London W6 7NA   081 740 9895

Malcolm Bullivant
9 Montrose Villas
Hammersmith Terrace
London W6 9TT   081 748 4146

Linda Butcher
39 Arlington Rd
Surbiton
Surrey KT6 6BW   081 390 9777

Sandie Bycroft
16 Mazenod Ave
London NW6 4LR

Angela Caird
Bracken Croft
Fern Way
Scarcroft
Leeds LS14 3JJ   0532 893231

Laura Cairns
Flat 2

7 Streathbourne Rd
London SW17 8QZ

Candid Casting
4 Samuels Court
South Bank
Lion Lane
London W6 9LT   081 748 0526

Cannon Dudley Associates
Top Floor
33 Cumberland Pl
London W1H 7LF
(Carol Dudley, Elaine Fallon)

Di Carling
52 Wardour St
London W1V 3HL   071 437 0841

Maggie Cartier
26 Lowther Rd
London SW13 9ND   081 748 1475

The Casting Company
9 Newburgh St
London W1V 1LH   071 734 4954
(Michelle Guish, Sarah Bird, Sarah Beardsall)

The Casting Directors
24 Cloncurry St
London SW6 6DS   071 731 5988
(Gillian Hawser, Caroline Hutchings, Kate Plantin)

The Casting House
9 Clifden Rd
Brentford
Middx TW8 0PB   081 995 3934
(Angela Grosvenor, Brian Wheeler)

Alison Chard (Head of Casting)
Deputy Head: Audrey Helps
RSC Barbican Theatre
Barbican Centre
London EC2Y 8BQ   071 628 3351

Charkham Casting
122 Wardour St
London W1V 3LA   071 734 0202
(Beth Charkham)

Chiltern Casting
2a Euston Rd
West Derby
Liverpool L12 7JJ   051 254 1686
(Collette Chiltern)

Leonie Cosman
14 Druid Stoke Ave
Stoke Bishop
Bristol BS9 1DD

Abi Cohen
Flat C
128a Fortress Rd
London NW6 2HP   071 284 2587

Linda Craig
Theatre Royal
Thames St
Windsor
Berks SL4 1PS   0753 863444

Margaret Crawford
81 Castelnau
London SW13 9RT   081 748 8929

Crowley Poole Casting
14 Goodwin's Court
London WC2N 4LL   071 379 5965
(Suzanne Crowley, Gilly Poole)

Mary Curran
RTE
Dublin   010 3531 64311

Roger Davidson
53 Park Rd
Hampton Wick
Surrey KT1 4AS

Jane Davies
c/o Noel Gay Television
6th Floor
76 Oxford St
London W1N 0AT   071 836 3941

Davis & Zimmermann Casting
31 King's Rd
London SW3 4RP   071 730 9421
(Noel Davis, Jeremy Zimmermann)

Paul de Freitas
2 Conduit St
London W1R 9TG   071 434 4233

Jane Deitch
BBC Sulgrave Hse
1 Woodger Rd
London W12   081 576 1906

Lesley de Pettit
2 Park View
Hatfield
Herts AL9 5HG   07072 64301

Malcolm Drury
c/o Cinema Verity
The Old Mill
Millers Way
1A Shepherd's Bush Rd
London W6 7NA   081 876 5686

Irene East Casting
40 Brookwood Ave
London SW13 0LR   081 876 5686

Denise Elder
56 Plympton Rd
London NW6 7EQ   071 326 2835

Liz England
86–88 Wardour St
London W1V 3LF   071 494 0728

Richard Evans
10 Shirley Rd
London W4 1DD   081 994 6304

Ann Fielden
52 Wardour St
London W1V 3HL   071 434 1331

Cornelia Fielden
Film Production
121–124 Rotherhithe St
London SE16 4NF   071 231 7251

Susie Figgis
46 Old Compton St
London W1V 5PB   071 287 9406

Bernice (Bunny) Fildes Casting
56 Wigmore St
London W1   071 935 1254

Nikki Finch (& Janie Fraser)
LWT
South Bank Television Centre
Upper Ground
London SE1 9LT   071 261 3338

Sally Fincher
Central Television
35–38 Portman Sq
London W1H 9AH   071 486 6688

Margaret Fisher
Wolsey Theatre
Civic Dr
Ipswich
Suffolk IP1 2AS   0473 218911

Alan Foenander
59 North Eyot Gdns
London W6 9NL   081 748 9641

Fothergill-Lunn Casting
18–21 Jermyn St
London SW1Y 6HP   071 287 6562
(Janey Fothergill, Maggie Lunn)

Celestia Fox
5 Clapham Common Northside
London SW4 0QW   071 720 6143

Jane Frisby
51 Ridge Rd
Crouch End
London N8 9LJ   081 341 4747

Caroline Funnell
25 Rattray Rd
London SW2 1AZ   071 326 4417

Joyce Gallie
37 Westcroft Sq
London W6 0TA   081 741 4009

GB Casting
1 Charlotte St
London W1   071 636 2437
(Karen Grainger)

Nina Gold
1st Floor
36 Notting Hill Gate
London W11 3HX   071 229 3990

Lesley Grayburn
74 Leigh Gdns
London NW10 5HP   081 969 6112

Marcia Gresham
12 Sherbrooke Rd
London SW6 7HU   071 381 2876

Judi Hayfield
Granada Television
TV Centre
Manchester M60 9EA   061 832 7211

Howard Harrison
Cameron Mackintosh
1 Bedford Sq
London WC1B 3RA   071 637 8866

Pat Hayley
58 Sheaf Way
Sandy Lane
Teddington
Middx TW11 0DQ   081 977 3036

Anne Henderson Casting
93 Kelvin Rd
London N2 2PL   071 354 3786

Serena Hill
National Theatre
Upper Ground
South Bank
London SE1 9PX   071 928 2033

Howard & Day Casting
37 Wharton St
London WC1 0PG   071 837 2978

Howard Field Associates
27 Neal St
London WC2H 9PR   071 240 0388

Rebecca Howard
37 Wharton St
London WC1X 9PG   071 837 2978

Hubbard Casting
6 Noel St
London W1V 3RB   071 494 3191
(John Hubbard, Ros Hubbard)

Sally Hughes
The Mill at Sonning
Sonning Eye
Reading RC4 0TW   0734 696039

Sarah Hughes
Stephen Joseph Theatre
Valley Bridge Parade
Scarborough
North Yorks YO11 2PL   0722 320117

Simone Ireland
32 Mornington Crescent
London NW1 7RE   071 383 7184

Sue Jackson
Yorkshire Television
TV Centre
Leeds LS3 1JS   0532 438283

Jennifer Jaffrey
136 Hicks Ave
Greenford
Middx UB6 8HB   081 578 2899

Pat Jarvis
120 Lancaster Court
London SW6 5TH   071 736 4051

Priscilla John
c/o Cinema Verity
The Old Mill
Millers Way
1A Shepherd's Bush Rd
London W6 7NA   081 743 8011

Marilyn Johnson
The Basement
115 Chesterton Rd
London W10 6ET   081 969 7128

Doreen Jones
c/o Cinema Verity
The Old Mill
Millers Way
1A Shepherd's Bush Rd
London W6 7NA   081 743 8011

Just Casting
128 Talbot Rd
London W11 1JA   071 229 3471
(Ms Leo Davis)

Kate Kagan
152 Campden Hill Rd
London W8   071 221 2009

Beverley Keogh
19 Old Broadway
Didsbury
Manchester M20   061 448 1524

Ivor Kimmel Casting
19 Premier Corner
London W9 3EG   081 964 2265

Amanda Kimpton
BBC
Sulgrave Hse
1 Woodger Rd
London W12   081 576 1906

Suzy Korel
20 Blenheim Rd
London NW8 0LX   071 624 6435

Leslie Lawton
Ray Cooney Productions
Shaftesbury Theatre
210 Shaftesbury Ave
London WC2H 8DP   071 379 3345

Jane L'Epine Smith
2 Chertsey Rd
St Margarets
Twickenham TW1 1JQ   081 891 1685

Sharon Levinson
30 Stratford Villas
London NW1 9SG   071 485 2057

Karen Lindsay-Stewart
27 Neal St
London WC2H 9PR   071 240 0388

Julia Lisney
501A Battersea Park Rd
London SW11 4LN   071 223 0293

Judy Loe
c/o BBC
Television Centre
Wood Lane
London W12 7RJ   081 743 8000

Joan McCann
3 Tyers Gate
London SE1 3HX   071 407 6004

Dorothy MacGabhann
2 O'Tranto Place
Sandycove Co
Dublin   010 3531 2807242

Geraldine McKeown
52 Dumbarton Rd
London SW2 5LU   081 671 0834

Sophie Marshall
Royal Exchange Theatre
St Anne's Sq
Manchester M2   061 833 9333

Jacqui Morris
20 Greek St
London W1V 5LF   071 437 9245

Sue Needleman
122 Wardour St
London W1V 3LA   071 287 5494

Joyce Nettles
16 Cressida Rd
London N19   071 263 0630

Pat O'Connell
86 King Edward's Grove
Teddington
Middx TW11 9LX   081 943 9749

Pam O'Connor
26 Millgreen Rd
Welwyn Garden City
Herts AL7 3XF   0707 336773

Sally Osoba
42 Dordrecht Rd
London W3 7TF

Jill Pearce
1st Floor
6 Langley St
London WC2H 9JL   071 240 0316

Stephanie Penall
Leicester Haymarket
Belgrave Gate
Leicester LE1 3YG   0533 530021

Patsy Pollock
21 First Ave
London SW14

Simone Reynolds
60 Hebdon Rd
London SW17 7NN   081 672 5443

Corinne Rodriguez
11 Lytton Ave
London N13 4EH

Maggi Sangwin
51 Ormiston Grove
London W12 0JP   081 740 9939

Laura Scott
The Basement
115 Chesterton Rd
London W10 6ET   081 969 7128

Mary Selway
Twickenham Studios
St Margaret's
Twickenham
Middx TW1 2AW   081 892 4477

Philip Shaw (in association with Allan Foenander)
29 Marden Gdns
Mitcham
Surrey CR4 4DH   081 715 8943

Rose Tobias Shaw
219 Liverpool Rd
London N1 1LX   071 609 9028

Hazel Singer
1 Newcastle Hse
Luxborough St
London W1M 3LF   071 935 9049

Michelle Smith
34 Willow Way
Didsbury
Manchester M20 0JS   061 445 9613

Suzanne Smith
138 Haverstock Hill
London NW3 2AY   071 722 2085

Stern & Parriss Casting
2nd Floor
91 Regent St
London W1R 7TB   071 734 5053
(Paddy Stern & Susie Parriss)

Gail Stevens Casting
7 Garrick St
London WC2E 9AR   071 379 3877

Liz Stoll
24 Corinne Rd
London N19 5ET   071 700 0724

Emma Style
Flat 7
115 Finchley Rd
London NW3 6HY   071 586 4946

Michael Syers
Garden Studios
11–13 Betterton St
London WC2 9PB   071 379 0344

Shirley Teece
106 North View Rd
London N8 7LP   081 347 9241

Gill Titmarsh
75 Thornton Ave
London W4 1QF   081 994 8173

Tessa Topolski
25 Clifton Hill
London NW8 8JY   071 328 6393

Sheila Trezise
25 Cavendish Mansions
Mill Lane
London NW6   071 435 8577

Kate Triscott
Duncan Wheldon Productions
Suite 4
Waldorf Chambers
11 Aldwych
London WC2B 4DA   071 836 0186

Alice Troughton
Man In The Moon Theatre
392 King's Rd
London SW3 5UZ   071 351 5701

Van Ost & Millington Casting
10 St Martin's Court
London WC2N 4AJ
(Valerie Van Ost, Andrew Millington)

Sally Vaughan
Churchill Theatre
High St
Bromley
Kent BR1 1HA   081 464 7131

Liz Vincent Fernie
2 Redway
Kerridge
Cheshire SK10 5BA

Lucille Wagner
Bill Kenwright Ltd
55–59 Shaftesbury Ave
London W1V 7AA

Sue Whatmough
26 Redfern
58 Ewell Rd
Surbiton
Surrey KT6 6JD   081 390 6225

Mela White & Lorna Cotton
29 Talbot Rd
Twickenham
Middx TW2 6SJ   081 894 3505

NB: Casting directors who do not have offices usually work from the offices of the production company. Letters can be sent to home addresses, but telephone numbers have not been given for casting directors who do not wish to be called at home.

Agents

Cooperative agencies (see text) are not included in this list. Asterisks denote membership of PMA (Personal Managers' Association).

A & B Personal Management*
5th Floor Plaza Suite
114 Jermyn St
London SW1Y 6HJ   071 839 4433

A.D.A.
346A Richmond Rd
E. Twickenham
Middx TW1 2DU   081 892 1716

AIM*
5 Denmark St
London WC2H 8LP

A&J Management
551 Green Lanes
London N13 4DR   081 882 7716

A M Artists
63C Randolph Avee
London W9 1BG   071 286 4852

Abacus Agency
31 Chesfield Rd

Kingston-upon-Thames
Surrey KT2 5TH   081 546 3463

Marjorie Abel
50 Maddox St
London W1R 9PA   071 499 1343

Act One Agency
Business Village
Broomhill Rd
London SW18 4JQ   081 871 5158

Acting Associates
Tempo House
15 Falcon Hse
London SW11 2PJ   071 924 3728

The Actors File
Sadler's Wells
Roseberry Ave
London EC1R 4TN   071 278 5927

Alander Agency
135 Merrion Ave
Stanmore
Middx HA7 4RZ   081 954 7685

Alexander Personal Management
16 Roughdown Ave
Hemel Hempstead
Herts HP3 9BN

Allsorts Casting
1 Cathedral St
London SE1 9DE   071 403 4834

Jonathan Altaras Associates
2 Goodwins Court
London WC2N 4LL   071 497 8878

Alvarez Management
86 Muswell Rd
London N10 2BE   081 883 2206

Amor Reeves Management
80 Crawthew Grove
London SE22 9AB   081 693 7733

Angel Star Theatrical Employment Agency
5 Lancaster Rd
London E11   081 539 7740

Susan Angel Associates*
12 D'Arblay St
London W1V 3FP   071 439 3086

Mary Arnold Management
12 Cambridge Park
East Twickenham
Middx TW1 2PF   081 892 4860

Artsworld International Management
Studio 101 Canalot
222 Kensal Rd
London W10 5BN   081 964 4434

BBP Ltd
36 Cambridge Rd
E Twickenham TW1 2HL   081 891 6366

BCC Ltd
144 Wigmore St
London W1H 9FF   071 486 1222

BR Management
7 Stonehill Mansions
8 Streatham High Rd
London SW16 1DD   081 677 9865

Paul Bailey Agency
22 Wolsey Rd
East Molesey
Surrey KT8 9EL   081 941 2034

Andrew Bancroft Associates
48 Mortimer St
London W1N 7DG   071 580 5839

Julian Belfrage
68 St James's St
London SW1A 1PH   071 491 4400

Audrey Benjamin Agency
51 Westbourne Terrace
London W2 3UY   071 402 3265

Blackburn Sachs Associates
37 Barnes High St
London SW13 9LN   081 878 3077

Rebecca Blond Associates
52 Shaftesbury Ave
London W1V 7DE   071 434 2010

Sheila Bourne Management
Greenwich Business Centre
49 Greenwich High Rd
London SE10 8JL   081 469 2726

Michelle Braidman Associates
3rd Floor Suite
10 Lower John St
London W1R 3PE   071 437 0817

Dolly Brook Agency
52 Sandford Rd
London E6 3QS   081 472 2561

Barry Brown & Partners
47 West Sq
Southwark
London SE11 4SP   071 928 1229

Joan Brown Associates
3 Earl Rd
London SW14 7JH   081 876 9448

Peter Browne Management
Pebro Hse
13 St Martin's Rd
London SW9 0SP   071 737 3444

Brunskill Management
Suite 8A
169 Queen's Gate
London SW7 5HE   071 581 3388

Richard Bucknall Management
Garden Studios
11–15 Betterton St
London WC2H 9BP   071 379 0344

Barry Burnett Organisation Ltd
Suite 24
Grafton Hse
2 Golden Sq
London W1   071 437 7048

The Business
86 York St
London W1   071 723 9009

CCA Management
4 Court Lodge
48 Sloane Sq
London SW1W 8AT   071 730 8857

CSM (Artistes)
49 Churchfield Rd
London W3 6AY   081 992 8668

Campbell Hinton Management
26 Delaware Mansions
Delaware Rd
London W9 2LH   071 266 3299

Roger Carey Associates
64 Thornton Ave
London W4 1QQ   081 995 4477

The Central Agency
112 Gunnersbury Ave
London W5 4HB   081 993 7441

Peter Charlesworth Ltd
68 Old Brompton Rd
London SW7 3LQ   071 581 2478

Chatto & Linnit Ltd
Prince of Wales Theatre
Coventry St
London W1V 7FE   071 930 6677

Elspeth Cochrane Agency
11–13 Orlando Rd
London SW4 0LE   071 622 0314

Shane Collins Associates
24 Wardour St
London W1V 3HD   071 439 1976

Collis Management
182 Trevelyan Rd
London SW17 9LW   081 767 0196

Conway Van Gelder Ltd
3rd Floor
18–21 Jermyn St
London SW1Y 6HP   071 287 0077

Jeremy Conway
109 Jermyn Street
London SW19 6HB   071 839 2121

Vernon Conway Ltd
5 Spring St
London W2 3RA   071 262 5506

Heidi Cook Personal Management
12A Vauxhall Bridge Rd
London SW1V 2SD   071 828 8185

Clive Corner Associates
PO Box 56
Hampton
Middx TW12 2XE   081 941 8653

Lou Coulson*
1st Floor
37 Berwick St
London W1   071 734 9633

Crawford Associates
2 Conduit St
London W1R 9TG   071 629 6464

Creative Talent Management
93 Hereford Rd
London W2 5BB   071 792 3411

Crouch Associates
9–15 Neal St
London WC2H 9PF   071 379 1684

Dacs Personal Management
14 Rusthall Ave
London W4 1BP   081 995 1995

DAS Theatrical Agency Ltd
31 Carnaby St
London W1V 1PQ   071 734 3121

Daly Gagan Associates
68 Old Brompton Rd
London SW7 3LQ   071 581 0121

Larry Dalzell Associates Ltd
Suite 12
17 Broad Ct
London WC2B 5QN   071 379 0875

The David Agency
153 Battersea Rise
London SW11 1HP   071 223 7720

Caroline Dawson Associates*
Apt 9
47 Courtfield Rd
London SW7 4DB   071 370 0708

Dee Hindin Associates
44 Royal Crescent
Holland Park Ave
London W11 4SN   071 603 3129

Felix de Wolfe
Manfield Hse
376 The Strand
London WC2 0LR   071 379 5767

Bryan Drew Ltd
Mezzanine
Quadrant Hse

80–82 Regent St
London W1R 6AU   071 437 2293

Paul du Fer Associates
12 Alfred Rd
London W3 9LH   081 896 0393

Evan Dunstan Associates
1B Montague Mews North
London W1   071 486 3479

Susi Earnshaw Management
5 Brook Place
Barnett
Herts EN5 2DL   081 441 5010

Joyce Edwards
275 Kennington Rd
London SE11 6BY   071 735 5736

Ellison Combe Associates
Rosedale Hse
Rosedale Rd
Richmond
Surrey TW9 2SZ   081 940 7863

Emanco Management
9 Gt Russell St
London WC1B 3NH   071 323 0821

Doreen English Agency
30 Sandal Court
Sandal Rd
New Malden
Surrey KT3 5AP   081 942 7515

June Epstein Associates
Flat 1

62 Compayne Gdns
London NW6 3RY   071 328 0864

Essanay Ltd
2 Conduit St
London W1R 9TG   071 409 3526

Jacque Evans Management
11A St Johns Wood High St
London NW8 7NG   071 722 4700

Evans & Reiss
221 New Kings Rd
London SW6 4XE   071 384 1843

Kate Feast Management
43A Princess Rd
London NW1 8JS   071 586 5502

Sheridan Fitzgerald Management
69B Credon Rd
London E13 9BS   081 471 9814

Fletcher & Boyce
1 Kingsway Hse
Albion Rd
London N16 0TA   071 923 0606

Focus Management
179 Lichfield Ct
Sheen Rd
Richmond
Surrey TW9 1AZ   081 332 6701

Frazer-Skemp Management
34 Bramerton St
London SW3 5LA   071 352 2922

G.M.M.
Canonbury Hse
Canonbury Sq
London N1 2NQ   071 359 8152

Kerry Gardner Management
15 Kensington High St
London W8 5NP   071 937 4478

Garricks
7 Garrick St
London WC2E 9AR   071 240 0660

Noel Gay Artists
6th Floor
76 Oxford St
London W1N 0AT   071 836 3941

David Graham Management
7 Teddington Business Park
Station Rd
Teddington
Middx TW11 9BQ   081 977 8707

Joan Gray Personal Management
29 Sunbury Court Island
Sunbury-on-Thames
Middx TW16 5PP   0932 783544

Green & Underwood
2 Conduit St
London W1R 9TG   071 493 0308

Stella Greenfield Agency
41 Bush Grove
Stanmore
Middx HA7 2DY   081 952 1805

Sandra Griffin Management
6 Ryde Place
Richmond Rd
E Twickenham
Middx TW1 2EH   081 891 5676

Group 3 Associates
79 Hornsey Rd
London N7 6DJ   071 609 9862

J. Gurnett Personal Management
2 New Kings Rd
London SW6 4SA   071 736 7828

HCA
Apt 1
20 Courtfield Gdns
London SW5 0PD   071 835 0136

Hamilton & Sydney
21 Goodge St
London W1P 1FD   071 323 1162

Lorraine Hamilton
19 Denmark St
London WC2H 8NA   071 836 3941

Hamper-Neafsey Management
4 Great Queen St
London WC2B 5DG   071 404 5255

Barry Hannah Management
The Steeles
97 Haverstock Hill
London NW3 4RL   071 483 3872

Harbour & Coffey
9 Blenheim St

New Bond St
London W1Y 9LE   071 499 5548

Stephen Hatton Management*
The Basement
142A New North Rd
London N1 7BH   071 359 3593

George Heathcote Management
10 St Martin's Court
London WC2N 4AJ   071 379 1081

Louise Hillman Associates
33 Brookfield
Highgate West Hill
London N6 6AT   081 341 2207

Hill-Urwin
48C Hutton Grove
London N12 8DT   081 343 7929

Hobsons Personal Management
Burlington Hse
64 Chiswick High Rd
London W4 1SY   081 747 8474

Hope & Lyne*
108 Leonard St
London EC2A 4RH   071 739 6200

Howes & Prior Ltd
66 Berkeley Hse
Hay Hill
London W1X 7LH   071 493 7570

Trudy Howson
67 Kynaston Rd
London N16 0EB   071 241 1996

Bernard Hunter Associates
13 Spencer Gdns
London SW14 7AH   081 878 6308

Hutton Management
200 Fulham Rd
London SW10 9PN   071 352 4825

ICM*
76 Oxford St
London W1R 1RB   071 636 6565

IMA Group
2 Hinde St
London W1M 5RH   071 486 3312

Independent Management Ltd
Panther Hse
38 Mount Pleasant
London WC1X 0AP   071 837 9460

International Artistes
Mezzanine Floor
235 Regent St
London W1R 8AX   071 439 8401

JB Agency
7 Stonehill Mansions
8 Streatham High Rd
London SW6 1DD   081 677 5151

J.G.M.
15 Lexham Mews
London W8 6JW   071 376 2414

JLM*
242 Acton Lane
London W4 5DL   081 747 8223

JM Associates
77 Beak St
London W1R 3LF   071 434 0602

JRA Agencies
103 Charing Cross Rd
London WC2H 0DT   071 439 8245

Richard Jackson Personal Management
59 Knightsbridge
London SW1X 7RA   071 235 3671

Carole James Management
2 Water Lane Hse
Water Lane
Richmond
Surrey TW9 1TJ   081 940 8154

Susan James Management
22 Westbere Rd
London NW2 3SR   071 794 8545

Joy Jameson Ltd
2.19 The Plaza
535 Kings Rd
London SW10 0SZ   071 351 3971

Jeffrey & White Management
5 Richmond Mews
London W1V 5AG   071 439 7876

Joseph & Wagg
Studio One
2 Tunstall Rd
London SW9 8BN   081 738 3026

Chuck Julian Associates
Suite 51

26 Charing Cross Rd
London WC2H 0DH   071 437 4248

Roberta Kanal Agency
82 Constance Rd
Twickenham
Middx TW2 7JA   081 892 2277

Kean & Garrick
Rayleigh Hse
2 Richmond Hill
Richmond
Surrey TW10 6QX   081 940 5559

Charlotte Kelly
9 Calabria Rd
London N5 1JB   071 359 3531

Ivor Kimmel
16 Premier Hse
Premier Corner
London W9 3EG   081 964 2265

Adrian King Associates
100 Fellows Rd
London NW3 3JG   071 722 1149

Knight Ayton Management
70A Berwick St
London W1V 3PE   071 287 4405

Rolf Kruger Management
121 Gloucester Place
London W1H 3PJ   071 224 4493

LWA
52 Wardour St
London W1V 3HL   071 434 3944

Michael Ladkin Personal Management
11 Southwick Mews
London W2 1JG   071 402 6644

Langford Associates
Garden Studios
11 Betterton St
London WC2H 9PB   071 379 7216

Tessa Le Bars Management*
18 Queen Anne St
London W1M 9LB   071 636 3191

Jane Lehrer Associates
26 Danbury St
London N1 8JU   071 226 2404

Leigh Management
14 St David's Drive
Edgware
Middx HA8 6JH   081 951 4449

Brian Lidstone
138 Westbourne Grove
London W11 2RR   071 727 2342

London Management
2–4 Noel St
London W1V 3RB   071 287 9000

Robert Luff Ltd
294 Earls Court Rd
London SW5 9BB   071 373 7003

McAllister & Co
Swan Centre
Fishers Lane
London W4 1RX   081 995 0900

Rae McIntosh Management*
Thornton Hse
Thornton Rd
London SW19 4NG   081 944 6688

McKenna & Grantham
1B Montague Mews North
London W1H 1AJ   071 224 4434

Bill McLean Management
23b Deodar Rd
London SW15 2NP   081 789 8191

McNaughton Lowe Representation
200 Fulham Rd
London SW10 9PN   071 351 5442

Ken McReddie
91 Regent St
London W1R 7TB   071 439 1456

Mahoney Gretton Associates
Suite 105
Southbank Hse
Black Prince Rd
London SE1 7SJ   071 587 1463

Hazel Malone Associates
26 Wellesley Rd
London W4 4BW   081 994 1619

Andrew Manson Personal Management
288 Munster Rd
London SW6 6BQ   071 386 9158

Markham & Froggatt Ltd
4 Windmill St
London W1P 1HF   071 636 4412

John Markham Associates
6 Dale Park Rd
London SE19 3TY   081 653 4994

Marmont Management
Langham Hse
308 Regent St
London W1R 5AL   071 637 3183

Billy Marsh Associates
19 Denmark St
London WC2H 8NA   071 379 4004

Ronnie Marshall Agency
66 Ollerton Rd
London N11 2LA   081 368 4958

Scott Marshall
44 Perryn Rd
London W3 7NA   081 749 7692

Martin Ashman Associates
6A Danbury St
London N1 8JU   071 359 3646

Carol Martin Personal Management
19 Highgate West Hill
London N6 6NP   081 348 0847

Mayer Management
Suite 44
Grafton Hse
2 Golden Sq
London W1R 3AD   071 434 1242

Milner Management
36 Lewisham Park Rd
London SE13 6GZ   081 244 4059

Montagu Associates
3 Bretton Hse
Fairbridge Rd
London N19 3HP   071 281 4658

Morgan & Goodman*
1 Old Compton St
London W1V 5PH   071 437 1383

William Morris*
31–32 Soho Sq
London W1V 5DG   071 434 2191

Muirsmith & Easton
484 Kings Rd
London SW10 0LF   071 352 1470

Elaine Murphy Associates
1 Aberdeen Lane
London N2 2EJ   071 704 9913

Narrow Road Company
22 Poland St
London W1V 3DD   071 434 0406

Toni Nelson Associates
42 Berrymead Gdns
London W3 8AB   081 993 2078

Nevs Agency
36 Walpole St
London SW3 4QS   071 730 0615

Jackie Nicholson Associates
Avon Hse
4th Floor
360 Oxford St
London W1N 9HA   071 493 1899

1984 Personal Management
54 Peartree St
London EC1V 3SB   071 251 8046

Dee O'Reilly Management
112 Gunnersbury Ave
London W5 4HB   081 993 7441

PBAM
11 Campden Hill Mansions
Edge St
London W8 7PL   071 243 2594

PBJ Management
47 Dean St
London W1V 5HL   071 434 0672

Lorraine Page Management
18 Hampton Rd
Twickenham
Middx TW2 5QB   081 898 7100

Al Parker Ltd
55 Park Lane
London W1Y 3DD   071 499 4232

Phyl Payne
7 Chesney Ct
Shirland Rd
London W9 2EG   071 286 1270

Peters Fraser & Dunlop*
503 The Chambers
Chelsea Harbour
Lots Rd
London SW10 0XF   071 352 4466

Frances Phillips Agency
49 Hendon Hall Court
Parson St
London NW4 1QY   081 203 4375

Hilda Physick
78 Temple Sheen Rd
London SW14 7RR   081 876 0073

Plunket Greene
21 Golden Sq
London W1R 3PA   071 434 3801

Portfolio Management
58 Alexandra Rd
London NW4 2RY   081 203 1747

Peter Prichard Ltd
Mezzanine Floor
235 Regent St
London W1R 8AX   071 352 6417

Prime Performers
The Studio
5 Kidderpore Ave
London NW3 7SX   071 431 0211

Profile Management
The Workhouse
6 Aberdeen Studios
22 Highbury Grove
London N5 2EA   071 354 0625

Quick Nine Associates
2nd Floor
12 Abingdon Rd
London W8 6AF   071 937 2117

Joan Reddin
Hazel Cottage
Wheeler End Common
Lane End
High Wycombe
Bucks HP14 3NL   0494 882729

John Redway Associates
5 Denmark St
London WC2H 8LP   071 836 2001

Caroline Renton
84 Claverton St
London SW1 3AX   071 630 9191

Stella Richards Management
42 Hazlebury Rd
London SW6 2ND   071 736 7786

Rigal Management
109 Albert Bridge Rd
London SW11 4PF   071 228 8689

Rossmore Associates
1A Rossmore Rd
London NW1 6NJ   071 258 1953

Royce Management
44 Nasmyth St
London W6 0HB   081 741 4341

Gillian Russell
124 Mayfield Rd
Wellington Court
London W12 9LU   081 459 2781

Saraband Associates
265 Liverpool Rd
London N1 1LX   071 609 5313

Scot-Baker Agency
The Quadrangle
Atlanta St
London SW6 6TU   071 937 3464

Tim Scott Management
South Bank Commercial Centre
140 Battersea Park Rd
London SW11 4NB   071 978 1352

Susan Shaper Management
19 Denmark St
London WC2H 8NA

James Sharkey Associates
21 Golden Sq
London W1R 3PA   071 434 3801

Vincent Shaw Associates
20 Jays Mews
London SW7 2EP   071 581 8215

Malcom Shedden Management
1 Charlotte St
London W1P 1DH   071 636 1876

Christina Shepherd Ltd
84 Claverton St
London SW1 3AX   071 630 9191

Elizabeth Shepherd
29 Eversley Cross
London N21 1EL   081 364 0598

Silvester Management
122 Wardour St
London W1V 3LA   071 734 7232

Pamela Simons
9 Lowlands
2–8 Eton Ave
London NW3 3EJ   071 483 0170

Simpson Fox Associates
52 Shaftesbury Ave
London W1V 7DE   071 434 9167

Stagestruck Management
57 Duke St
London W1M 5DH   071 629 2334

Stellaris Management
12A Vauxhall Bridge Rd
London SW1 2SD   071 828 6826

Rennee Stepham Ltd
2 Arthur Court
Queensway
London W2 5HW   071 221 5550

Annette Stone Associates
9 Newburgh St
London W1V 1LH   071 734 0626

Richard Stone Partnership
25 Whitehall
London SW1A 2BS   071 839 6421

Success
Suite 74
3rd Floor
Kent Hse
87 Regent St
London W1R 7HF   071 734 3356

Michael Summerton Management
336 Fulham Rd
London SW10 9UG   071 351 7777

Talents Artists
4 Mews Hse
Princes Lane
London N10 3LU   081 444 4088

Thomas & Benda Associates
361 Edgware Rd
London W2 1BS   071 723 5509

Nick Thomas Associates
11–13 Broad Court
London WC2B 5DN   071 240 5052

David Thompson
50B Neal St
London WC2H 9PA   071 836 3988

Jim Thompson
1 Northdown Rd
Belmont
London SM2 6DY   081 770 3511

Tobias Management
77 Oxford St
London W1R 1RB   071 734 8367

Trends Management
54 Lisson St
London NW1 6ST   071 723 8001

Gary Trolan Management
30 Burrard Rd
London NW6 1DB   071 431 4367

Tommy Tucker Agency
43 Drury Lane
London WC2B 5RT   071 497 2113

Roxane Vacca Management
8 Silver Place
London W1R 3LJ   071 734 8085

Michael Vine Associates
Flat N
61 Shepherd's Hill
London N6 5RE

Thelma Wade Personal Management*
54 Harley St
London W1N 1AD   071 580 9860

Walmsley Horne Associates
36 Aybrook St
London W1M 3JL   071 487 3534

Janet Welch Personal Management
32 Hill St
Richmond
Surrey TW9 1TW   081 332 6544

David White Associates
2 Ormond Rd
Richmond
Surrey TW10 6TH   081 940 8300

Michael Whitehall Ltd
125 Gloucester Rd
London SW7 4TE   071 244 8466

David Wilkinson Associates
115 Hazlebury Rd
London SW6 2LX   071 371 5188

April Young Ltd*
The Clockhouse
6 St Catherine's Mews
Milner St
London SW3 2PX   071 584 1274

Organisations

British Actors' Equity
Guild House
Upper St Martin's Lane
London WC2H 9EG   071 379 6000

British Council
11 Portland Pl
London W1N 4EJ   071 930 8466

British Film Commission
70 Baker St
London W1M 1DJ   071 224 5000

British Film Institute
21 Stephen St
London W1P 1PL   071 255 1444

Broadcasting Entertainment Cinematograph
   Theatre Union (BECTU)
111 Wardour St
London W1V 4AY   071 437 8506

Children's Theatre Association
Unicorn Theatre
Gt Newport St
London WC2H 7JB   071 437 6567

Department of National Heritage
4th Floor
2–4 Cockspur St
London SW7 5DH   071 211 6445

Directors Guild of Great Britain
Suffolk Hse
1–8 Whitfield Pl
London W1P 5SF   071 383 3858

ITC (Independent Theatre Council)
4 Baden Place
Crosby Row
London SE1 1YW   071 403 1727

Independent Television Commission
33 Foley St
London W1P 7LB   071 225 3000

London Theatre Council
Bedford Chambers
The Piazza
London WC2E 8HQ   071 836 0971

National Association of Youth Theatres
Unit 1304
The Custard Factory
Gibb St
Digbeth
Birmingham B9 4AA   021 608 2111

New Playwrights Trust
Interchange Studios
Dalby St
London NW5 3NQ   071 284 2818

PACT (Producers Alliance for Cinema and Television)
Gordon Hse

Greencoat Pl
London SW1P 1PH   071 233 6000

Personal Managers' Association
Rivercrofts
1 Summer Rd
E. Molesey
Surrey KT8 9LX   081 398 9796

Society of British Fight Directors
56 Goldhurst Terrace
London NW6 3HT   071 624 1837

The Spotlight
7 Leicester Place
London WC2H 7BP   071 437 7631

Standing Conference of Young People's Theatre (SCYPT)
Collar & Tie Theatre
Hereford Education Centre
Blackfriars St
Hereford HR4 9HS   0432 353851

Theatrical Management Association (TMA)
Bedford Chambers
The Piazza
London WC2E 8HQ   071 836 0971

The Theatre Museum
1E Tavistock St
London WC2E 7PA   071 836 7891

Personal Notes

PEOPLE I HAVE MET

Production	Casting Director	Director	Company	Date

PEOPLE I HAVE WORKED WITH

Production	Casting Director	Company	Date	Transmission Date	Role